MW01044653

PAINTING
THE PLATE

To my father Martin,
who taught me to dream big.

He would have loved this book.

Felicity Souter

PAINTING THE PLATE

52 recipes inspired by
great works of art from Mark Rothko,
Frida Kahlo and many more

PRESTEL
Munich · London · New York

CONTENTS
—

INTRODUCTION
—

The close relationship between food and art stretches back thousands of years. From the earliest cave paintings to still-life oils and conceptual performance art, artists have repeatedly turned to food as both subject matter and medium.

I consider food to be a powerful tool to connect with formidable artists and their practices, from a different, more relatable perspective; one you don't find in art history books. And in researching this book, the more I looked, the more I found weird and wonderful ways in which food and art are linked through artists' work. The Futurists banned pasta; Dieter Roth turned literature into sausages; Olafur Eliasson turned ingredients into pigments; and Alison Knowles made salad into a performance.

Just like the rest of us, artists have to eat, and many have significant relationships with food and drink outside of the studio too. Gordon Matta-Clark opened a restaurant; George Segal ran a chicken farm; Henri de Toulouse-Lautrec concealed alcohol in his walking stick; and Jackson Pollock baked prize-winning apple pies.

Painting the Plate is both a book about art history and a cookbook. It explores fifty-two artists' unique connections to food, with accompanying easy-to-make recipes inspired by an artwork from their career. Before we even take a bite, we first eat with our eyes; these are not just artistic-looking dishes, but recipes that visually reference specific works of art, without sacrificing flavour; an experience of the artwork in a different medium.

Over the last few years, I have delved into the work and lives of artists from different countries and eras, working in a variety of art movements and mediums, from the 1600s to the present day, in Europe, Asia and North America. But there are also a number of artists I couldn't include. For some, we couldn't access the image rights for the artwork, while for others, there simply wasn't a point of contact available. Unfortunately, many artists, particularly women and those of ethnic minorities, are underrepresented, and because of their inaccessibility this vicious cycle is perpetuated. Western art history lacks diversity and the limited exposure of these important artists makes the inequality even more extreme; it is not only harder to share their work in a publication but harder to research and learn about them too. Nevertheless, I remain fascinated by all of the artists we have been able to include, and I hope this book introduces you to some new people, movements and artworks, or else helps you to consider them from a new perspective.

But most of all, I hope you simply enjoy the book. *Painting the Plate* has been a labour of love that I have been planning, refining and creating on and off for fifteen years. And although it's designed to be informative, it's also a bit of fun. Art doesn't have to be deeply serious all the time, and I hope this book helps you to connect to it in a different way – even if just for one meal. So, get out your chopping board and pick a recipe. It's time to feast on art.

HOW TO USE THE BOOK

—

Painting the Plate is divided by dish type – *Starters and Sides, Mains, Desserts* and *Drinks* – and includes dishes from a variety of cuisines, for a variety of diets.

These simple recipes have been designed so that the food truly is the art. There's no need for fancy plates but white and cream do work best to really showcase the colours and textures of the food – much like a blank canvas – while some dishes are served in the pan or baking dish for visual impact. And although presentation is obviously important, you don't have to be a chef or an artist to make these edible masterpieces. Each recipe is designed to be easy to cook and assemble. Just follow the instructions, reference the photos, and go for it! After all, art is subjective, so if you do make a mistake, you can always claim it as your own creative interpretation.

To make this book accessible to cooks on both sides of the Atlantic, I have included oven temperatures in both centigrade and Fahrenheit, along with the temperatures for both if you prefer to cook with the fan on (that is, using the convection setting). However, conversions are not always as neat as one might like and many ovens don't allow for such precise temperatures and instead offer temperatures in 5° increments. But don't worry, extreme precision isn't required for these recipes, so I've rounded the temperatures up or down slightly, which is why some conversions may not appear exactly precise. Every oven is unique and may run a little hot or cold; it's always best to follow the visual cues and keep an eye on what you're cooking so that you can adjust the time or temperature as needed.

I've also included a *Menu Planner* at the back of the book, in case you feel inclined to throw an artful dinner party. Most of the recipes are designed to be served at the table, making them ideal for sharing, and their visual impact and connection to an artwork is a great way to spark conversation. For most people, sharing an opinion on food is less intimidating than sharing one on art. Food breaks down barriers and sitting down at the dinner table with friends is a great way to ease into art if you're a newbie, or to get a deeper discussion started among more seasoned art lovers.

But ultimately, *Painting the Plate* is designed to help you pour a little creativity into your culinary world and have fun making something beautiful in the kitchen. And who knows, maybe it'll inspire you to come up with your own edible artworks.

STARTERS AND SIDES

LOUISE BOURGEOIS

On Saturdays, Louise Bourgeois would invite her friends over from six to eleven o'clock – between the art galleries closing and the jazz clubs opening – and cook for them, using food from the freezer and her eight much-loved pressure cookers. She embraced cooking for others and created what she called *'cuisine à l'improviste'*, serving improvised but simple recipes. In 1977, she was invited to contribute to *The Museum of Modern Art Artists' Cookbook*, and in the short interview that introduces her eleven recipes she outlined how her relationship to food and cooking had changed throughout her life.

Bourgeois enjoyed cooking as an adult and created simple dishes using French delicacies such as lamb kidneys and herring roe. *Veal Blanquette Lippe* – a simple dish of pressure-cooked veal with a cream cheese sauce – was a firm favourite at her dinner parties and the first recipe she included in the cookbook. Her prized pressure cookers made cooking quicker and easier, allowing her to spend more time with her guests. It was perhaps her own way of rebelling against what she saw as a social requirement for women to slave away in the kitchen for men, as she had been forced to do as a child.

Bourgeois is widely known to have been affected by her difficult childhood, and the traumas she experienced heavily influenced her artistic practice. But they also impacted her relationship with the kitchen. When she was young, she assisted her sick mother with the housework and cooked dinner for her father. But when she learned that her father was having an affair, she started to resent cooking. 'It wasn't easy', Bourgeois said. 'He often came home very late. I waited hours to make sure the food stayed hot and fresh – and I became expert at just that. When my father appeared and wanted a steak, I cooked it for him. In those days a man had the right to have his food ready for him at all times.'

Despite this negative early association, she transformed her approach to cooking as an adult, not only making the time with friends and family more important than the actual act of cooking, but incorporating it into the experience: 'You see how the present repeats the past – only now I wait for friends instead of my family, and I don't have to wait by the stove any more. When my friends arrive, I begin my cooking and I do it in the nicest way I can.'

There are many connections between Bourgeois' relationship with cooking and her artistic practice. Through her work she explored her experience of being a woman, unpicking ideas of the self and the body as both a child and an adult, such as domesticity and motherhood – which often link back to her challenging relationship with her father. One of her most famous sculptures, *The Destruction of the Father* (1974), is a womb-like space that resembles a dining room. The cavity is filled with undulating, bodily forms which the artist cast from large chunks of beef and mutton before covering them in a pink latex. Bourgeois suggested that the work came from a childhood fantasy she had about her family sitting around the dinner table. Tired of her father's jokes, her brother, sister and mother dismember and eat him. In the video clip titled *How To Peel an Orange*, the then eighty-seven-year-old Bourgeois explains how her father had insisted that each family member provided a source of entertainment at dinner time, such as reading or singing. His own trick was to create a little figure out of a tangerine skin, which Bourgeois demonstrates, first drawing the figure onto the fruit – explaining exactly where each body part should be placed – before carefully cutting the outline with a knife. On peeling back the figure her father would reveal his big joke. When he reached the pelvis, the skin would pull the white core out with it like a little penis sticking out from the body, on which occasions he would say to his mortified child, 'I thought she was my daughter, but obviously she's not … because my daughter has nothing there.'

For Louise Bourgeois, the dining table could be a battleground. But, with the help of technology, she discovered a love for quick and simple dishes that not only allowed her to dedicate more time to her art practice, but perhaps made the dinner table, surrounded by friends, become a place of sharing and healing.

Louise Bourgeois, *Les Fleurs*, 2007
Gouache on paper, suite of 18, 59.6 × 45.7 cm
Private collection

CHERRY AND JAMBON DE BAYONNE BRUSCHETTA WITH HOMEMADE RICOTTA

—

One of the eleven recipes Louise Bourgeois submitted to *The Museum of Modern Art Artists' Cookbook* was a simple cucumber salad served with crusty bread, much like bruschetta. This recipe uses cherries not only to contrast with the salty ham, but because the history of the cherry is a little…juicy. Cherries have been considered an erotic fruit since the prehistoric era and have been used symbolically throughout art history. I like to think that Bourgeois would appreciate their fleshy connotations.

The individual elements of this dish can be prepared in advance and quickly assembled to give you more time with your guests, just as Bourgeois would have wanted it.

SERVES 4–6

FOR THE RICOTTA
560 ml (2¼ cups) full fat milk
250 ml (1 cup) double cream (heavy cream)
½ teaspoon fine salt
2 tablespoons fresh lemon juice

FOR THE BRUSCHETTA
1 loaf baguette / ciabatta
80 g (2¾ oz) jambon de Bayonne or Parma ham
15–20 fresh sweet cherries

For the ricotta, bring the milk and double cream to a boil in a medium-sized saucepan, preferably nonstick, stirring regularly to stop it from scalding. Stir in the salt and immediately remove the pan from the heat. Add the lemon juice and stir gently. Once the mixture starts to curdle, set it aside to stand for 10 minutes.

Line a colander or sieve with 2 layers of muslin, cheesecloth or a clean tea towel and set over a bowl. Carefully pour in the curdled milk and put it in the refrigerator to chill for at least 30 minutes and up to 12 hours – the longer you leave it, the thicker the ricotta will become. Once it's reached a thick, spreadable consistency, transfer the ricotta to a lidded dish and store it in the refrigerator until needed.

(Freeze the whey collected in the bowl for future recipes – it makes a delicious savoury addition to soups.)

For the bruschetta, cut the bread into roughly 2 cm (¾ in) thick slices and toast them in a hot dry pan for 1 minute on each side, or until golden brown. Set aside on a wire rack to cool.

Once cooled, spread a generous layer of ricotta onto each piece of toast. Don't worry about being neat, as any texture will help the toppings stay in place.

Tear each slice of ham in half and place one half onto each slice of toast in a ruffle shape.

Halve most of the cherries and remove the stones. Place 2 or 3 cherry halves onto each slice.

Arrange the bruschetta on a platter with some whole cherries scattered artfully around the plate.

Use any excess juice from the cherries to drizzle over your masterpiece (you may need to crush a couple to get some more juice) and serve.

ODILON REDON

—

For the first half of his career, Odilon Redon gave faces to the invisible terrors that haunted his generation – germs. Although often interpreted as simply depictions of his own dreams, Redon's nightmarish creatures were fantastical renderings of the French public's anxieties in the late nineteenth century. Illnesses were common and many were caused by contaminated water and food, and proliferated by a lack of understanding of scientific hygiene principles. As scientists' knowledge of these microscopic dangers began to increase, so did the public's fears; Redon's haunting creatures bloomed into life.

Redon grew up on his uncle's wine estate, Château Peyre-Lebade in the Bordeaux region, where he produced some of his most famous paintings and first discovered an interest in death and decay. Fermentation is at the heart of wine production, a process we now understand due to Redon's hero, biologist Louis Pasteur, who discovered that yeasts cause fermentation. Fermentation has been used as a preservation method for millennia, but it was not yet fully understood in the mid-nineteenth century when France experienced a catastrophic national crisis – sour wine. A vital export for the nation, the economy took a significant hit. But after much research, Pasteur discovered not only that undesirable yeasts were the cause but also that they could be controlled. He went on to establish the process of pasteurisation, a method through which bacteria are destroyed by heating a liquid to a certain temperature to kill off any unwanted organisms, before allowing it to cool. This method was quickly applied not only to wine production but also to drinking water, saving countless lives. The food industry was also transformed. Eliminating pathogens from food extended its shelf life and created a predictable end product, without damaging it in the process. Pasteurisation continues to be used today, particularly in dairy, to ensure product consistency and safety.

Redon was first introduced to Pasteur's microbial studies when he moved to Paris as a young man. In the 1870s, he attended numerous lectures at scientific institutions to learn about the world of microbes which, in turn, influenced his art. In 1883, he sent a letter of praise to Pasteur, accompanied by a copy of *The Origins*, a set of lithographic prints inspired by the scientist's research. These were part of his *Noirs* series: dark, black-and-white images depicting death and decay in the form of hybrid creatures – plants with human faces, vast black spiders and bodiless heads – monsters Pasteur once described as 'fit to live'.

But in the late 1890s, Redon's work took a radical turn as he abandoned monochrome for colour, creating vibrant pastel works and paintings that sit somewhere between realism and abstraction. There's no pinpoint moment that sparked this change, but it was certainly well received by the public and Redon received more commissions than ever before. In 1899, the Baron de Domecy commissioned seventeen decorative panels for his dining room at Château de Domecy-sur-le-Vault in Burgundy. Far removed from his heavy *Noirs*, the 2.5-metre-high (8 foot) panels are predominantly yellow, resembling Japanese folding screens and with a far more palatable source of inspiration than the world of microbes. Flowers, landscapes and mythological scenes appear in hazy moments on the canvas, with delicate washes of paint so thin, they're almost transparent. A daydream rather than a nightmare: far removed from the world before pasteurisation.

Odilon Redon, *The Birth of Venus*, c. 1912
Oil on canvas, 143.2 × 62.5 cm
Museum of Modern Art, New York

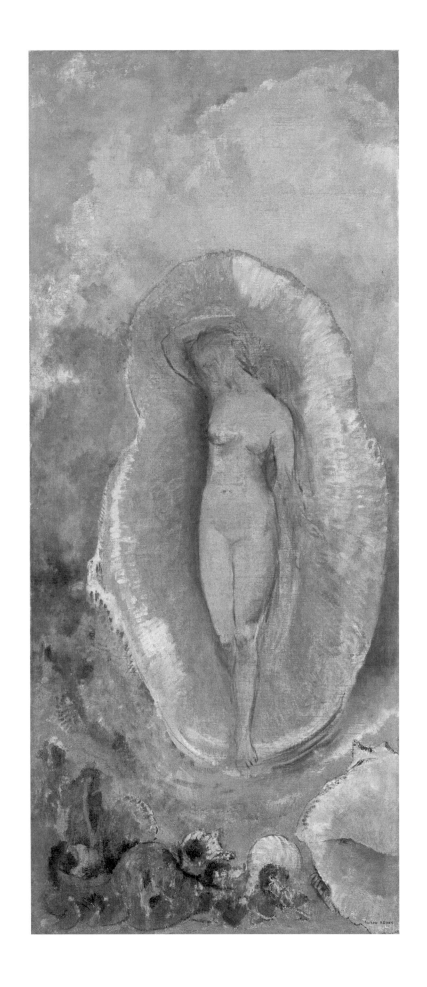

OYSTERS WITH A PICKLED GINGER AND SHALLOT DRESSING

—

Much like the later work of Odilon Redon, this is a French classic with a subtle, Japanese-inspired twist.

SERVES 3–4

FOR THE DRESSING
1 echalion shallot
    (banana shallot)
1 tablespoon drained
    pickled ginger slices
75 ml (5 tablespoons)
    rice vinegar
½ teaspoon cracked
    black pepper
Fine salt

12 fresh oysters

For the dressing, very finely chop the shallots and pickled ginger and put them in a small bowl with the rice vinegar, pepper and a pinch of salt. Stir and have a taste. Some pickled gingers are sweeter than others, so adjust with additional salt and/or vinegar to get it to your liking. Cover the dressing and put it in the refrigerator to allow the flavours to intensify for at least 2 hours and for up to 2 days before using.

Carefully shuck the oysters with an oyster knife. Fold a tea towel lengthways into a thick rectangle. Put an oyster, curved-side down, on one end, and wrap the rest of the towel around your hand to protect it as you hold the oyster in place.

Using an oyster knife, put the tip at the base of the hinge. Push down and then twist to pop open the shell. Slide the knife down the length of the top shell to separate the oyster and remove the top shell. Detach the oyster meat from the bottom shell.

To serve, lay the oysters over ice with the dressing in a small bowl with a spoon.

JUDY CHICAGO

—

In 1979, Judy Chicago unveiled her iconic feminist artwork *The Dinner Party* at the Museum of Modern Art in San Francisco: a vast triangular table featuring thirty-nine place settings, each dedicated to a prominent female figure in Western history and mythology. Her 'guests of honour' include Egyptian pharaoh Hatshepsut, the Minoan snake goddess, and artists Artemisia Gentileschi and Georgia O'Keeffe, with the names of an additional 999 women celebrated on the white-tiled base of the installation, including the artists Adélaïde Labille-Guiard, Mary Cassatt and Barbara Hepworth.

The setting is almost altar-like. Atop the long white tablecloths, each artist's place is defined by a large, overhanging placemat, intricately embroidered to reflect the woman's achievements, with their name written in gold thread. Cutlery and a drinking goblet frame each plate, which are variations on the vulva, uniquely designed to reflect the woman each place honours. Rounded and colourful, these flower-like plates gradually become more three-dimensional as they progress in time around the table, occasionally falling and rising again, as a metaphor for the undulating history of women's liberation. But a consistent rise occurs after the nineteenth century, with the sculptural designs reaching up off the table because, as Chicago puts it, 'women don't belong on a table'. Using the traditionally feminine crafts of embroidery and china painting, painstakingly executed by more than 400 volunteers, Chicago wanted the work to 'express the way women had been confined' and 'thus reflect both women's achievements and their oppression'. It is her own version of *The Last Supper*, as seen 'from the point of view of women, who, throughout history, had prepared the meals and set the table'. At this dinner party, each female diner holds equal importance; all the women sit facing the centre, maintaining the integrity of the triangle.

The Dinner Party was an important work in the feminist art movement during the second wave of feminism, which took place from the 1960s to the 1980s. Food played an essential role in how artists and writers campaigned for equality. They rejected traditional ideas about the role of women that had been set by society and endorsed by such books as *American Cookery*. The first American cookbook, it was written in 1796 by Amelia Simmons 'for the improvement of the rising generation of *Females* in America', and intended to help make women into 'good wives, and useful members of society'. Fifty years later, the first wave of feminism began, followed by the second wave one hundred years after that. In the late-twentieth century, brands jumped on the bandwagon, launching convenience foods and TV dinners, advertised as offering 'Women's Liberation'; food supposedly designed to free up women's time.

But what the adverts missed was that many feminist women wanted to achieve equality in the division of labour, taking the kitchen as a starting point for the rest of society. Much of their messaging was less about women throwing down their oven gloves and more about men picking them up; it wasn't that they hated cooking, they wanted it to be a gender-neutral activity. Many American feminist groups produced and sold cookbooks as a way of raising funds for their campaigns. These books encouraged men to cook and advocated for all children to be taught domestic skills, not just girls. They also spearheaded vegetarianism, comparing the oppression and commodification of women and their bodies to that of meat animals. They strived to achieve great social change by starting in the kitchen – hoping to create a society in which everyone met as equals around the dinner table.

Judy Chicago, *Let it All Hang Out*, 1973
Sprayed acrylic on canvas, 203.2 × 203.2 cm
New Orleans Museum of Art, New Orleans

BEETROOT-PICKLED DEVILLED EGGS

—

A contemporary twist on the 70s classic, this dish is a kaleidoscope of colour and flavour. It's the perfect hors d'oeuvre to kick off a dinner party.

SERVES 8

FOR THE PICKLED EGGS
8 eggs
200 ml (¾ cup plus
  1 tablespoon) white wine
  vinegar
2 tablespoons caster sugar
  (superfine sugar)
10 whole black
  peppercorns
1 bay leaf
1 beetroot, raw
  (pre-cooked beetroot
  also works)

FOR THE FILLING
2 tablespoons mayonnaise
1 teaspoon English mustard
2 tablespoons olive oil
Fine salt

TO SERVE
Paprika

For the pickled eggs, bring a saucepan of water to a boil. Add the eggs and boil them for 9 minutes. Drain the eggs, then put them in a bowl of ice water. Once cooled slightly, shell the eggs and return them to the ice water while you prepare the pickling liquor.

Put the saucepan over medium heat. Pour in 100 ml (⅓ cup plus 1 tablespoon) of cold water, followed by the white wine vinegar, caster sugar, peppercorns and bay leaf. Stir until the sugar is dissolved. Quarter the beetroot and add this to the pan. Bring the liquid to a boil, then immediately turn off the heat and set aside to cool and infuse for 10 minutes.

Stir to pull out as much colour from the beetroot as possible before removing it from the liquid and discarding. Leave in the aromatics.

Put the eggs in a sterilised 1 L (4 cup) glass jar with an airtight lid. Pour the warm pickling liquid over the eggs (they should be fully submerged), seal the lid and refrigerate. Leave for 12 hours for a perfect pink border or 2–3 days if you want the eggs to be pink all the way through. The eggs will keep in the refrigerator for a month, if fully submerged, getting pinker and pinker.

For the filling, remove the eggs from the jar and halve them lengthways. Carefully remove the yolks and add them to a bowl with the mayonnaise and mustard. Drizzle in the olive oil, whisking to create a smooth paste. Season with salt.

Arrange the egg halves on a serving plate.

Transfer the yolk mixture to a piping bag with a star nozzle and pipe the mixture into each egg half. Squeeze the bag to fill the yolk cavity and lift up as you release to create a point.

Sprinkle with paprika and serve.

HELEN FRANKENTHALER

—

Helen Frankenthaler's cheese grater was used more often in her studio than in her kitchen. She claimed she created her best work when she followed a strictly healthy diet, and cheese was not often on the menu. 'My usual regime is no fat, no salt, no butter, no sugar, no bread, no cream', she said, 'I count calories and carbohydrates and then I have a blast and I go all out and then start again with the diet.'

Frankenthaler's idea of junk food was a good chunk of processed cheese, cheap sardines, kosher dill pickles and peanut butter. But on the rare occasion she decided to host a dinner party, her food became a little more luxurious. Frankenthaler was a talented cook and she often kicked off a party with her *Quick Heavenly Hors d'Oeuvres* – mushrooms filled with red lumpfish caviar, topped with parsley and poppy seeds. The main event included dishes such as poached fish or chicken with wild rice, served with big bowls of salad. These were followed by slightly more decadent desserts of pear tart and macaroons. But this was a once-every-two-years kind of occasion for Frankenthaler, who found hosting highly stressful. She claimed to plan dinners three weeks in advance, setting aside multiple days for shopping and preparation and creating a huge mess in the process.

In the studio, however, she was always calm. This is also where she most often put her cheese grater to work. Frankenthaler prepared many of her paintings with a method she called 'guzzying', distressing the surface of wooden boards with an array of tools, including cheese graters, to create small marks and indentations. She then thinned down paint with turpentine and poured it directly onto the surface from a coffee can, allowing it to soak into the grain of the wood. She called this technique a 'soak-stain', a new method which opened up the possibilities of abstract painting as she transitioned from Abstract Expressionism to Colour Field painting.

The modern European cheese grater was invented in the 1540s by Francois Boullier in France, or perhaps by Isaac Hunt in England (a point hotly debated by food historians). However, other designs have been discovered in archaeological sites dating back as far as 700 BC. Graters in Ancient Greece were perforated sheets of bronze or terracotta, created to use up the ends of hardened cheeses. One such grater even makes an appearance in Homer's *Iliad*: 'Therein the woman resembling the goddesses mixed them a potion – Prámneian wine she used, and upon it grated some goat cheese with a bronze grater, a fine white barley meal sprinkled upon it.' It definitely wouldn't make it onto Frankenthaler's menu but she might have appreciated knowing that her artistic tool of choice came from such a long and poetic culinary tradition.

Helen Frankenthaler, *Untitled*, 1979
Acrylic on canvas, 23.8 × 54.8 cm
Syracuse University Art Museum, Syracuse

WATERMELON, RADISH AND CUCUMBER SALAD WITH GOAT'S CHEESE

—

This salad is exactly what you want on a hot summer's day. Refreshing and energising, it's sure to get your creative juices flowing. I recommend storing the ingredients in the refrigerator until ready to serve the salad to make it extra refreshing.

SERVES 4, AS A SIDE

FOR THE DRESSING
2 tablespoons extra-virgin olive oil
1 tablespoon white wine vinegar
1 tablespoon lemon juice
Fine salt

FOR THE SALAD
200 g (7 oz) radishes
1 cucumber
400 g (14 oz) watermelon (prepared weight)
1 small handful fresh mint leaves
100 g (3½ oz) soft, rindless goat's cheese

For the dressing, in a small bowl, whisk together the olive oil, white wine vinegar, lemon juice and a pinch of salt and set aside.

For the salad, very finely slice the radishes so that they are semi-transparent, cutting them along their length and width for variation.

Use a peeler to thinly slice the cucumber lengthwise into long ribbons.

Slice the watermelon flesh into thin, bite-size pieces of different shapes and sizes for textural variation.

Pluck off some of the smallest mint leaves and set aside. Finely chop the rest of the mint.

To serve, use the back of a spoon to make swirls of the goat's cheese on an oval or rectangular serving plate. Artfully arrange the radishes and watermelon on top in overlapping slices. Add the cucumber to show a mix of pink and green shades, arranging it in curls for visual texture.

Sprinkle over the chopped and whole mint leaves.

Drizzle with the dressing and serve.

MARINA ABRAMOVIĆ

—

For her 2010 performance *The Artist is Present*, Marina Abramović sat on a chair for eight hours a day for nearly three months, staring into the eyes of one thousand strangers. She had no breaks and ate no food during the 600 hours of performance. How did she achieve this extraordinary feat? Extensive preparation, mental resilience and lentils.

Food is a vital element of Abramović's performances; whether eating an entire raw onion as she recites the things she's tired of (*The Onion*, 1995), or as essential preparation for her more physically taxing performances, some of which involve fasting for days at a time. For her legendary performance *The House with the Ocean View* (2002), the artist fasted for twelve days, as she lived in three open-sided rooms mounted on the gallery wall.

In order to complete these extraordinary performances, Abramović works with renowned holistic doctor, Linda Lancaster, to prepare her body – or as the artist puts it, 'elevate my health into another galaxy!' To get her ready for the gruelling challenge of *The Artist is Present*, Lancaster created a detailed eating plan for Abramović: Slow-cooked lentils, tomatoes and high-quality olive oil were prioritised, simple ingredients that the artist said made her 'fall in love with food again'. In the morning before each day's performance, she ate her lentils with rice, but no seasoning – not even salt – and at the end of each day she had another serving of lentils, along with a whole grain, a vegetable and a light consommé. Abramović prepared for the performance for a year, removing lunch from her routine to train her body not to expect it.

But even when not preparing for a performance, Abramović is disciplined and continues to observe small and personal rituals in her daily life. Having grown up in former Yugoslavia, she cherishes her routine of drinking Turkish coffee and recalls fond childhood memories of her grandma roasting the beans at home. She also revels in the ritual of eating alone. So much so that she designed a dinner set for one with the French porcelain company Bernardaud in 2014. Entitled *Misfits for the Table*, the two plate sets featured four plates: a high-sided red or white plate in the shape of the five-pointed communist star (a symbol she engraved into her own stomach in her early performances); a larger plate printed with an image of textured gold or silver leaf; and two white plates, one printed with her family crest, the

other a cropped photograph of her lips, taken from her 2009 performance *Golden Lips*, where she covered her face in a mask of honey and gold leaf.

Almost two decades earlier, Abramović produced *Spirit Cooking* (1996), a book of 'essential aphrodisiac recipes'. The unusual 'recipes' – which share more with spellcraft than cooking – are accompanied by a collection of aquatint etchings that continue the theme of the artist's use of her own body in her work. The printing plates were prepared with soft ground so that Abramović could work directly onto the surface with her own body, affecting it with her nails and fingertips. She also worked with spitbite, a printing technique that creates a softer, more painterly mark, diluting the nitric acid with her own saliva to paint on the plate to continue the physical connection.

The 'recipes' read like poetic potions that are more magical than practical: *to be consumed on a solar eclipse* requires you to steam '13 leaves of uncut green cabbage with 13,000 grams of jealousy' before drinking '3 glasses of water that a ruby has been soaking in for 3 days'. This is perhaps a more appetising prospect than *essence drink*, a cocktail of 'fresh breast milk with fresh sperm milk' to be drunk on 'earthquake nights'. Her recipe for *pain* (or perhaps a cure – its purpose is unclear) says to 'keep a small meteorite stone in your mouth', while *fire food* instructs the reader to use a sharp knife to cut into their own hand and 'eat the pain'. None have the makings of a dinner party.

But as we know, even Abramović doesn't live purely off such things as a paste of 'one grain of cooked rice, one grain of fresh pollen' and 'one spoonful of tears'. She follows the guidelines of Dr Lancaster, eating nutritious foods, such as her favourite soup recipe, originally taken from a cookbook by Austrian doctor, Nonna Brenner, which she contributed to *Wallpaper** magazine's Artist's Palate series in 2021. Containing just five ingredients – flax seeds, oats, oat bran, a pinch of herb salt and zest from a frozen lemon – it's a simple soup designed to be eaten on the first day of fasting, which the artist says 'keeps your mind peaceful and clear.' Best eaten alone, perhaps?

Marina Abramović, *The Onion*, 1995
Performance for video, 10 minutes
(photo based on performance, 2006)

FRIED ONION FLOWERS WITH RED PEPPER DIPPING SAUCE

—

These onion flowers are a great sharing starter for a dinner party but can, of course, be eaten alone, if you prefer Marina Abramović's approach to eating. Although the onions are deep-fried, the dipping sauce (inspired by *Ajvar*, a Serbian roast pepper sauce) is tangy enough to cut through the fattiness of the batter, keeping it light and fresh.

SERVES 4

FOR THE DIPPING SAUCE
225 g (8 oz) jarred roasted
   red peppers, drained
1 small garlic clove
2 tablespoons extra-virgin
   olive oil
1 teaspoon white wine
   vinegar
Fine salt

FOR THE ONION FLOWER
4 medium onions
100 g (¾ cup) plain flour
   (all-purpose flour)
2 teaspoons paprika
1 teaspoon fine salt
½ teaspoon ground cumin
½ teaspoon cracked black
   pepper
60 ml (¼ cup) full fat milk
1 egg
Flaky sea salt

FOR DEEP FRYING
Sunflower oil
   (about 750 ml / 3 cups)

For the dipping sauce, put the red peppers, garlic, olive oil and white wine vinegar in a food processor or blender and blitz until smooth. If your jar of peppers has some vinegar in its ingredients list, omit the vinegar from the recipe until after you've blended and tasted, so that you can judge how much you need – the sauce should be quite zingy to lift the fried onion. Season the dip with salt, then transfer it to a small bowl and put it in the refrigerator until ready to serve.

For the onion flowers, chop off the top of an onion and peel it, keeping the root end intact. Put it on a chopping board, cut-side down and root-side up. Using a sharp knife, make 4 evenly spaced cuts down the sides of the onion, starting about ½ cm (⅙ in) away from the root and going all the way to the cut side. Make another 3 cuts between the original 4 cuts to create 16 sections. Flip the onion over and gently fan out the petals. They should still be secured at the base of the onion. Repeat with the remaining 3 onions.

Combine the plain flour, paprika, salt, cumin and pepper in a bowl large enough to fit an onion. In another bowl large enough to fit an onion, whisk together the milk and egg.

Fill a deep pan halfway with the sunflower oil and heat the oil to 175°C (345°F).

As the oil heats, coat an onion in the dry mixture. Dunk it into the wet mixture to fully coat it and shake off the excess. Coat it in the dry mixture again.

Use a slotted spoon to carefully place the coated onion into the hot oil with the root side up to help the petals fan out. Fry the onion, occasionally spooning hot oil over the base, for 3–4 minutes, or until brown and crispy. Carefully flip over the onion and fry for 2 more minutes, or until golden and soft throughout. Adjust the heat as needed to keep the oil between 170 and 190°C (340 and 375°F).

Remove the onion from the oil and place it on paper towels to cool and absorb excess oil while you fry the other onions.

To serve, arrange the onion flowers on a platter with the dipping sauce and plenty of napkins. Sprinkle with sea salt flakes. Pluck off individual petals and dunk them in the sauce.

LEE KRASNER

—

When Lee Krasner first met Jackson Pollock, she didn't cook. In fact, according to the fictionalised version of their love story (*Pollock* starring Ed Harris and Marcia Gay Harden), her culinary skills were so limited that on Pollock's first visit to Krasner's studio, she asked her future husband if he would like a cup of coffee and took him to the local cafe saying, 'You don't think I make it here?'

The couple met in 1942 when they participated in a group show in New York. At the time, Krasner was a more established artist than Pollock but, recognising the potential of his 'drip paintings', she would go on to help make his name as one of the most celebrated painters of the twentieth century. The couple moved to rural East Hampton three years later and, far from any cafes, Krasner had no choice but to make her own coffee. They bought a gas stove and over the years, she learnt to cook and became known for making beautiful meals for friends and collectors. She regularly invited influential people from New York to ensure she stayed connected with the city's art world and to promote Pollock's work.

As an artist, it's not surprising that she was interested in the presentation of her food, but Krasner took this to extremes. If she asked friends to bring a dish to dinner, she would tell them exactly how she wanted it; how it should be cooked and served, even which ingredients to use. Her attention to detail was noted by many of her guests as she would make everything she could from scratch, from homemade bread to lobster bisque, one of Pollock's favourites.

Despite not having an interest in cooking when she was younger, Krasner had links to good food and produce from childhood as her parents sold fresh fruit, vegetables and fish at a market stand in Brooklyn. And once they were settled in their new home, she and Pollock established an abundant vegetable garden. The couple were very proud of their home-grown produce and would often give it away to friends and visitors as gifts. Pollock enjoyed fishing with friends and after a particularly successful trip, Krasner celebrated the catch by rubbing the large tarpon in ink before pressing it onto a sheet of paper. The print still hangs in the kitchen of their home today, which is now a museum and study centre.

Natural forms fascinated Krasner. Moments like this inspired her, and as she developed her practice ingredients began to feature in her work. In her earlier career, she had worked on a relatively small scale, mostly in collage. But after Pollock's death she moved into his studio, which was much larger than her own, where she was able to start working on a bigger scale and shifted her practice to create action-based paintings that required greater physical effort. The vast 2-by-5-metre (6.5 × 16.4 feet), green and pink canvas *The Seasons* (1957), features a pomegranate, apple and pear which are sensual and bodily in form. Made in the year following her husband's death, the gestural drip marks and brown undertones hint at decay and death, suggesting the cycle of rebirth.

Ultimately, Krasner reduced these shapes down to focus on the true essence of the forms. *Vernal Yellow* (1980), features rounded shapes in vivid shades of purple and yellow. She's known to have loved the colours of the garden and these shades could easily be inspired by the beetroot she grew there. She also became more and more engrossed by the textural quality of her works and beneath the swipes of paint you can see ripped up pieces of her own paintings and drawings that make up the shape of the composition – a resourcefulness and attention to detail that she applied to all aspects of her life as an artist, a homemaker and a cook.

Lee Krasner, *Vernal Yellow*, 1980
Oil on canvas, 150 × 178 cm
Museum Ludwig, Cologne

BEETROOT, HALLOUMI AND CHICORY SALAD WITH TAHINI-YOGHURT DRESSING AND POMEGRANATE MOLASSES

—

Lee Krasner created a variety of beautiful meals from her homegrown produce. She was particularly fond of beetroots and created a range of dishes to celebrate their vibrant pink colour. Just like the layered, textural collage *Vernal Yellow* (1980), this dish is an explosion of colour and texture, with layer upon layer of flavour. Earthy beetroot, sharp and crisp chicory, sweet butternut squash and salty, chewy halloumi are topped with a creamy tahini dressing and a generous drizzle of fruity pomegranate molasses.

Serve this salad hot or cold, depending on the occasion and time of year – both are equally delicious. I recommend preparing the vegetables and dressing in advance and frying the halloumi at the last minute for an easy but impressive side dish.

SERVES 4–6, AS A SIDE

FOR THE SALAD
3 golden beetroots
2 red beetroots
350 ml (1¼ cups)
   just-boiled water
1 small butternut squash
1 tablespoon olive oil
Flaky sea salt
225 g (8 oz) halloumi
   cheese
2 heads red chicory

FOR THE DRESSING
60 g (¼ cup) natural
   (regular) yoghurt
1 tablespoon tahini
½ small lemon, juiced
Flaky sea salt

TO SERVE
2 tablespoons
   pomegranate molasses

Preheat the oven to 180°C / 160°C fan (350°F / 320°F fan).

For the salad, put the whole golden and red beetroots with their skins on in a deep baking dish. Pour just-boiled water from the kettle to come one-third of the way up the sides of the beetroots. Bake for 15 minutes, then turn the beets, and continue baking for another 10 to 15 minutes, or until softened.

Meanwhile, peel the butternut squash. Halve, deseed and cut the squash crosswise into ½ cm (⅙ in) thick slices. Toss the squash with the olive oil, spread it in a single layer on a baking tray and sprinkle with a pinch of salt. Roast for 10 minutes, then flip the squash and bake for another 10 minutes, or until soft.

Rinse the beetroot under cold water until cool enough to handle and scrape off the skin with a spoon. Cut each beetroot into 8 wedges.

For the dressing, in a small bowl, whisk together the yoghurt, tahini, lemon juice and a pinch of salt until smooth. Whisk in a little cold water to make the dressing just thin enough to pour.

Cut the halloumi into ½ cm (⅙ in) thick slices.

In a dry nonstick frying pan over medium-high heat, fry the halloumi for 1–2 minutes on each side, or until crisp and speckled brown. Set aside.

To serve, chop the base off the chicory bulbs and snap off the leaves. Arrange them on a large, flat serving plate, overlapping them with the two colours of beetroot, the butternut squash and the halloumi. Drizzle the dressing over the salad, followed by the pomegranate molasses, and serve.

OLAFUR ELIASSON
—

On the roof of his vast studio in Berlin, Olafur Eliasson keeps a vegetable garden. Not only for himself but for his staff, who sit down for lunch together four days a week to eat nutrient-rich food. The aim: sparking creative conversation.

Eliasson's interest in food is multifaceted and interwoven into every aspect of his work and practice. For many, he is probably best known for his unforgettable installation *The weather project* (2003) at Tate Modern, London, to which two million people flocked to bask in the glow of the artificial sun. Fascinated by the sun and solar energy, Eliasson sees food as a vital source of sunlight; a way for us to soak up the sun's energy. The studio rooftop isn't quite large enough to feed ninety hungry employees, however, so his team sources the rest of their energy-giving food from organic farms within a 10-kilometre (6.2 mile) radius of the city.

A team of five female cooks runs the kitchen, using the carefully selected ingredients to create an array of vegetarian Eliasson-approved dishes for his staff, to not only fuel and nourish them but to create a sense of community and a healthy space for collaboration. Forget the heart of the home, this kitchen is the heart of the studio. After cooking a plethora of dishes over the years, tried and tested by the staff members, *Studio Olafur Eliasson: The Kitchen* was published; a collaborative cookbook and art project, created by the whole Eliasson team. Shot in black and white, with only the food in colour, the book features over 100 vegetarian recipes with plenty of poetic anecdotes about how the recipes came about and what conversations were sparked as they were eaten. Some recipes are simpler than others. Some take only a few minutes, while others (like the recipe for fermented miso) take six months. The recipe for *Umeboshi* (salted Japanese plums) requires you to know that 'at least 4 consecutive sunny days' are coming before you can even get started.

But Eliasson takes food to another level within his studio. It's not just for eating. For him, food is an art form in itself, and a way to make the consumer part of an artwork. 'Normally, we touch the world with our outsides,' he said, 'but with eating, we turn ourselves inside out. The people eating it are very much a part of the artwork.'

The food isn't confined to the kitchen at Studio Olafur Eliasson. Recently, his team have been experimenting with methods of painting, by dehydrating and grinding vegetables to create pigments and produce what Eliasson calls 'ecologically infused watercolours' – think leek green, red onion grey and carrot yellow. Working constantly to achieve sustainability within all areas of the studio, the powder is so natural it can even be sprinkled over bread and butter for an artful snack. For Eliasson, energy, art and food are all part of the same fluid system.

Olafur Eliasson, *The weather project*, 2003
Monofrequency lights, projection foil, haze machines,
mirror foil, aluminium, scaffolding, 26.7 × 22.3 × 155.4 m
Tate, London

TURMERIC HUMMUS WITH BLACK SESAME AND SEAWEED CRACKERS

—

Just like the food served at Olafur Eliasson's studio, this recipe is full of goodness and is a great lunchtime dish.

The recipe makes more chilli oil than is needed. Store it in the bottle in a cool, dark place and it will last for weeks. You can also use it for *Golden ramen-style soup with soy-cured quail egg yolks* (page 70) inspired by the work of Sakai Hōitsu or *Spinach pancakes with eggs and feta* (page 138) inspired by the work of Gabriel Orozco.

SERVES 4–6

FOR THE CHILLI OIL
250 ml (1 cup) olive oil
1 tablespoon dried chilli
  flakes

FOR THE CRACKER DOUGH
2 sheets dried nori
200 g (1½ cups) plain flour
  (all-purpose flour)
5 tablespoons black
  sesame seeds
2 teaspoons cracked black
  pepper
1 teaspoon fine salt
1 teaspoon caster sugar
2 tablespoons olive oil

FOR THE TOPPING
1 tablespoon cracked black
  pepper
1 tablespoon black sesame
  seeds
1 teaspoon flaky sea salt

FOR THE HUMMUS
400 g (14 oz) canned
  chickpeas, drained with
  liquid reserved
60 ml (¼ cup) tahini
3 tablespoons olive oil
1 tablespoon lemon juice
1 small garlic clove
2 teaspoons ground
  turmeric
1 teaspoon fine salt

For the chilli oil, heat the olive oil in a small saucepan over low heat for 1 minute. Add the chilli flakes and heat gently for 3 more minutes. It should not sizzle. Turn off the heat and set aside to cool completely. Transfer the chilli oil to a sterilised glass bottle and screw on the lid. The oil is already hot and ready to use, but the longer it sits, the hotter it gets.

Preheat the oven to 200°C / 180°C fan (400°F / 350°F fan).

For the cracker dough, rip the nori into pieces, then blitz it in a food processor until superfine. Transfer to a large bowl, then add the plain flour, sesame seeds, pepper, salt and caster sugar and mix thoroughly. Pour in the olive oil and mix again until combined. Add 125 ml (½ cup) of cold water and mix with your hands to form a dough. You may need to add a drop or two more water if the dough feels a little dry – it should be fully mixed and smooth but not sticky. Cover the bowl with a tea towel and leave the dough to sit for 10 minutes.

For the topping, combine the pepper, sesame seeds and salt in a small bowl.

Once the dough has rested, cut it into four equal pieces. On a lightly floured surface, use a rolling pin to roll out each piece of dough into a rectangle. The thinner the dough, the crispier the crackers will be. I recommend rolling them out into rectangles about the thickness of the sesame seeds for the perfect snap. Arrange the pieces on two baking trays lined with parchment paper.

Use a pastry brush to brush each sheet of dough with a little water, then sprinkle with the topping mixture. Bake for 7 minutes. Use a spatula to very carefully flip the dough rectangles, then turn off the oven. Leave the crackers in the oven as it cools with the door closed for 30 minutes for the best texture. Alternatively, bake for a further 10 minutes and set aside to cool for 5–10 minutes.

Snap the crackers into pieces.

For the turmeric hummus, in a blender or food processor, combine the chickpeas, 75 ml (5 tablespoons) of the reserved liquid from the chickpeas (add more for a thinner consistency if needed), the tahini, olive oil, lemon juice, garlic, turmeric and salt. Blend until smooth.

To serve, transfer the hummus to a bowl and use the back of a spoon to create a swirl in the surface. Drizzle with 2 teaspoons of the chilli oil and serve with the black sesame and seaweed crackers.

REMEDIOS VARO

—

Three vampires huddle together in a windowless chamber, feasting on their victims: a tomato, a rose and a slice of watermelon. These are vegetarian vampires – *Vampiros Vegetarianos* (1962) – conjured up by the surrealist artist Remedios Varo. Shrouded in gold flames, the winged trio sits around a small bistro table, sucking the 'blood' through long, thin straws.

Varo created this extraordinary work in Mexico City, where she fled from Paris during the German Occupation (having arrived only a few years earlier, fleeing from Madrid during the Spanish Civil War). Mexico City offered refuge for many Europeans, and Varo soon established one of the most important friendships of her life there. Varo and British Surrealist artist Leonora Carrington shared a wicked sense of humour, and together they enjoyed cooking for and pranking their friends – often at the same time. At a particularly raucous dinner party at Varo's home, the devious duo tricked the poet Octavio Paz, serving him tapioca pearls spritzed with squid ink, in place of caviar. Much to the artists' delight, he fell for it. But this was a tame prank by their standards: Carrington once fed a guest an omelette containing their own hair.

The pair also shared a keen interest in the supernatural. They believed that women have an alchemical power, seeing the kitchen, which is a traditionally female space, as a place to create and transform things. According to art historian Kelly Wacker, 'both Carrington and Varo saw food, whether vegetable or animal, as having a distinctive life force.' The kitchen table became an alchemist's lab for the two artists in their everyday lives, as well as figuring as a key motif within their paintings. Working in their kitchens, they concocted potions and practised their very own spellcraft; along with the photographer Kati Horna, they were nicknamed the three *brujas* (witches).

Varo's work sits between three realms: religion, science and magic. Daughter of a Catholic mother and a Universalist father, who worked as an engineer, her work is a combination of religious motifs and precise architectural drawing. It possesses an overall sense of mystery, often in reference to her other fascination – dreams. Her recipe *To Induce Erotic Dreams* is a complex series of instructions which requires an equally baffling list of ingredients: 'a kilo of horseradish, three white hens, a head of garlic, four kilos of honey, a mirror, two calf livers, a brick, two clothespins, a whalebone corset, two false mustaches and hats to taste.' Among the many instructions, the method states that the maker must spread their bedsheet with all four kilograms of honey, before covering it with the hen's feathers. Then, they must put on the corset, sit in front of the mirror and smile while sipping broth and trying on the different hats and moustaches. It's certainly unusual, but arguably more appealing than her recipe *To Dream you are King of England*, where the maker must paint their entire body with egg white in order to become a royal for the night.

With the assistance of her Surreal friendship, Remedios Varo turned domestic moments into magical ones, transforming the kitchen into a spellbinding hub of creativity, as reflected in her extraordinary paintings.

Remedios Varo, *Vampiros Vegetarianos*, 1962
Oil on canvas, 85.7 × 60.3 cm
Private collection

CHIPOTLE PRAWNS

—

This recipe is ridiculously easy but a real showstopper. Make sure to provide your guests with plenty of napkins and some crusty bread to mop up the buttery sauce.

SERVES 4–6

FOR THE PRAWNS
200 g (7 oz) unpeeled raw king prawns
400 g (14 oz) peeled raw king prawns
50 g (3½ tablespoons) salted butter
2 tablespoons olive oil
1½ tablespoons chipotle paste
3 garlic cloves, thinly sliced

TO SERVE
1 small red chilli, thinly sliced
1 small handful fresh coriander (cilantro) leaves, finely chopped
1 lemon, cut into wedges

For the prawns, devein the peeled and unpeeled prawns, if preferred. Insert a toothpick into the centre of the back of the prawn, going in just below the vein. Pull up to break through the shell and lift up the vein. Gently pull with your fingers to remove it in one piece.

Put a large frying pan over high heat. Add the butter, olive oil and chipotle paste and once the butter is melted, add the garlic. Cook for 30 seconds, then add the prawns. Cook, tossing constantly in the chipotle butter, for 1–2 minutes, or until the prawns turn pinky-orange on both sides.

To serve, arrange the prawns on a serving platter. Sprinkle with the red chilli and coriander and serve straight away with lemon wedges on the side.

I suggest serving this dish with some bread, such as the Barbara Hepworth *Crusty bread* (page 44) to soak up the buttery sauce.

BARBARA HEPWORTH

—

Barbara Hepworth's life and career were dramatically shaped by war. She experienced World War I as a child and was an established artist aged thirty-six when World War II broke out. Not only was she faced with financial instability – when people's money was spent anywhere but on large-scale sculptures – but she would worry about providing enough nutritious food for her young family.

Her friend and art critic Adrian Stokes and his wife Margaret Mellis had moved to St Ives the previous year and, once war broke out, Stokes worked as a market gardener for the Home Guard. They had a large vegetable garden where they grew a variety of staple root vegetables as well as lettuce and mushrooms, they kept chickens and Mellis had begun beekeeping. Shortly before war was declared, the couple opened their home to Hepworth, who by this time was married to fellow artist Ben Nicholson, bringing with them their four-year-old triplets, their nanny and cook. The painter William Coldstream also soon arrived with his wife. Stokes and Mellis, and their maid Martha, suddenly had twelve mouths to feed.

Tensions ran high and Hepworth and Nicholson moved to a small home of their own nearby, four months after leaving London. But with rationing in place, they had to lay-off their cook. The nanny remained to help care for the children, but Hepworth had to take over the housework herself, planting her own vegetable garden to feed the family, utilising the skills she had learnt from her time with Stokes. Nicholson continued to paint and bring in sporadic income, but Hepworth didn't have enough space to sculpt. Their financial troubles were pressing, and she was particularly concerned about her family's health and her ability to provide a nutritious diet for them as she and her children were becoming ill too often for her liking. American art dealer Curt Valentin sent food parcels from America to help her during the rationing: 'If you need anything in the way of food, let me know … I can charge your account and will take some of yours or Ben's work some day', he said in a letter. The artist gratefully accepted this lifeline as she and Nicholson often gave the children their own rations.

But in 1942, things were looking up. The family moved again, and Hepworth finally had a studio space of her own, which in turn gave her room to establish the balance between her identities as a mother and an artist.

'A woman artist is not deprived by cooking and having children, nor by nursing children with measles (even in triplicate)', she said, 'one is in fact nourished by this rich life, provided one always does some work each day; even a single half hour, so that the images grow in one's mind.' In a letter to art writer E. H. Ramsden, she outlined her technique for achieving this equilibrium: 'I've slowly discovered how to create for 30 mins, cook for 40 mins, create for another 30 & look after children for 50 & so on through the day. It's a sort of a miracle to be able to do it – I think the secret lies in not resisting the chores & drudges & in carrying the creative mood on within oneself while cooking so that it's unbroken … Normally I used to need 8 hrs continuous work to really create something.'

Although many of her earlier works explored the relationship between mother and child, by the end of World War II her work had shifted into a much more abstracted style, exploring the relationships between non-representational forms. Her pierced sculptures were breakthrough works of abstraction, allowing her sculptures to be viewed not only from the outside, but also from within, encouraging the viewer's gaze to move in and around the work. *Oval Sculpture* (1943) epitomises her newly abstracted style and showcases her accomplishment of piercing the shape, examining the relationship between negative spaces within one form.

Just like her maternal need to prioritise her family, Hepworth's approach to creating work was always instinctive. She considered the medium she used to be the most important aspect of her practice and strived to showcase the essence of the material. Using a chisel as an extension of her own body, she worked in repetitive rhythmic movements to reveal the sculpture within the stone or wood: 'The strokes of the hammer on the chisel should be in time with your heartbeat. You breathe easily. The whole of your body is involved. You move around the sculpture, and the whole of you, from the toes up, is concentrated in your left hand, which dictates the creation'. This meditative, hands-on approach to creating was undoubtedly therapeutic for Hepworth and her own way of finding that balance between motherhood and artistry she worked so hard to achieve.

Barbara Hepworth, *Oval Sculpture*, 1943
Plane wood with painted concavities, 34.9 × 46.2 × 29.9 cm
The Pier Arts Centre, Stromness

CRUSTY BREAD

—

As both artist and cook, I love taking a material or ingredient and transforming it into something else and there's nothing more satisfying than baking a perfect loaf of bread. With a little practice (and a fair amount of patience) you can turn flour, water and yeast into an edible sculpture. This recipe requires ten minutes of diligent kneading to create a springy, elastic dough – a repetitive motion that echoes the techniques Hepworth used to create her masterpieces. I enjoy how it connects me to her techniques and practice. Try scoring the loaf in a different pattern each time to create your own series of sculptures.

MAKES 1 LOAF

1½ tablespoons caster
    sugar (superfine sugar)
7 g (2 ¼ teaspoons) active
    dry yeast
450 g (3 ¼ cups) strong
    white bread flour
1 teaspoon fine salt
2 tablespoons, plus
    1 teaspoon olive oil

In a small bowl, dissolve the caster sugar in 60 ml (¼ cup) of lukewarm water (approx. 45°C / 115°F). Sprinkle the yeast over the surface and stir. Cover with a tea towel and leave the bowl in a warm place for 15 minutes, or until puffed up and slightly bubbly.

In a large bowl, combine the flour and salt and stir well. Make a well in the centre and pour in the yeasty mixture. Use a butter knife to start mixing. Once the yeast mixture has been absorbed, gradually add 250 ml (1 cup) of lukewarm water (approx. 45°C / 115°F), mixing thoroughly until the water has been incorporated and a dough is beginning to form. It should still be quite crumbly at this stage. Tip the mixture out onto a floured surface and use your hands to bring it together.

Knead the dough for 10 minutes, using the heel of your hand to push the dough away from you and your fingers to pull it back towards you. I recommend alternating your hands with each knead to help you get into a rhythm. Put a timer on and get lost in the repetitive motion to form a smooth, elastic dough. It should be tacky, not sticky. If it sticks to the surface as you're kneading, sprinkle more flour over it.

Put the dough in a large, clean bowl with enough room to rise and pour the 2 tablespoons of olive oil over it. Using your hands, roll the dough to coat it in the oil and spread any remaining oil up the sides of the bowl to prevent the dough from sticking as it rises. Cover with a tea towel and leave the bowl in a warm place to rise for 1½ – 2 hours, or until doubled in size.

Knock back the dough by punching your fist down into the bowl to deflate the largest air bubbles. Tip the dough out onto your surface and pull and stretch the dough over itself a few times to get rid of any large pockets of air. Shape the dough into a round by moving your hands clockwise around the dough, scooping downwards slightly to make a perfect rounded loaf.

Put the loaf onto a baking tray lined with parchment paper, cover loosely with a tea towel and let it sit in a warm place for 30 minutes.

Meanwhile, preheat the oven to 180°C / 160°C fan (350°F / 320°F fan).

Brush the top of the loaf with the remaining 1 teaspoon of olive oil and use a bread lame or sharp knife to score a few cuts in a rounded pattern of your own design. Put the bread on the baking tray on the middle rack of the oven and bake for 45 minutes. To test if it's ready, knock on the base of the loaf with your knuckle. If cooked, it should sound hollow. If you're unsure, put the loaf back in the oven for 5 more minutes.

Remove the loaf from the oven and let cool on a wire rack for 15–20 minutes. I recommend digging in before it's entirely cold and slathering your first slice with high-quality butter and a sprinkling of sea salt to taste the bread at its best.

LOWELL BLAIR NESBITT
—

The art world can be a place of extremes. While some artists struggle to put food on the table, others are able to hire live-in chefs. Lowell Blair Nesbitt did the latter. The artist lived in a lavish 18,000-square-foot (1672 m²) apartment in the meat-packing district of New York. Previously a police stable (and a slaughterhouse before that), it was renovated to Nesbitt's own design with a dazzling four-storey atrium, complete with swimming pool, jacuzzi and a goldfish pond.

For a while, Nesbitt's cuisine of choice was Chinese, and he hired a full-time chef to cook authentic, fresh dishes for him and for his friends, who often came round to sample the goods. But the extensive renovations proved to be too much for the chef, who soon left complaining about the dust. After that, a new chef came in once a week to prepare meals for the weekends, mostly for Nesbitt's dinner parties. But the artist was also capable of cooking for himself, often opting for French-style cuisine, such as his *Waste Not Want Not Stew Nesbitt*. This stew, featured in *The Museum of Modern Art Artist's Cookbook* in 1977, uses a variety of traditional ingredients such as beef, bouillon, onions, turnips and potatoes, with a few unexpected additions such as Hungarian rose paprika and the chopped rind of a grapefruit.

But regardless of who was cooking, Nesbitt had very particular ideas on how his food should taste and especially how it should look. 'The way food looks is ninety percent of its appeal to me', he said, 'I would almost sacrifice taste to looks.' He certainly took his culinary presentation seriously. Nesbitt is famous for painting vast Photorealist flowers but in his household, florals weren't reserved for canvases. One of his favourite dishes to serve dinner guests was *pasta primaflora* – spaghetti with edible flower petals (roses, day lilies, nasturtiums and violets) in a pine nut and cream sauce.

Nesbitt's dream meal was an edible Eden: a fantasy menu of exotic hors d'oeuvres, which he turned into a reality in 1982, as documented in an article by *New York Magazine*. Dressed in a dazzling white suit with pink accents, the artist is photographed behind a spectacular garden of canapés, centred around a large pink lily

sculpture. Guests could forage for devilled eggs from a field of marigold flowers, pluck cheese skewers from the edible trees and feast on beer-infused shrimp from the iced 'snowfields'. This host didn't do anything by half. His events were always flowing with champagne, which he claimed to drink 'like other people drink wine'. And when he did drink wine, it was, of course, only the best. Almost always a bottle of Chambertin, an expensive French wine from Burgundy, known to have also been a favourite of Napoleon Bonaparte, who once said, 'nothing makes the future look so rosy as to contemplate it through a glass of Chambertin'. Clearly Nesbitt agreed.

Perhaps influenced by his own gastronomic interests, Nesbitt started a new series of paintings in the 1970s, temporarily moving away from his iconic flower works, to focus on still lifes of fruits and vegetables. Unlike the florals, which were painted on flat backgrounds of plain colour or black-and-white patterns, these scenes have a more traditional art approach. Featuring heaps of produce lying on patterned rugs as though they have just been tipped out of a shopping bag, the paintings have a sense of depth, distance and perspective, with a highly saturated aesthetic. Like his flower pieces, they are colossal, with grapes the size of golf balls and lemons bigger than your head. Nesbitt enjoyed working on an oversized scale; his biggest painting was 10.6 metres (35 feet) long. In his vast home, the artist lived a larger-than-life existence that extended into his artworks, which – like Nesbitt himself – are no wallflowers.

BEETROOT-CURED SALMON WITH HOMEMADE BLINIS

—

This recipe creates bouquets of hors d'oeuvres, so beautiful that no one would ever guess how simple they are to make. Start the salmon a couple of days before you need it and prepare the blinis in advance, so that you can quickly assemble them before your guests arrive.

SERVES 10–12

FOR THE SALMON
1 teaspoon ground coriander
1 teaspoon cracked black pepper
3 beetroots, peeled and coarsely grated
200 g (¾ cup) coarse sea salt
200 g (1 cup) Demerara sugar
1 whole side of salmon, skin off and pin-boned (about 600 g / 21 oz)

FOR THE BLINIS
125 g (¾ cup plus 2 tablespoons) plain flour (all-purpose flour)
1 teaspoon baking powder
Fine salt
1 egg plus 1 egg yolk
250 ml (1 cup) full fat milk
Unsalted butter, for cooking

TO SERVE
2 unwaxed lemons
200 ml (¾ cup plus 1 tablespoon) thick crème frâiche
1 teaspoon cracked black pepper, plus more for garnish
Fine salt

Start the salmon at least 48 hours before you want to serve it. Tip the coriander and pepper into a large bowl, along with the grated beetroot, salt and Demerara sugar and mix well to combine. I recommend using gloves to avoid staining your hands.

Arrange three layers of cling film over a baking dish that is large enough to hold the salmon and has sides that are at least 2.5 cm (1 in) deep and leave some cling film hanging over the sides. Tip out half of the salt mixture and spread it evenly over the bottom of the dish. Lay the salmon on top and cover it with the rest of the salt mixture, making sure it is completely covered. Wrap the overhanging cling film over the salmon like a parcel and add another layer or two as needed to completely wrap the salmon.

Put the baking dish in the refrigerator and use cans or whatever you have on hand to evenly weigh down the salmon.

After 24 hours, tip out and discard any liquid from the baking dish that has escaped from the cling film, then flip the salmon, still wrapped in cling film, and weigh it down again. Return the baking dish to the refrigerator.

After another 24 hours, discard the beetroot salt mixture and briefly rinse the fish under cold water to remove any excess.

Use a sharp knife to slice the salmon so thinly that the slices are translucent when held up to the light. Serve the salmon as a starter with the sauce on the side, or as a canapé, as described below.

For the blinis, combine the plain flour, baking powder and a pinch of salt in a large bowl. Make a well in the centre and tip in the egg and egg yolk. Slowly pour in the milk, whisking as you go, until you have a smooth batter. Leave it to sit for 10 minutes.

Heat a nonstick frying pan over medium-low heat and grease it with a little butter. Drop spoonfuls (about 1 tablespoon) of the batter around the pan to create bite-size rounds – you should get about 40 – and cook, flipping once the top side starts to set, for about 90 seconds on each side. Transfer to a wire rack to cool. Repeat to cook the rest of the blinis.

When ready to serve the canapés, cut 1 of the lemons into wedges and set aside. Zest and juice the other lemon. Set aside some of the zest for garnish then combine the remaining zest with 1 teaspoon of the lemon juice, the crème frâiche, pepper and a pinch of salt.

Spread the blinis with a swirl of the crème frâiche mixture and place 1 or 2 thin slices of the salmon on top, arranging the fish like the petals of a flower. Finish with a sprinkle of lemon zest and pepper and serve with the lemon wedges on the side.

Notes: You can make the blinis a few hours in advance or freeze them if making them a few days ahead. Leave them on the counter to defrost for a couple of hours before you need them.

To store the salmon, wrap it in cling film and keep it in the refrigerator for up to 4 days.

GEORGE SEGAL

—

George Segal started his career not as an artist but as a chicken farmer. Growing up during the Great Depression, his parents had a kosher butcher shop in the Bronx before moving to New Jersey to run a poultry farm. When World War II began, his brother was drafted into the military, but Segal stayed with his parents to help on the farm, attending university in the evenings in New York, graduating in art education. In time, he started his own chicken farm and began to look for jobs as an art teacher to make extra money for his family.

Eventually, Segal took up an art practice of his own. Fascinated by Abstract Expressionism, he started his career as a painter. However, his enjoyment of the physical aspects of farm work soon led him to pursue the more physical medium of sculpture, utilising materials from the farm, such as chicken wire and burlap. 'I never liked chickens', he said, 'I liked building the chicken houses.' Opting for art over poultry, Segal disposed of his flock and transformed his farm into something like an artists' residency, hosting artist friends and converting farm buildings into studios. In 1961, he created his first body-cast figure, *Man Sitting at a Table*, using a casting technique with plaster that he continued to employ for the rest of his career. By making casts directly from human figures, he was able to create sculptures that expressed tangible human emotions, using real gestures and body language.

Although Segal's work is associated with the Pop Art movement because of its references to mass culture, his work has a feeling of intimacy that separates it from other pieces of the era. For example, many of his prints and drawings focus on cropped parts of the body to depict subtle, familiar gestures, magnifying tiny, everyday moments. Labelled by the artist as 'assembled environments', Segal's sculptures focus on moments and emotions experienced by the masses through the lens of the individual: a woman sits in solitary contemplation (*Woman in a Restaurant Booth*, 1961); a man orders from a hot dog vendor (*Hot Dog Stand*, 1978); a waitress pours coffee for a customer (*The Diner*, 1964–1966). The moments Segal captures are familiar and relatable, but they also have a unique, almost ridiculous, sacredness to them; a quietness you wouldn't want to disturb.

As such, Segal's work has a serious tone that lends itself to commemorating dark moments in history. As the artist was well aware, the Great Depression had been a challenging time for the nation, and in 1991, he was commissioned to create a sculpture to commemorate the hardship experienced by many Americans living in urban areas who suffered from hunger during the 1930s. *Depression Bread Line* shows five desperate and hungry men standing in line, waiting for food. Although they stand together, each figure is isolated and tilts their head to hide their face with their hat. Despite one in four workers being unemployed, it was still considered shameful to accept charity and the figures' destitution is palpable. The men are plaster casts of four of Segal's friends, as well as himself. They are anonymous, yet still so personal. Unlike many of his works which remain forever as white, ghostly plaster, this piece was cast in bronze to ensure its durability outside. And now, the men have been waiting for so long, they've started to weather. A testament to their resilience and in turn, the resilience of art: a powerful form of expression that can come out of anywhere. Even a chicken farm.

George Segal, *Human by Rattan*, 1978
Color serigraph, 88.9 × 81.28 cm
Private collection

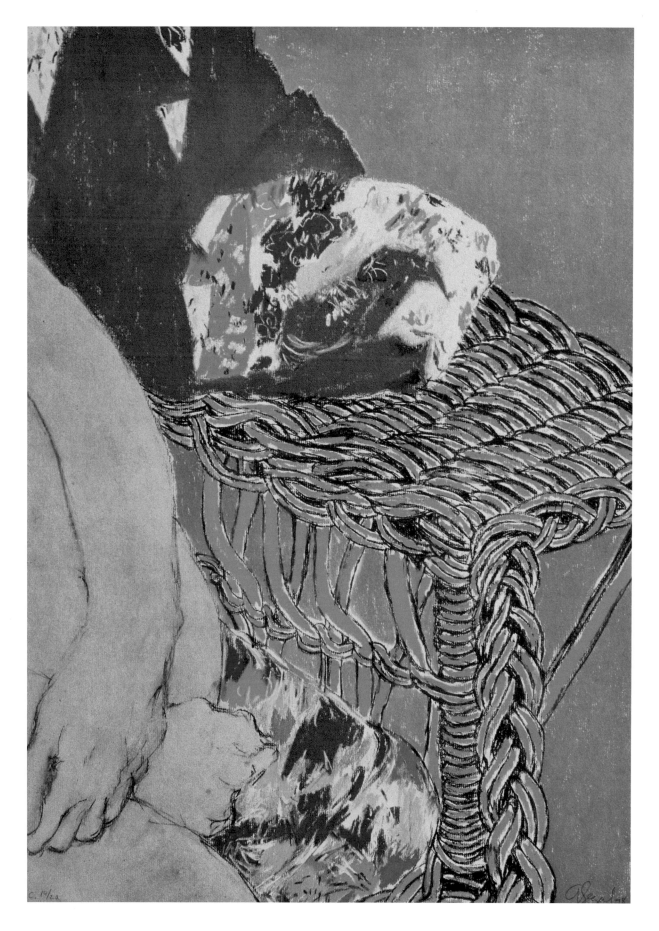

C. 19/20

BRAIDED SUN-DRIED TOMATO AND FETA BREAD

—

Inspired in part by challah, this loaf is rich and fluffy, with a filling of pesto, sun-dried tomatoes and feta cheese. It's particularly good served with eggs for a unique and satisfying breakfast.

MAKES 1 LOAF

FOR THE DOUGH
3.5 g (1⅛ teaspoons) active dry yeast
2 teaspoons caster sugar (superfine sugar)
100 ml (⅓ cup plus 1 tablespoon) full fat milk, warm (about 35°C / 100°F)
2 tablespoons unsalted butter, melted
½ teaspoon fine salt
2 eggs
350 g (2½ cups) plain flour (all-purpose flour)
1 teaspoon olive oil

FOR THE FILLING
100 g (½ cup) red tomato pesto
100 g (3½ oz) drained sun-dried tomatoes
100 g (3½ oz) feta cheese

TO SERVE
1 small handful fresh basil leaves, roughly chopped

Combine the yeast and caster sugar in a small bowl. Pour over the warm milk and let it stand in a warm place for 10 minutes; it should look quite foamy.

Add the melted butter, salt and eggs. Whisk until fully combined.

Fold in the plain flour. Once the dough starts coming together, tip it out onto a floured surface and knead it for 2–3 minutes, or until it becomes smooth and elastic. It will feel quite dense at this point. Sprinkle over small pinches of flour as needed to prevent sticking.

Drizzle the olive oil in a large clean bowl, add the dough and move it around to coat the dough and the sides of the bowl to prevent sticking as the dough rises. Cover the bowl tightly with cling film and put it in a warm place for 1–2 hours, or until the dough has doubled in size.

Line a 900 g (2 lb) loaf tin with parchment paper, leaving 2–3 cm (about 1 in) hanging over the sides to make it easier to remove the loaf later.

Punch down the dough to deflate it and tip it out onto a lightly floured surface.

Use a rolling pin to roll out the dough into a 30 × 25 cm (12 × 10 in) rectangle. Spread the pesto over the surface, leaving a 2 cm (¾ in) border around the edges. Roughly chop the sun-dried tomatoes and scatter them over the top. Crumble over the feta.

Starting on one of the long sides, tightly roll the dough around the filling to create a log and pinch the ends to seal them.

Use a sharp knife to halve the dough lengthwise, then turn each half to face upwards so you can see the layers. Pinch the top of the two strands together. Carefully wrap the strands over each other to create a twist, keeping the layers facing upwards – this can be a messy process. Pinch the bottom ends together and tuck both ends underneath the loaf for a neater look.

Carefully transfer the braided loaf to the prepared loaf tin, with the braid facing up and cover it loosely with a clean tea towel. Leave it to rise again for 40 minutes.

Set a rack near the bottom of the oven and preheat the oven to 180°C / 160°C fan (350°F / 320°F fan).

Set the tin on a baking tray, set it on the lower oven rack and bake for 35 minutes, or until a skewer inserted in the centre comes out clean – check a few spots to ensure it is evenly cooked. If the exposed filling starts to brown too much, cover the bread lightly with a piece of parchment paper.

Set the bread on a wire rack to cool in the tin for 20–30 minutes before slicing. Sprinkle over the chopped basil and serve.

MAN RAY
—

In 1961, Man Ray's *Menu for a Dadaist Day* was published in *The Artists' and Writers' Cookbook*. He created recipes for breakfast, lunch and dinner. All were totally inedible.

Dadaists were interested in exploring the bizarre, the illogical and the irrational, and this 'menu' is no exception. To create Man Ray's breakfast the chef must 'take a wooden panel of an inch or less thickness, 16–20 inches in size. Gather the brightly coloured wooden blocks left by children on the floors of playrooms and paste or screw them on the panel.' Lunch, on the other hand, mentions food, if only to discard it: 'Take the olives and juice from one large jar of prepared green or black olives and throw them away. In the empty jar place several steel ball bearings. Fill the jar with machine oil to prevent rusting. With this delicacy serve a loaf of French bread, 30 inches in length, painted a pale blue.' Man Ray also created this blue loaf as a separate artwork: *Blue Bread – Favourite food for the Blue Birds* (1958/1966). Originally a real painted bread loaf (as per the recipe), the work had to be remodelled in plaster for its buyer in 1964, after mice discovered its predecessor. The Dadaist day ends with a feast of wooden eggs on skewers served in a pan covered in cling film.

When he wasn't crafting these recipes / performance artworks, food continued to influence much of Man Ray's work and personal life. He was knowledgeable about food and wine and went only to the best restaurants, often enjoying lengthy, luxurious lunches with his lover and muse, photographer Lee Miller. Man Ray had a significant influence on Miller, not only on her practice but on her culinary life too: 'Man Ray taught me how to eat', she said. But it wasn't until a few years later, once she had married artist Roland Penrose, that Miller really learnt how to cook. Naturally gifted, she hosted countless dinner parties, coming up with artistic (and often surreal) recipes for her guests, some of which were intended to be included in a cookbook she was working on. *Entertaining Freezer* was to be a book dedicated to helping women achieve impressive dinner party menus with ease by fully utilising the freezer and preparing many of the elements in advance.

Among the list of unusual dishes of Miller's invention, were such delicacies as *Gold Fish* (whole cod covered in a mound of grated carrot and onion), *Gold Chicken* (roast chicken, covered with gold leaf), *Persian Carpet* (a chilled orange and rose-water dessert, inspired by her travels in North Africa), *Cauliflower Breasts* (cauliflower domes with pink mayonnaise, topped with an egg slice and caviar), *Melted Tomato Thing* (a baked tomato and tapioca concoction) and *Tomato Soup Cake* (which is exactly as it sounds).

But even with her drive to experiment, Miller was a particularly attentive host and made note of her guests' likes, dislikes and their dietary requirements to make sure everyone was taken care of. Man Ray's name was annotated with 'no salt'. After years of lavish dining, his diet had taken a dramatic turn. He began to follow the Hay Diet which, according to Miller, meant eating nothing more than 'four lettuce leaves and a piece of bacon'. She was not impressed by the restrictions the diet imposed: 'You could never eat potatoes or starch on the same day you ate fruit, or fruit on the same day you ate meat. Talk about food taboos!' Better than wooden play blocks, I suppose.

Man Ray, *Pisces*, 1938
Oil on canvas, 60 × 73 cm
Tate, London

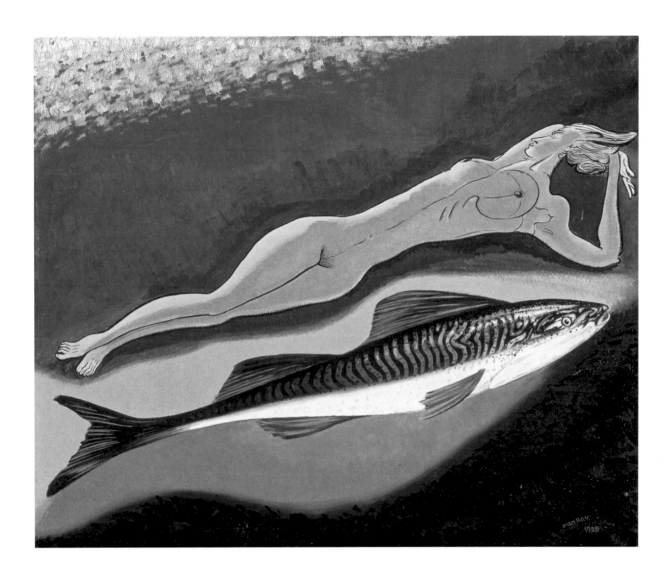

RHUBARB-SOUSED MACKEREL

—

This beautiful dish embraces rhubarb's natural sharpness to enhance the flavours of the pickling liquor. If you like mackerel and you like pickles, this is really worth a try. Serve the fish fillets whole as part of a grazing board or slice them into small pieces to create elegant canapés.

SERVES 4–12,
AS A SNACK OR CANAPÉ

3 pink rhubarb stalks (about 250 g / 8 ¾ oz)
1 small red onion
200 ml (¾ cup plus 1 tablespoon) white wine vinegar
3 tablespoons caster sugar (superfine sugar)
8 whole black peppercorns
2 bay leaves
1 teaspoon fine salt
4 mackerel fillets, skin on and pin boned

Chop the rhubarb crosswise on a diagonal into 2.5 cm (1 in) pieces and set aside.

Halve the red onion, cut it into thin half-moons and put them in a medium saucepan. Add the white wine vinegar, caster sugar, peppercorns, bay leaves and salt, then put the pan over medium heat and bring to a simmer. Add the rhubarb, reduce the heat slightly and cook for 3–4 more minutes, or until the rhubarb is slightly softened but still holding its shape. Remove from the heat.

Arrange the mackerel fillets, skin-side up and in a single layer, in a shallow dish. Pour over the hot pickling liquid and let cool to room temperature.

Once cool, cover the dish with cling film and refrigerate for 24 hours.

Serve the mackerel as you wish – with crème fraîche and crackers; on blinis as a canapé; on top of a watercress salad; or as part of a grazing board.

MAINS

ANDY WARHOL
—

Andy Warhol was a sugar addict. Alongside Pepsi and Coca-Cola, he lived on sweets, chocolate and 'anything with red dye #2 in it'. His favourite treat was chocolate; from the luxurious 'Frrrozen hot chocolate' at the New York restaurant Serendipity3, where he spent almost two thousand dollars in 1966 (equivalent to over twenty thousand today), to his own budget recipe for 'cake', which consisted of nothing more than a bar of chocolate between two slices of white bread.

But, apart from these indulgent moments, Warhol often didn't eat much at all. He suffered from body dysmorphia and obsessed over being thin. He often made it his goal to avoid eating altogether if he could help it, with the added help of diet pills: 'I like to go to bad restaurants, because then I don't have to eat', he said. 'When I order...I order everything that I don't want, so I have a lot to play around with while everyone else eats'. He was particularly reluctant to eat meat and only ate it to make himself look 'normal': 'I'm only kidding myself when I go through the motions of cooking protein: all I ever really want is sugar...People expect you to eat protein and you do so they won't talk.'

Keeping up appearances, in 1982 Warhol agreed to take part in Jørgen Leth's film 66 Scenes from America, in which he eats a fast-food burger – the footage of which was later used by Burger King for their ad campaign during the 2019 Super Bowl. He doesn't seem to enjoy it. No matter how hard he tried, this sugar addict always wanted something sweet: 'I'll buy a huge piece of meat, cook it up for dinner, and then right before it's done I'll break down and have what I wanted for dinner in the first place – bread and jam.' The artist's other dream meals included such delicacies as toast and tea, boiled chicken, corn on the cob and of course, Campbell's canned soup – or, as Warhol called it, 'the food of life' – which, according to the artist, he ate every day for twenty years.

Warhol's love for this red and white can also took centre stage in his artwork. He repeatedly drew on branded packaging from his everyday life and diet and the Campbell's soup can became one of his most iconic images, alongside bananas, Coca-Cola bottles, Lifesavers sweets, Kellogg's Cornflakes and Heinz Tomato Ketchup, which Warhol considered to be his 'big sin'. Interested in mechanical reproduction, his creative process mimicked the production line of this industrially produced food,

resulting in a style that became as instantly recognisable as the cans of soup on the shelves.

Unexpectedly, this lover of mass-produced food had in fact created a cookbook earlier in his career. In 1959, Warhol self-published *Wild Raspberries*, a colourful collaboration with Suzie Frankfurt, an interior designer who had discovered Warhol's work at an exhibition at his favourite restaurant Serendipity3. Described by Frankfurt as 'a funny cookbook for people who don't cook', the book is a feast for the eyes, with some truly unique recipes (if you can call them that). *Roast Iguana Andalusian* requires ingredients that are only found on the Galapagos Islands; *Omelet Greta Garbo* states it should be 'eaten alone in a candlelit room'; and *Chocolate Balls à la Chambord* demands the purchase of chocolate truffles from a specific pastry shop in New York, which, once acquired, are only to be served 'to very thin people'. Transforming food into art, each page features a large and joyful illustration of the otherworldly dishes by Warhol with Frankfurt's recipe instructions scrawled into the remaining space by Warhol's mother in beautiful calligraphy. Wanting the book to be hand coloured, the pair hired four young boys who lived upstairs to colour in the designs, but it took so long that they only produced 34 copies in total. Not quite the money-making masterpiece they'd hoped for.

Of course, this didn't hinder Warhol's eventual rise to fame. But as his fame increased, his health deteriorated, and the artist was forced to dramatically improve his diet. He swapped Coca-Cola for carrot juice and stopped eating anything that came out of a can, but it was too little, too late. Warhol was in poor health. An operation on his gallbladder found it to be full of gangrene from a gun wound he had sustained nearly twenty years earlier. He died in hospital aged fifty-eight. He was never to be forgotten as the man who turned basic shop ingredients into internationally recognised icons; they, in turn, made him one of the most famous artists in history. A testament to the power of marketing, the power of art and the power of food.

Andy Warhol, *100 Cans*, 1962
Casein, spray paint and pencil on cotton, 182.88 × 132.08 cm
Buffalo AKG Art Museum, Buffalo

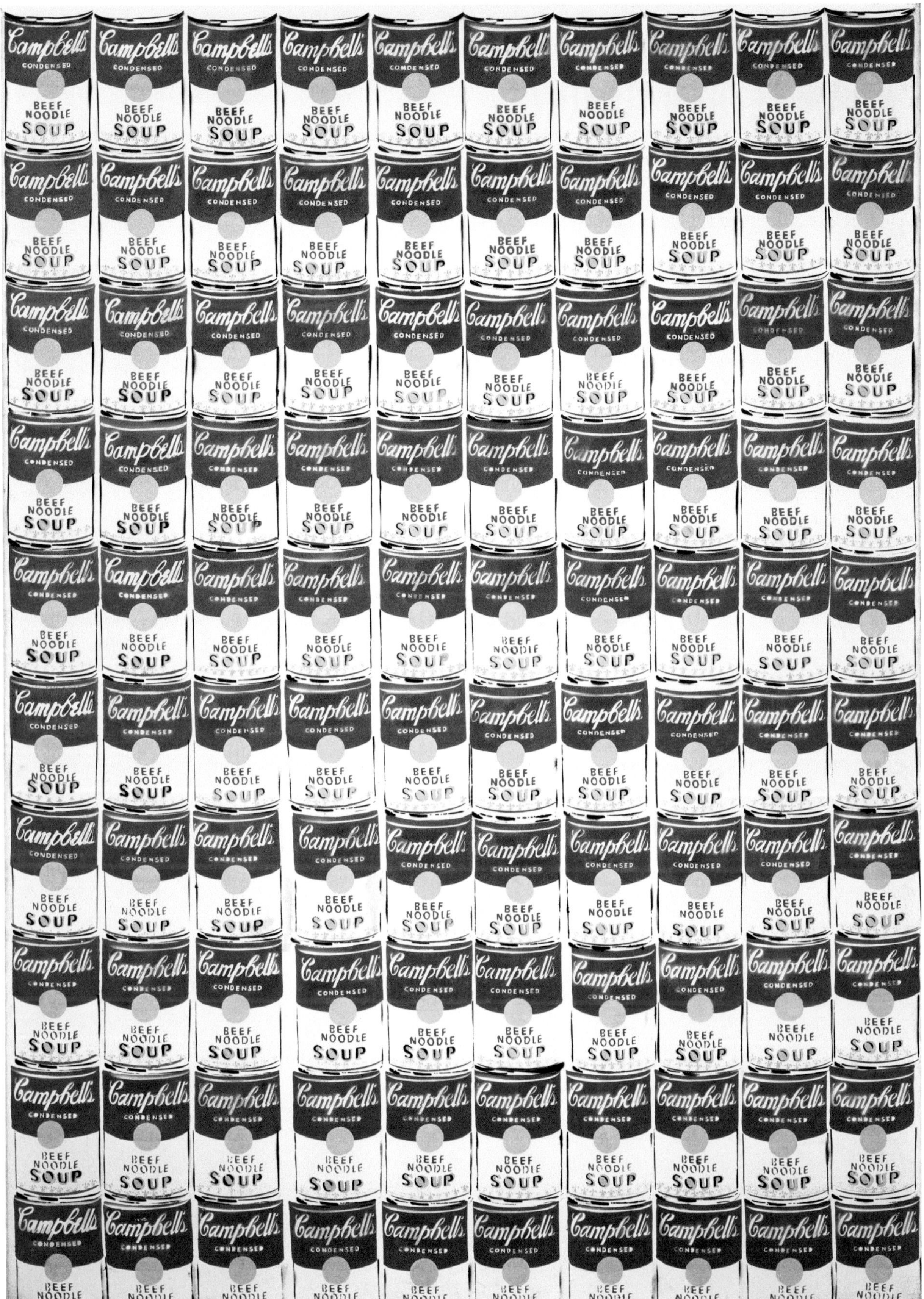
Campbell's
CONDENSED
BEEF
NOODLE
SOUP

TOMATO AND MOZZARELLA GALETTE WITH CARAMELISED ONIONS

—

This dish embodies the flavours of Andy Warhol's favourite tomato soup and with a base of caramelised onions, it's sure to have appealed to the artist's sweet tooth.

MAKES 1 TART-WORK SERVES 4–8, AS MAIN OR STARTER

2 tablespoons unsalted butter
2 tablespoons olive oil
4 large onions, finely chopped
Fine salt
1 tablespoon balsamic vinegar
375 g (12½ oz) puff pastry (thawed, if frozen)
250 g (8¾ oz) fresh mozzarella
6 yellow cherry tomatoes
5 large red tomatoes
High-quality extra-virgin olive oil, for drizzling
Cracked black pepper
Flaky sea salt

In a large frying pan, warm the butter and olive oil over high heat until the butter is melted. Add the onions and sprinkle in 2 pinches of salt. Stir and reduce the heat to low. Cook, stirring regularly, for 30–40 minutes, or until the onions are caramelised and jammy. Stir through the balsamic vinegar and cook for another minute. Season with additional salt and set aside to cool.

Preheat the oven to 180°C / 160°C fan (350°F / 320°F fan).

On a lightly floured surface, use a rolling pin to roll out the puff pastry into a 30 × 25 cm (12 × 10 in) rectangle. Carefully transfer the puff pastry to a baking tray lined with parchment paper. Use a knife to score a line around the edge of the pastry to create a 2 cm (¾ in) border. Prick inside the border with a fork.

Place a piece of parchment paper over the pastry, covering the entire sheet, and pour baking beans into the central rectangle. Bake for 15 minutes. Remove the beans and paper, turn the tray around so that the opposite edge is facing the back of the oven this time, and bake for 10 more minutes. Transfer the pastry on the parchment paper to a wire rack to cool.

Cut the mozzarella and tomatoes across their equator into ½ cm (⅙ in) thick slices.

Spread the jammy onions across the entire centre of the tart, keeping the border clean. Arrange a row of 4 mozzarella slices on top of the onions and across one of the shorter sides. Add a row of 3 yellow cherry tomato slices, placing them on top of where the mozzarella slices meet. Top with a layer of 4 red tomato slices, overlapping them with the other toppings. Repeat until you have covered the onion to create a scale-like pattern.

To serve, drizzle with a little of the olive oil and sprinkle with a generous crack of black pepper and flaky sea salt.

GUSTAV KLIMT
—

During his holidays at Lake Attersee, Gustav Klimt prepared himself for a long day of painting with a hearty portion of whipped cream.

He spent his days by the lake enjoying the luxuries of the great outdoors – painting and swimming – and always carving out plenty of time to eat to fuel his creativity. The artist outlined his daily routine in a detailed letter to his lover Marie (Mizzi) Zimmermann: 'In the early morning I get up, usually at 6 o'clock – sometimes a little earlier, sometimes a little later. If the weather is good I go into the nearby wood – there I am painting a small beech forest (in the sun) with a few conifers mixed in. This takes until 8 o'clock. Then I have breakfast and after that a swim in the lake, taken with all due caution. Then I paint again for a while … Then it's midday. After lunch I have a short nap or read – until the afternoon snack. Before or after tea I go for a second swim in the lake – not always but usually. After tea it's back to painting … Dusk falls – supper – then early to bed and early to rise the next morning.'

For his first meal of the day, the artist would often walk four kilometres (2.4 miles) to Tivoli, a dairy and cafe, where he was joined by friends, such as fellow artists Egon Schiele, Wilhelm Dessauer and Carl Moll. According to Moll, Klimt would reward his morning exercise with a hearty breakfast of *gugelhupf* – a bundt-like sponge cake – and 'a huge portion of whipped cream … to get him through the day.' Discussions about art were forbidden; this was a time for eating.

For lunch, Klimt often ate alone, either a picnic in the woods while he worked or in the house before his nap. He spent a lot of time painting in the forests surrounding the lake and the locals came to call him *'Waldschrat'* ('Forest Demon') as he would often be seen disappearing into the trees in his flowing robes, lugging a large supply of painting materials with him. *Beech Forest I* (1902) was created during his 6 a.m. painting sessions in the woods before breakfast, capturing the orange morning sun glinting through the trees.

He enjoyed this secluded lifestyle. Klimt had risen to fame in Vienna for his highly stylised figurative paintings with opulent decoration. His most famous work *The Kiss* (1907/08), is the epitome of his lavish style, with gold leaf, silver and platinum embellishment. But as Klimt aged, he sought out a more isolated existence. He spent much of his time on the banks of Lake Attersee, painting the landscape more for his own personal pleasure than financial gain. Unadorned, these paintings might appear to be a stark contrast to his figurative pieces, but despite the lack of gold leaf they are just as rich, exhibiting the lushness of nature with a profusion of leaves and flowers in jewel-like tones.

One critic, who reviewed Klimt's retrospective exhibition in 1903, said, 'Klimt's landscapes should be in an exhibition on Mars or Neptune; thank God things look somewhat different on our planet.' You can see what he meant. The explosion of life, through small pointillist dabs of paint, seems to be in almost hyper-focus. Klimt was known to use binoculars to zoom in on the scene to paint chosen elements in greater detail, which creates a sense of being both up close to, and far away from, the view. Many of the flowers look edible, as if candied. When he wasn't painting the forest, he zoomed in on the fruit orchard to paint the apple trees or the church at Unterach which he affectionately described as onion shaped.

As an artist who applied himself with such energy to the canvas, sitting out in the elements, it's no surprise that Klimt required such a calorific breakfast. It is, after all, the most important meal of the day – made even better, no doubt, by a large dollop of whipped cream.

Gustav Klimt, *Beech Forest I*, 1902
Oil on canvas, 100 × 100 cm
Albertinum, Galerie Neue Meister, Dresden

WARM FOREST MUSHROOM AND WILD RICE SALAD

—

A combination of autumnal woodland produce and earthy and zesty flavours, this fresh and comforting dish celebrates the abundance of wild mushrooms that can be found in the forest, including around Austria's Lake Attersee where Gustav Klimt made so much of his work. It is quite simply autumn on a plate.

SERVES 4

FOR THE DRESSING
1 large handful fresh dill
60 ml (¼ cup) white wine vinegar
60 ml (¼ cup) extra-virgin olive oil
Fine salt

FOR THE RICE
Fine salt
250 g (8¾ oz) wild rice blend (a mix of wild, brown and red rice)
1 fresh rosemary sprig
360 g (12 oz) mixed wild mushrooms
60 ml (4 tablespoons) olive oil
2 echalion shallots (banana shallots)
1½ tablespoons unsalted butter
2 garlic cloves
120 g (4 oz) chestnut (cremini) mushrooms
100 g (3½ oz) pecans

Preheat the oven to 180°C / 160°C fan (350°F / 320°F fan).

For the dressing, finely chop the dill and set aside about 3 tablespoons for garnish. Put the remaining dill in a jar and add the white wine vinegar, oil and a pinch of salt. Screw on the lid and shake to mix everything together. Set the dressing aside to infuse, giving it a good shake every now and then to get as much flavour as possible out of the dill.

For the rice, combine 500 ml (2 cups) of water and 1 teaspoon of salt in a large saucepan and bring to a boil. Add the rice and rosemary sprig and reduce the heat to a gentle simmer. Cover the pan with a lid and cook for 35–40 minutes, or according to the packet instructions.

As the rice cooks, toss the wild mushrooms with 2 tablespoons of the olive oil in a baking dish. Roast for 15–25 minutes, depending on the type and size of the mushrooms, or until softened and golden.

Meanwhile, finely chop the shallots. Melt the butter and the remaining 2 tablespoons of olive oil in a frying pan over medium-low heat. Add the shallots and sauté for 3–5 minutes, or until translucent. Crush in the garlic and cook for 1–2 more minutes.

As the shallots cook, chop the chestnut mushrooms into quarters. Add them to the pan and turn up the heat slightly. Cook, stirring regularly, for 5–7 minutes, or until the mushrooms are softened and slightly browned. Transfer to a bowl and set aside.

Put the pan over medium heat and toast the pecans, stirring frequently to prevent burning, for 2–3 minutes, or until lightly browned. Remove from the heat and roughly chop.

Remove the rosemary from the rice and discard. The rice should now be fluffy and dry. Gently fold in the shallot and chestnut mushroom mixture, along with most of the pecans. Pour over the dressing and mix gently.

To serve, tip the hot, fragrant rice onto a serving platter. Scatter the wild mushrooms and reserved pecans over the top. Finish with the reserved dill leaves and serve.

SAKAI HŌITSU
—

During the eighteenth century the Zen Buddhist diet was adopted across most of Japan and the now-classic flavours of miso, soy sauce and wasabi became staples. It was the Edo period, a time of peace and economic growth with innovation in the arts and in food, which would influence Japanese culture forever.

Ogata Kōrin was an artist of the Rinpa School (also spelled Rimpa), whose style Sakai Hōitsu would go on to revive. Its members were recognised for their dynamic depiction of nature, making highly decorated paintings, ceramics and screens inspired by Japanese literature and poetry. But Kōrin had not always been a devoted artist. Born into a wealthy family, he inherited money from his father, which he spent with great enthusiasm. The extravagance of his lifestyle is humorously summed up by the story of a grand picnic he held with his friends. Each guest presented beautiful dishes one by one, all edible works of art, encased in lacquered boxes. But Kōrin provided the grand finale and presented his dish wrapped in bamboo skins which were decorated with gold leaf on the inside. After the meal, as a further demonstration of his opulence and wealth, he threw the leaves into the river. This was not only shocking but against the law and the dramatic young man was banned from Kyoto. It was only once his inheritance ran out that he turned to art as a career and developed his own style – using plenty of gold leaf – which Hōitsu would adopt.

Hōitsu was also born into wealth. His family were influential daimyos who had been patrons of Kōrin's work; when Kōrin first came to Edo, they had supported him with a rice allowance large enough for ten people. Hōitsu was the second son and did not inherit the family fortune. But, being the son of a daimyo, he was expected to study the military arts as well as haiku poetry and the tea ceremony. His elder brother had studied under the great tea master Matsudaira Fumai and was a keen collector of tea utensils, including pieces of lacquerware and pottery created by Kōrin, and his enthusiasm likely sparked Hōitsu's interest in the ritual.

The tea ceremony is a tradition steeped in Zen Buddhist teachings that dates back to the twelfth century. In the medieval period, the samurai class used the ritual to build political alliances, but today it is practised as an art form and preserved as a unique cultural tradition. The ceremony is a spiritual exchange between the host and their guest. The host prepares the tea; by drinking it, the guest takes in the sentiments and well wishes of the host, and they come together in respect and tranquillity.

After studying the tea ceremony, Hōitsu went on to become a Buddhist priest and spent twenty-one years in seclusion, dedicating his time to painting, poetry and calligraphy. He studied the work of Kōrin, which in turn inspired his own artwork, eventually developing his own Edo method. The Edo Rinpa School was more heavily focused on natural imagery with a particular emphasis on the four seasons and the changes they bring. *Persimmon Tree* (1816), depicts a small persimmon tree laden with fruit and the delicate movement of grasses blowing in the breeze below. His work also often includes references to the tea ceremony. *Fan Painting – Camellia and Tea Bowl* (late 18th century) is a beautiful example of Hōitsu's sensitive approach to objects, rituals and the natural world.

As art was developing in the tranquillity of nature, food was changing in the chaos of the cities. The Edo period was a particularly influential moment in culinary history. Eating out became popular due to urbanisation alongside an increase in general wealth, and food stalls popped up around the capital Edo (now Tokyo). Street vendors innovated to serve fast food such as soba and tempura. Soba, which was once the food of temples, became more widespread, the noodles cut shorter to make them easier to eat quickly standing up. Sushi also appeared, along with unagi (charcoal grilled eel) and nori (dried seaweed). These dishes remain firmly in the Japanese diet to this day and have travelled overseas to Europe and beyond, influencing other cuisines.

The Edo period also had a significant impact on European art. The work of the Rinpa and Edo Rinpa Schools reached Europe in the nineteenth century and Kōrin and Hōitsu's paintings heavily influenced the Post-Impressionists and artists of the Art Nouveau, who were all capturing their own experiences of nature, over eight thousand miles away. A power of influence Hōitsu or Kōrin could never have predicted.

Sakai Hōitsu, *Persimmon Tree*, 1816
Two-panel folding screen; ink and
color on paper, 143.7 × 143.8 cm
The Metropolitan Museum of Art, New York

GOLDEN RAMEN-STYLE SOUP WITH SOY-CURED QUAIL EGG YOLKS

—

The history of ramen and its origin are heavily debated. According to the Shin-Yokohama Ramen Museum, this famous noodle dish arrived in Japan in the late 1800s, brought over by Chinese immigrants. Like the work of the Edo Rinpa School, which came as a development of the original Rinpa School, Japanese ramen is an adaptation and has been developed over time to become one of the most popular dishes in Japan.

Ramen is a true craft that can take years to learn, with some chefs dedicating their entire careers to mastering the dish. I will not insult these great culinary artists by claiming this to be an authentic ramen recipe, but I have instead developed my own adaptation and created a ramen-style noodle soup with a British twist of peppery watercress and creamy cured quail egg yolks. You can, of course, serve one normal hen's egg yolk per bowl if you prefer – just double the curing time.

SERVES 4

FOR THE CURED EGG YOLKS
8 quail egg yolks
80 ml (⅓ cup) soy sauce, plus more as needed

FOR THE RAMEN
3 cm (1¼ in) piece fresh ginger
2 garlic cloves
1 tablespoon sunflower oil
5 whole black peppercorns
2 star anise pods
1 cinnamon stick
1 tablespoon white miso paste
560 ml (2¼ cups) vegetable stock
60 ml (¼ cup) soy sauce
2 tablespoons mirin
1 teaspoon lemon juice
200 g (7 oz) ramen noodles

TO SERVE
4 teaspoons chilli oil (see page 36)
1 handful fresh watercress

For the cured egg yolks, place the egg yolks in a shallow bowl that is wide enough to keep them all separate. Pour in the soy sauce to cover the bottom halves of the yolks, adding more as needed, and place in the refrigerator for 1 hour, then delicately turn them over with a spoon and return to the refrigerator for 1 more hour.

For the ramen, finely chop the ginger and garlic.

Heat the sunflower oil in a large saucepan over a medium heat. Add the garlic and ginger and fry for 1–2 minutes. Add the peppercorns, star anise and cinnamon and fry for 30 more seconds.

Dissolve the miso paste in 560 ml (2¼ cups) of hot (but not boiling) water from the kettle and add it to the pan. Pour in the stock and simmer, stirring regularly and making sure it doesn't boil, for 5 minutes.

Pour in the soy sauce, mirin and lemon juice. Turn off the heat and leave it to infuse for 30 minutes. Strain through a sieve to remove the spices, return the broth to the saucepan and bring to a simmer but do not boil.

Bring a large pan of water to a boil. Add the noodles and boil for 2–3 minutes, according to the packet instructions, or until cooked through. Drain.

To serve, use tongs to divide the noodles among 4 bowls, twist the tongs slightly before removing them to create a neat pile of noodles in the centre of each bowl. Pour over the broth to almost cover the noodles.

Remove the egg yolks from the soy sauce with a spoon and carefully drain off any excess liquid. Place 2 egg yolks on top of each bowl of noodles. Drizzle a little chilli oil over the broth, add 2–3 stems of fresh watercress and serve immediately.

CLARA PEETERS

—

Clara Peeters' paintings reflect the time in which she lived; her still lifes forever preserve the foods of the seventeenth-century Netherlands. Peeters worked during the Dutch Golden Age, a period of great prosperity during which Dutch trading and art were some of the most acclaimed in Europe. Showcasing wealth, she depicted an array of luxurious ingredients, such as salt (elegantly stored in silver salt cellars), almonds, raisins and figs imported from the Mediterranean and locally baked breads. The Dutch ate four meals a day and all included bread, which was served with butter and cheese or meat, or else stirred into porridge. Peeters depicted expensive wheat breads in her paintings (poorer people ate heavy, rye-based breads), as well as pretzels, which were eaten by the rich and poor alike.

Pretzels were associated with fasting and the period of Lent in Christianity, appearing across many eras of Dutch art, as far back as medieval manuscripts. Made without dairy or eggs, their looped shape represents a pair of hands brought together in penitential prayer. Cheese was also a large part of the Dutch diet at this time. High in fats, it was an important source of calories. Cheese was relatively affordable as it was produced locally but it was also a major export item, along with butter. Dairy was prohibited during the period of Lent, but in many of Peeters' compositions, cheese and pretzels appear side by side. A number of her still-life scenes are dominated by three vast wheels of cheese stacked on top of one another. For example, in *Still Life with Cheeses, Almonds and Pretzels* (1615), a cheese tower is topped with a plate of butter curls, defying the Dutch saying that 'dairy product on dairy product brings the devil.' It could be that Peeters is referring to the period between Shrove Tuesday and Lent, inspired by Bruegel's famous painting *The Fight between Carnival and Lent* (1559); in a chaotic scene of two hundred characters, pretzels, meat and fish are depicted together as people say goodbye to meat before the fast.

Perhaps symbolising the end of fasting – or else another defiance of the rules of Lent – Peeters' paintings often include wine, displayed in ornate Italian glasses. Most Dutch meals were washed down with local beer, which was safer than water. Wine was reserved for the wealthy, imported from Germany, France and Italy. Blue-and-white Chinese porcelain dishes were also brought to the Netherlands by the Dutch East India Company and these appear alongside shining metal plates and goblets in Peeters' compositions; a variety of surfaces and textures demonstrating her prodigious skill.

But it could be that Peeters was slightly ashamed of the wealth of the Golden Age and the indulgence it inspired. A silver knife sits in the foreground of *Still Life with Cheeses, Almonds and Pretzels* with the word *'Tempa'* ('temperance') engraved into its handle. An exhortation for moderation and restraint in a time of such abundance, perhaps? The artist also engraved her own name down the side of the handle. She often included her signature within her compositions – a huge help for art historians to confidently identify the works of one of the few female artists of the era. Very little is known about this female master, but it seems she wanted to be known. In addition to her signature, in many of her paintings she appears as tiny reflections, her bonneted head popping into view in the lid of a jug or curve of a goblet. She was one of the first artists in northern Europe to use this technique. In *Still Life with Cheeses, Artichoke, and Cherries* (c. 1625) she appears in a warped, miniature self-portrait, not only demonstrating her skill, but also leaving no doubt that this work was painted by a woman. In the midst of a man's world, Clara Peeters found a way of leaving behind her own subtle feminist statements – seventeenth-century style.

Clara Peeters, *A Bouquet of Flowers*, c. 1612
Oil on wood, 46 × 32 cm
The Metropolitan Museum of Art, New York

FIVE-SPICE DUCK LEGS WITH PLUMS AND KALE

—

This edible bouquet celebrates some of the spices that arrived in the Netherlands during the Dutch Golden Age. It's an easy but luxurious dinner for two, with minimal washing up.

SERVES 2

2 tablespoons hoisin sauce
2 teaspoons Chinese five spice powder
1 teaspoon honey
2 duck legs
6 baby potatoes
3 small echalion shallots (banana shallots)
80 g (2¾ oz) kale leaves, roughly chopped
4 plums (red and purple varieties work best)

TO SERVE

2 tablespoons fresh coriander (cilantro) leaves

In a large bowl, whisk together the hoisin sauce, Chinese five spice powder and honey.

Add the duck legs and use your hands to coat them fully in the mixture. Cover and put in the refrigerator to marinate for 2 hours.

Preheat the oven to 180°C / 160°C fan (350°F / 320°F fan).

Put the duck legs in a ceramic roasting dish and pour any marinade left in the bowl over the meat. Cover the dish tightly with foil and roast for 1 hour.

Bring a small pan of salted water to a boil. Halve the potatoes, add them to the boiling water and parboil them for 5–10 minutes, or until cooked through. Drain and leave in the colander to steam.

Peel and halve the shallots lengthwise. Add them, along with the potatoes, to the roasting dish, arranging them around the duck legs. Stir the shallots and potatoes to coat them in the rendered duck fat, then return the dish to the oven and continue roasting uncovered for 20 more minutes.

Add the kale, using a fork or tongs to carefully distribute it around the dish and coat it in the fat. Halve and de-stone the plums and nestle them, cut-side up, around the duck legs. Return the dish to the oven, raise the temperature to 200°C / 180°C fan (400°F / 350°F fan) and roast for a final 10–15 minutes, by which point the duck should be falling off the bone and have deliciously crisp skin.

Finely chop the coriander leaves and sprinkle them over the dish. Serve in the baking dish.

HENRI DE TOULOUSE-LAUTREC
—

For Henri de Toulouse-Lautrec, cooking was as much an art form as painting or drawing. And he believed that food, like art, was something that should be shared and enjoyed with others. It's well known that Toulouse-Lautrec enjoyed attending parties; his dynamic works capture snapshots of the most raucous nights at the Moulin Rouge. But he also enjoyed being the host and regularly invited friends to his studio for elaborate dinners. During one particularly memorable evening, the artist dramatically summoned his guests to follow him into another room, where he revealed a painting by Edgar Degas, saying, 'there is your dessert'.

After presenting their invitations hand-drawn by the artist, arriving guests would be presented with a cocktail from the bar, which was always well stocked. *The Earthquake* cocktail was one of his specialties; a lethal combination of absinthe and cognac. Quite a way to start a meal. Toulouse-Lautrec believed cocktails were essential for viewing art and always had the tools on his person to ensure he never ran dry. He walked with a stick which was cunningly designed to be hollow, allowing him to carry a drink at all times, whether in front of a painting or not. He also carried a whole nutmeg and a tiny grater in his pocket to flavour his port, which flowed wherever he went.

His cooking was surprisingly sober. Toulouse-Lautrec was a talented cook and enjoyed making grand but simple dishes that often took hours to prepare. Symbolist poet Paul Leclercq, who was a regular dinner guest, said of the artist, 'He was a great gourmand … He loved to talk about cooking and knew of many rare recipes for making the most standard dishes … Cooking a leg of lamb for seven hours or preparing a lobster à l'Américaine held no secrets for him.' After Toulouse-Lautrec's untimely death, aged just thirty-six, another close friend, Maurice Joyant, created the cookbook *The Art of Cuisine* in memory of the many meals the two had shared together. The book documents numerous recipes invented by the artist, with sketches and menu designs interspersed throughout the pages to bring his two art forms together.

Surprisingly, despite living a party lifestyle in central Paris, Toulouse-Lautrec was knowledgeable about hunting and foraging, which he learnt from his father as a young man. Indeed, many of the recipes focus more on how to catch and prepare the food than how to actually cook it. *Whole Sheep Roasted Out of Doors* requires digging a hole 'one meter fifty by one meter and one meter deep' before cooking the whole animal in it, while *Dandelion Salad* requires some patient foraging.

There are some unusual meats included too. Squirrel and heron sound almost normal next to *Fillets of Porpoise* and *Stewed Marmot,* a particularly unusual recipe with some uncomfortable instructions: 'Having killed some marmots sunning themselves belly up in the sun with their noses in the air one sunrise in September, skin them and carefully put aside the mass of fat which is excellent for rubbing into the bellies of pregnant women … Cut up the marmot and treat it like stewed hare which has a perfume that is unique and wild.'

Some of the most intriguing and 'Toulouse-Lautrec' recipes of all are stashed at the very back, in a chapter entitled *Ultima ratio finis* (The ultimate plan of the end). For example, there is a very strange recipe for *Saint on the Grill:* 'When you have whipped him, lay him on the grill over a big bed of charcoal … if he is a real saint, he himself will ask to be turned over in order to be grilled to a turn on both sides'.

It's safe to say, no one will ever really know what went on in Toulouse-Lautrec's booze-filled head – we can only wish to have been a fly on the wall at a dinner party!

Henri de Toulouse-Lautrec, *La Troupe de Mademoiselle Eglantine*, 1895
Lithograph, 61.2 × 79.4 cm
The Metropolitan Museum of Art, New York

LAMB CUTLETS WITH YOGHURT SAUCE AND A SAFFRON DRESSING

—

While this dish is simple to make, it maintains a sense of luxury that Henri de Toulouse-Lautrec would have enjoyed. Its unexpected flavours are sure to impress your dinner party guests.

I recommend pairing this dish with blanched green beans and whole roasted baby potatoes.

SERVES 4

FOR THE LAMB
12 lamb cutlets, French-
    trimmed
250 g (1 cup) natural
    (regular) yoghurt
1 garlic clove, crushed
2 teaspoons fine salt
Olive oil, for frying

FOR THE SAFFRON DRESSING
Pinch of saffron threads
1 tablespoon just-boiled
    water
2 anchovy fillets, in oil
1 small garlic clove, peeled
100 ml (⅓ cup plus 1
    tablespoon) extra-virgin
    olive oil
2 tablespoons sherry
    vinegar
Fine salt

FOR THE YOGHURT SAUCE
Fine salt
250 g (1 cup) natural
    (regular) yoghurt
2 teaspoons cornflour
    (cornstarch)
1 egg

Start the lamb cutlets at least 5 hours before serving. If your chops haven't been trimmed, clean the bones by using a sharp knife to carefully remove any meat from the top 5 cm (2 in) of bone.

Combine the yoghurt, garlic and salt in a bowl, add the lamb and use your hands to rub the marinade into the meat. Cover and put in the refrigerator to marinate for at least 4 hours.

Remove the lamb from the refrigerator 30 minutes to 1 hour before cooking to bring the meat up to room temperature. I recommend warming an oval serving plate during this time, to keep everything hot once served.

For the saffron dressing, tip the saffron into a small bowl or jug and pour over the just-boiled water. Leave it to soak for about 5 minutes to get that rich yellow colour. Once infused, add the anchovy fillets, garlic, olive oil, sherry vinegar and a pinch of salt. Use an immersion blender to blitz it into a smooth dressing.

For the yoghurt sauce, in a small saucepan over medium heat, combine 100 ml (⅓ cup plus 1 tablespoon) of water and ½ teaspoon salt and bring to a simmer. Turn off the heat.

In a bowl, whisk 3 tablespoons of the yoghurt with the cornflour until smooth. Add the egg and the remaining yoghurt and whisk again. Slowly pour the hot water into the bowl, whisking as you go. Once smooth, pour the yoghurt mixture back into the pan, put over medium-low heat and cook, stirring constantly, for about 5 minutes, or until thickened. Remove from the heat and set aside.

Add 1 tablespoon of olive oil to a frying pan over medium-high heat. Once hot, use your hands to wipe off the excess marinade from the lamb cutlets and cook them in batches for 3 minutes on each side, for a pink centre. Transfer the lamb to a plate and loosely cover with foil to rest for 5 minutes.

To serve, pour the yoghurt sauce into the base of your warmed serving platter and drizzle over the saffron dressing. Arrange the lamb cutlets on top with the bones all facing one side of the plate. Serve immediately.

MARK ROTHKO
—

In the 1940s, Mark Rothko established his iconic painting style, using vibrant shades of yellow, red and pink to create glowing beacons of colour. He developed his technique over the following decade and in 1958 was offered a $35,000 commission (nearly $300,000 today) to create over 500 square feet (46.45 m²) of mural-scale canvases for the Four Seasons restaurant at the Seagram Building in New York. This commission marked a turning point in Rothko's career as he created his first ever series of dark burgundy paintings. Despite having space for only seven works, he created more than thirty large-scale canvases for the project as he constantly changed his mind about which paintings were to be used.

But, after going to the restaurant to have dinner, Rothko refused to follow through with the commission. Coming from a humble background, he was appalled by the lavish experience and the cost of the meal, saying to a friend, 'Anybody who will eat that kind of food for those kind [sic] of prices will never look at a painting of mine.' The commission was cancelled and nine of the works are now on permanent display at London's Tate Modern.

This series of moody, meditative paintings, pulsing with colour and emotion, might seem a strange backdrop for a busy restaurant; likely, as he feared, to fade into the background. For Rothko, creating art was a religious act of communication and the mural sized canvases seem better suited to a gallery setting, where they can be suitably worshipped. He was devoted to his painting process and using a variety of materials such as egg, glue and dammar resin to alter the texture and finish of the paint. He built up his iconic swathes of colour through a series of thin, almost transparent, layers. Each layer was a subtly different texture and finish enabling him to create the distinctive depth of tone and texture he is so famous for, making the canvases appear to glow from within.

The progression of Rothko's paintings and colour palette have been analysed extensively, including through the unlikely medium of food. In 1981, the somewhat serious journal *October* published an unusually light-hearted article by the art historian E. A. Carmean titled 'The Sandwiches of the Artist'. The piece made an expansive analogy between sliced white bread and painters' canvases, examining the colourful history of the 'sandwiches' Rothko made over the course of his career. Carmean writes, 'Rothko's sandwiches of the 1950s, his most popular, are marked by the free use of colourful ingredients: mustard, ketchup and lettuce.' Carmean is referring, of course, to some of Rothko's most famous works, such as his vibrant 1956 painting *Orange and Yellow*. In fact, by substituting 'painting' for 'sandwich', the article provides a handy summary of Rothko's oeuvre.

It also suggests the ease with which it is possible to switch between the vocabulary of art and food. As Rothko started creating paintings much darker and deeper in colour, he was also struggling with his physical and mental health. Many art historians have linked this shift in colour palette to his personal struggles. Carmean's tongue-in-cheek article suggests his sandwiches changed too: 'His last works, the brown and gray sandwiches, combine liverwurst and peanut butter.' Unpleasant but powerful.

Mark Rothko, *Orange and Yellow*, 1956
Oil on canvas, 231.14 × 180.34 cm
Buffalo AKG Art Museum, Buffalo

ROASTED PEPPER TART WITH A PARMESAN CRUST

—

This recipe celebrates the versatile egg. Just as Rothko used it to combine paint pigments, the egg binds the ingredients together to create a vibrant tart-work with layers of flavour, framed in a Parmesan pastry crust.

**MAKES 1 TART-WORK
SERVES 6–8**

FOR THE PASTRY
300 g (2 cups plus
    2 tablespoons) plain flour
    (all-purpose flour)
Fine salt
150 g (½ cup plus
    2 tablespoons) unsalted
    butter, chilled
50 g (1 ¾ oz) Parmesan
    cheese
2 egg yolks
Cold water, as needed

FOR THE FILLING
3 red bell peppers
2 yellow bell peppers
1 small onion
4 garlic cloves
2 tablespoons olive oil
1 teaspoon turmeric
1 teaspoon smoked paprika
1 teaspoon Dijon mustard
Fine salt
200 ml (¾ cup plus
    1 tablespoon) passata
2 eggs plus 2 egg yolks

For the pastry, in a large bowl, combine the flour and a pinch of salt. Cut the butter into small cubes and use your fingertips to rub it into the flour mixture until it resembles fine breadcrumbs. Finely grate in the Parmesan and stir to incorporate. Add the egg yolks and use your hands to bring the mixture together into a smooth dough, adding a little cold water, as needed, until the dough leaves the sides of the bowl clean. Wrap the pastry in cling film and put it in the refrigerator to chill for 30 minutes.

Preheat the oven to 180°C / 160°C fan (350°F / 320°F fan).

For the filling, deseed and chop the red and yellow bell peppers into 5 cm (2 in) pieces and spread them on separate baking trays. Chop the onion into quarters and add 2 quarters to each baking tray. Crush or finely chop the garlic cloves. Add half of the garlic, along with 1 tablespoon of the olive oil and the turmeric to the yellow bell peppers and mix thoroughly. Add the rest of the garlic, along with the remaining 1 tablespoon of olive oil and the paprika to the red bell peppers and mix thoroughly. Place both baking trays in the oven and roast for 15 minutes, then stir and roast for another 15 minutes.

On a lightly floured surface, use a rolling pin to roll out the chilled pastry dough into a rectangle approx. 35 × 25 cm (14 × 10 in). Carefully lift the pastry and lay it over a 30 × 20 cm (12 × 8 in) loose-bottomed tart tin. Use your knuckles to press the pastry into the edges and corners of the tin to create a sealed lining. Don't worry if the pastry crumbles. If it is too difficult to lift as one piece, take small pieces and push them into place. Trim off any excess and put the pastry shell in the refrigerator to chill for another 30 minutes.

Once the pastry shell is chilled, set the tin on a baking tray to make it easier to lift. Line the bottom of the pastry shell with parchment paper, pour in baking beans or rice and blind bake for 15 minutes. Remove the beans and paper and bake for 10 more minutes, or until the pastry is lightly golden. If the base puffs up at all, remove from the oven and wait a couple of minutes for it to deflate before adding the fillings.

Meanwhile, tip the roasted yellow pepper mixture into a blender or food processor. Add the mustard and blend until smooth. Season with salt and transfer to a bowl, scraping out as much as you can. Tip the red pepper mixture into the blender (no need to rinse it). Add the passata and blend until smooth. Season with salt and transfer to a second bowl.

In a third bowl, whisk together the eggs and yolks. Pour one-third of the egg mixture into the yellow purée and the remaining two-thirds into the red purée. Stir both mixtures until each is fully combined.

Preheat the oven to 160°C / 140°C fan (320°F / 275°F fan).

Pour the red pepper purée into the bottom half of the pastry shell and around the edges of the top half, leaving a gap in the centre for the yellow purée. Carefully pour the yellow pepper purée into the gap to make a rectangular shape, then use a fork to slightly blend the colours into each other for a more painterly look. Shake the tin gently to make the surface level. Bake for 30–35 minutes, or until the tart is set, checking on it regularly to make sure the top doesn't brown. If it starts to brown, turn the oven down slightly and loosely cover the tart with a piece of parchment paper.

Leave the tart to cool completely, then chill in the refrigerator for 30 minutes. You can eat this tart warm, but I prefer it cold, with a side salad. Remove it from the tin and serve it whole at the table before slicing it into portions.

FRIDA KAHLO
—

When Frida Kahlo first married Diego Rivera, she couldn't cook. But she did learn. In fact, she learnt her culinary skills from someone quite unexpected – Diego's second ex-wife, Lupe Marín, who for a while lived with their two daughters in a flat above the newlyweds. Kahlo wanted to be a good wife and thought it important that she should know how to cook for her food-loving husband, whose bad temper could only be remedied with a good meal. So, the unusual teacher-student pair worked together, cooking traditional Mexican dishes in earthenware and copper pots over wood fires to satisfy his appetite.

A proud Mexican, Rivera was passionate about upholding traditions and the couple's wedding menu celebrated not only their marriage, but their heritage too: oyster soup, white rice with plantains, huauzontles (a Mexican herb) in green sauce, chiles stuffed with picadillo, black mole from Oaxaca and red hominy stew from Jalisco were followed by flan and a show-stopping finale of a multi-tiered wedding cake with white icing doves and roses, topped with a little model of the newlyweds. Continuing with tradition, and in solidarity with the poor, Diego demanded that all the dishes should be eaten with tortillas rather than a knife and fork. There was also plenty of tequila to drink.

The wedding had a profound impact on Kahlo. From that point on, she wore indigenous clothes, began to explore Mexican aesthetics and traditions through her artistic practice, and learnt to cook local dishes. She felt these activities enhanced her 'Mexicanness' of which she was very proud. She loved to celebrate special occasions, from birthdays to saints' days, and having mastered the cuisine, she would regularly host dinners with the help of their cook Eulalia. When not hosted outside, these dinners took place in the dining room, the floor of which Kahlo painted a happy, sunshine yellow. Guests were often artists, academics and leftists, keeping Kahlo and Diego, who were both members of the Communist Party, at the centre of Mexico City's social and political circles.

Kahlo often created vibrant table settings that were works of art in themselves. She did this every day as a demonstration of her love for Diego, transforming the table into a still life for his meals or, if he was out painting a mural, taking him lunch in a basket lavishly decorated with fruit and flowers from the garden.

But as her health deteriorated, Kahlo often became bed-bound for days at a time. Ever the hostess, she would invite guests to her bedroom, where she also continued to paint – still with plenty of tequila on hand. Thanks to Eulalia, the food remained impeccable, no matter the location, with extensive menus of twelve or more dishes. Mescal, mole, tamales and tacos were often served, alongside deeply flavoured soups, escabeche and sumptuous desserts that celebrated ripe, local fruits, such as pineapple, guava and prickly pears, as well as fritters and churros. All of this was achieved over a wood fire; Kahlo never ordered a modern stove.

Many of Kahlo's favourite ingredients ended up in her studio, where she captured the abundance of local produce in paint. Watermelons, coconuts, papayas, corn and limes feature heavily in her work. As they were often painted cut open, some critics of the time interpreted them as being simply erotic symbols, but for Kahlo they held deeper meanings. In the painting *Viva la Vida, Watermelons* (1954), Kahlo depicts a group of vibrant watermelons, each cut into a different shape, at a different stage of ripeness. The words 'VIVA LA VIDA (LONG LIVE LIFE) Frida Kahlo – Coyoacán 1954 Mexico' are inscribed into a slice of melon at the bottom of the composition. Watermelons have long been used during *Dia de los Muertos* (Day of the Dead), to symbolise a connection to the dead or death. It seems Kahlo was predicting her own: this is considered to be one of the last paintings she ever made.

Frida Kahlo, *Sun and Life*, 1947
Oil on masonite, 41 × 51 cm
Private collection

BIRRIA-STYLE TACOS WITH FETA

—

Birria tacos went viral on social media a couple of years ago and I got swept up in the craze. Birria comes from the region of Jalisco in Mexico and is traditionally served as a stew made with goat meat. I have watched countless videos of people from all over the world preparing their version of this delicious recipe with beef or pork and after some trial and error, came up with my own variation. Many birria tacos are filled and then fried or made into *quesabirria* with the addition of melted cheese. But I prefer the texture of the tortilla when it's fried by itself before being filled at the table. The addition of feta is also not traditional (or Mexican), but there's something about the cold, zingy cheese that contrasts so beautifully with the rich, saucy beef. Thank you, internet, for bringing this heavenly food into my life.

SERVES 4–6

FOR THE FILLING
3 dried guajillo chillis
3 dried chipotle chillis
1 dried ancho chilli
2 large tomatoes, roughly
chopped
1 large onion, roughly
chopped
5 large garlic cloves,
roughly chopped
4 tablespoons olive oil
Fine salt
1.4 kg (3 lb) bone-in beef
short ribs
3 bay leaves
1 tablespoon cumin seeds
1 tablespoon whole black
peppercorns
1 tablespoon dried oregano
1 small cinnamon stick
750 ml (3 cups) beef stock

FOR THE TACOS
16 taco-size flour tortillas
1 small onion, finely
chopped
1 handful fresh coriander
(cilantro) leaves, finely
chopped
200 g (7 oz) feta cheese
2 limes, cut into wedges

For the filling, remove the stems and seeds from the guajillo, chipotle and ancho chillis. Roughly chop them, along with the tomatoes, onion and garlic.

Heat 2 tablespoons of the olive oil in a large, cast-iron pan (for which you have a lid) over high heat (you can use a regular saucepan if you'd rather use a slow cooker later). Generously salt all sides of the beef, then use tongs to add the meat to the pot, one rib at a time, and sear it, turning, until browned on all sides, about 1 minute on each side. Remove the beef and set aside (or put it in a slow cooker), leaving the oil and any rendered fat in the pan.

Turn down the heat slightly. Add the remaining 2 tablespoons of olive oil, along with the onion and garlic. Cook, stirring continuously, for 5 minutes, or until browned. Add the bay leaves, cumin, peppercorns, oregano, cinnamon stick and chopped chillis. Cook, stirring, for 3 more minutes, or until fragrant.

Add the tomatoes and cook for 1 more minute, crushing them slightly as they begin to break down. Pour over the beef stock and bring to a simmer. Leave to cook for 30 minutes.

Preheat the oven to 140°C / 120°C fan (275°F / 250°F fan) or turn a slow cooker to high.

Remove the cinnamon stick from the sauce and blend with an immersion blender or in a regular blender or food processor until smooth.

Return the meat to the pan in a single layer and pour over the sauce. Pour in enough water to fully submerge the meat in the liquid, cover the pan with a lid and put it in the oven (or add to the slow cooker) to cook for 6–8 hours. You'll know it's cooked to perfection when the meat is falling off the bone.

Once cooked, remove the meat from the sauce and use a fork to shred it in a large bowl. Depending on the beef you have, you may want to remove some of the fat before shredding the meat. Including some fat makes the filling delicious, but if your cut is particularly fatty it can be a bit heavy to include it all (this is, of course, personal preference!). Discard the bones or keep them to make stock another day.

Season the sauce (known as consomé) with salt, then pour enough sauce over the meat to just coat it (1 or 2 ladles) and mix to coat. Cover to keep warm and set aside.

For the tacos, heat a frying pan over high heat. Briefly dunk a tortilla into the remaining sauce, covering both sides, and transfer it to the pan. Fry on each side for 1–2 minutes, or until browned. Transfer to a warm serving plate and repeat with the remaining tortillas to make a stack.

Serve the warm tortillas and the meat at the table with bowls of chopped onion, coriander, crumbled feta and lime wedges. Pour the leftover consomé into bowls to dip your tacos in. Fill up a tortilla with all the goodies and dig in.

UMBERTO BOCCIONI

—

In 1910, Umberto Boccioni joined the revolutionary art movement that would go on to declare war – not on another movement, but on pasta. He became a leading Futurist artist, creating the sculptural masterpiece of the movement *Unique Forms of Continuity in Space* in 1913. Twenty years later, following the example of Mussolini's efforts to convert Italians to eating rice, *The Futurist Cookbook* was released, crafted by their poetic leader Filippo Tommaso Marinetti. Part joke, part serious manifesto, it declared there would be 'no more spaghetti for the Italians'. With a sinister, Fascist undertone, this movement intended on 'changing radically the eating habits of our race', removing the 'absurd Italian gastronomic religion' they claimed made men 'heavy, brutish', 'slow' and 'pessimistic', and instead seeking a more optimistic and forward-looking approach to eating, in response to the Great Depression.

The Futurist Cookbook focused more on the shape, colour and texture of food than its taste; a rebellion against traditional cooking in order to achieve 'absolute originality in the food.' Recipes were relabelled as 'formulas' and were cooked with unusual implements: ultraviolet ray lamps to irradiate food, litmus paper to indicate the pH of dishes and electrolysers to 'decompose juices and extracts, etc., in such a way as to obtain from a known product a new product with new properties.'

The first ever Futurist restaurant, Taverna del Santopalato (Tavern of the Holy Palate), opened in Turin in 1931. At its opening dinner it served fourteen extraordinary Futurist dishes, including: *Sunshine Soup; Aerofood, tactile, with sounds and smells; Elasticake;* and the famous spectacle *Sculpted Meat.* Described as 'a synthetic interpretation of the orchards, gardens and pastures of Italy,' *Sculpted Meat* was a cylinder of veal mince stuffed with eleven types of cooked green vegetables. According to the diagram that accompanies the formula, the stuffed tube of meat stood on its end, balancing on top of three spheres of chicken meat, supported by a ring of sausage, with a thick layer of honey on top – quite an architectural feat.

Aerofood, tactile, with sounds and smells, was a more multi-sensory experience. While eating the edible offerings of a black olive, a slice of fennel and a kumquat with their right hand, the diner was asked to move their left hand over sandpaper, silk and velvet as waiters sprayed their neck with a perfume,

all to the cacophonous sound of a piece by Bach set against the drone of an aeroplane motor. The Futurists were obsessed with air travel as the transport of the future and many of the formulas reference planes and aeronautics.

Although elaborate, these Futurist dinners were surprisingly affordable, which must have been a great comfort to the diners, who seem to have eaten little. According to Marinetti, 'in the ideal Futuristic meal, a certain number of dishes will be passed beneath the nose of the diner in order to excite his curiosity or provide a suitable contrast, and such supplementary courses will not be eaten at all.'

When diners were invited to eat the food, however, it wasn't always very pleasant. During one dinner, guests were served stuffed olives with small pieces of paper hidden inside which they had to spit out, unfurl and read aloud. At another, they were served *Timbale of Tomorrow* which featured a newborn calf's head in the middle of a display of pineapple, nuts and dates (the latter were stuffed with anchovies), followed by *Taste Buds Take Off*, an unappetising mix of meat stock, champagne and rose petals.

But if anyone wasn't put off by this and wanted to host their own Futurist dinner, the cookbook provides numerous 'dinner programmes' to help you achieve the ultimate 'provocative and evocative' Futurist dinner party. These dinner plans are more poetic than practical: the *Nocturnal love feast* requires diners to be on a terrace in Capri in August, while for the *Autumnal musical dinner*, the host must enlist a peasant woman to do the cooking. Meanwhile, the *extremist banquet* lives up to its name. Not only does it require a purpose-built villa, set on a piece of land dividing 'the most lake-like of lakes', for the venue, but it calls for many unusual props, including three edible sculptures equipped with vaporizers which look and smell like such things as 'a ship made of fried aubergines sprinkled with vanilla, acacia flowers and red pepper.' An added twist: this all had to be eaten without cutlery, too.

Umberto Boccioni, *States of Mind III*, 1911
Oil on canvas, 70.8 × 95.9 cm
Museum of Modern Art, New York

Not tempted? The *improvised dinner* might be more appealing. Yes, it does involve moving carpets around during the meal, but its ultimate goal is that 'EVERY PERSON HAS THE SENSATION OF EATING not just good food but also WORKS OF ART.' It's good to be shocked out of dinner table monotony occasionally.

HANDMADE GREEN TAGLIATELLE WITH CAVOLO NERO PESTO

—

Defying the wishes of the Futurists, this recipe is a true celebration of pasta, in all its glory.

SERVES 4

FOR THE PASTA

120 g (4 oz) frozen spinach, thawed (or 80 g / 2¾ oz fresh)

2 eggs plus 2 egg yolks

240 g (8½ oz) pasta flour, plus more for rolling the pasta

Finely ground semolina (about 100 g / 3½ oz)

Fine salt

FOR THE PESTO

1 large bunch cavolo nero (about 200 g / 7 oz)

Fine salt

200 ml (¾ cup plus 1 tablespoon) extra-virgin olive oil, plus more as needed

40 g (1½ oz) pine nuts, lightly toasted

40 g (1½ oz) Parmesan cheese, finely grated, plus more to serve

1 large garlic clove, peeled

1 tablespoon capers, plus more to serve

1 teaspoon dried chilli flakes

Start the pasta a few hours before you need it. Squeeze excess water from the spinach. (If using fresh spinach, wilt the leaves in a hot pan with a little water, cool and do the same). Tip the spinach into a food processor with the eggs and egg yolks and blitz until smooth.

Heap the pasta flour on a clean work surface and make a well in the centre. Add the egg mixture and use a fork to start incorporating the flour, slowly bringing it in from the sides as you go. Once you can't do anymore with the fork, use your hands to knead the mixture into a pliable dough that bounces back slowly after you push your thumb into it – this should take 2–3 minutes. Wrap the dough in cling film and put it in the refrigerator for 30 minutes. Once chilled, cut into eight equal pieces. Work with one piece one at a time, keeping the others covered.

Flatten a piece of dough to about 1.25 cm (½ in) thick with the palm of your hand. Set your pasta machine to the widest setting (no. 7) and run the pasta through it. You will need to sprinkle extra pasta flour as you go to stop it sticking. Arrange the dough on your work surface with the long edge towards you. Fold the left and right sides over and on top of each other to make the piece a third of its length. Flatten it slightly with your hand to help seal it back together and run it through the pasta machine again, feeding one of the open ends into the machine first. Repeat this process two more times to make a nice smooth dough. Keep rubbing it with flour as needed.

Adjust your pasta machine to be on setting no. 5. Run the dough through the machine, catching it underneath with your hand to stop it from crumpling. Adjust the setting to no. 3 and run it through again. Adjust to no. 1 (the thinnest) and run it through again. The dough should now be thin enough to show light through it when you hold it up. Hang the sheet over a balanced broom handle or the back of a chair to dry slightly as you repeat the entire process with the remaining pieces of dough.

Next, add your tagliatelle cutter to your machine. Take the first pasta sheet and pass it through. If you don't have a tagliatelle cutter, sprinkle the dough with a generous amount of flour, gently roll it up and use a sharp knife to cut it across the roll. Tip a few spoonfuls of semolina onto a baking tray and toss the pasta strands in it to stop them from sticking. Wrap the tagliatelle around your hand to create little nests. Repeat with the rest of the pasta and set aside to dry for 30 minutes or more.

For the pesto, remove the stems from the cavolo nero. Bring a large pan of water to a boil and add 1 teaspoon of salt. Blanch the leaves for 2–3 minutes. Transfer them to a bowl of ice water. Squeeze out most of the water. Finely chop the leaves and transfer them to a food processor or blender. Add the olive oil, pine nuts, Parmesan, garlic, capers and chilli flakes. Pulse to create a smooth paste, adding more olive oil as needed to thin the pesto. Season with salt to taste.

Once ready to serve, bring a large saucepan of water to a boil and add at least 1 tablespoon of salt. Add the pasta and stir to stop it from sticking together. Boil for 2–3 minutes, or until just al dente. Drain the pasta in a colander set over a large mug to reserve some of the water. Transfer the pasta back to the pan. Pour over the pesto and mix. Add as much pasta water as needed to make a creamier sauce. Taste and season with salt.

To serve, use tongs to transfer the pasta to a serving plate, twisting to make beautiful mounds. Scatter over the capers and serve with a block of Parmesan so guests can serve themselves.

GEORGETTE CHEN
—

Georgette Chen is revered for her vibrant paintings of the produce of Singapore. Fascinated by the wiry fruits that gave her the nickname 'the rambutan specialist', she painted countless still lifes of these and the many other fruits she discovered in the country she would call home.

Before her final move to Singapore in 1953, Chen had spent her life moving back and forth between China, Paris and New York, both for her education and to avoid war; she lived through two Chinese revolutions and both World Wars. Chen was born into a family who encouraged her artistic talent, and she was tutored in both European-style painting and Chinese ink painting.

In 1926, she enrolled at the Art Students League of New York, before returning to Paris the following year to continue formal training in academic painting. She also attended free studios, where the feel of an artwork held greater importance than its technical accuracy. She developed some of the stylistic traits of the Post-Impressionists, but her painting style remained unique as she drew technical and aesthetic inspiration from both East and West. The excellence of her work was recognised and exhibited in many Parisian salons during her career, and she held multiple solo shows; an impressive achievement for a female painter at the time.

But politics soon took hold of Chen's life. In the early 1930s, she and her husband Eugene Chen were itinerant between Paris, Hong Kong and Shanghai. He was the first foreign minister of the Fujian People's Government, a Chinese anti-Nationalist government which had been defeated. And once Hong Kong fell to Japan in 1941, the couple were placed under house arrest there, before being kept under surveillance in Shanghai for four years. But this period was surprisingly productive for Chen. She never stopped painting and used the time to refine and improve her techniques. She created many portraits of her husband and developed her still-life paintings, creating scenes of the foods available to her, predominantly in dark, moody tones.

Years later, Chen ended up in Singapore where she would spend the rest of her life. Enlivened by the warm weather and the tropical fruits, she had fresh subject matter to paint, using more vibrant colours than ever before. 'It is perhaps the fruits with their unexpected forms that intrigue me the most at the moment', she wrote in a letter to a friend, soon after her arrival in Penang in 1951, 'And there's so much variety that I forget their names as soon they [sic] are taught. Their colours are warm and intense and their fragrance strong.' Many of her still lifes focused on rambutans with their red, wiry exterior and milky innards.

In addition to her painting, Chen was well known in her community for being a skilled cook. She predominantly prepared dishes from her days in France and would paint menus for the dinner parties she hosted. These included French classics such as oyster soup, filet mignon steak and her speciality *Crêpes Georgette*; a far cry from the Singaporean foods she served up in her paintings.

Singapore has a unique culinary history. In the 1800s, it was a thriving port city that attracted people from present-day India, Malaysia, Indonesia, China and beyond. And with these migrants came new foods. People brought culinary traditions from their home countries and adapted dishes to include the ingredients of the region, merging cuisines to create a rich food scene, centred around its hawker culture. Hawkers work out of mobile kitchens, serving up one or two dishes, often perfected over generations. A popular dish is satay, a grilled skewered meat served with a sauce, which Chen captured in her painting *Satay Boy* (1964–1965). After World War II, many people became hawkers as a way to make money and the city was overrun with food carts. But after Singapore's independence in 1965, the year before Chen became an official citizen, the government introduced licences and dedicated areas in the city for them to work from, keeping roads clear and improving sanitation. Hawkers remain an essential part of Singaporean cuisine today. Some have received Michelin stars.

Chen witnessed the social and political developments of Singapore first-hand, just as she had in so many other places. Her life was peppered with moments of dramatic change and upheaval which moved her across borders and exposed her to many different cultures. This was reflected in her art; her oeuvre offers us unique insight into this turbulent time in history. Today, she is celebrated as one of the most important Singaporean artists of all time.

Georgette Chen, *Rambutans*, c. 1965
Oil on canvas, 55.3 × 38.2 cm
Collection of National Gallery Singapore

SINGAPOREAN-INSPIRED LAKSA WITH FISH BALLS

—

Georgette Chen's work celebrates the vibrant food culture of Singapore, capturing the abundance of its produce in rich, vivid tones. This Singaporean-inspired laksa is warming and energising, with bold oranges and reds that contrast the pearly fish balls – a visual nod to the rambutans Chen so often painted.

SERVES 4

FOR THE LAKSA PASTE
5 large garlic cloves, peeled
1 shallot, peeled
1 lemongrass stalk
1 fresh red chilli
2.5 cm (1 in) piece fresh galangal root (or 2.5 cm / 1 in piece fresh ginger root if you really can't find galangal)
2.5 cm (1 in) piece fresh turmeric root (or 1 heaping teaspoon ground turmeric if you really can't find fresh turmeric)
3 tablespoons dried shrimp, soaked in cold water for 5 minutes, then drained
2 tablespoons sunflower oil (or any neutral oil), plus more as needed
1 teaspoon smooth peanut butter
½ teaspoon dried chilli flakes

FOR THE LAKSA SOUP
2 tablespoons sunflower or coconut oil
400 ml (1½ cups plus 2 tbsp) full fat coconut milk
750 ml (3 cups) chicken stock
1 tablespoon fish sauce, plus more as needed
1 tablespoon palm sugar
Fine salt
12 raw king prawns, peeled and deveined
8 fish balls
200 g (7 oz) flat rice noodles

TO SERVE
80 g (2 ¾ oz) bean sprouts
2 tablespoons fresh coriander (cilantro) leaves
1 fresh red chilli sliced
1 lime, cut into wedges

For the laksa paste, use a rolling pin to whack the garlic, shallot, lemongrass, red chilli, galangal and turmeric root to release their aromas and roughly chop them. Transfer to a food processor, along with the dried shrimp, sunflower oil, peanut butter and chilli flakes, and blitz into a smooth paste. Add a little extra oil if the mixture is too dry to blend.

For the soup, warm the sunflower or coconut oil in a large saucepan over high heat. Add the laksa paste and fry, stirring constantly for 2–3 minutes, or until fragrant. Add the coconut milk and give it a whisk to fully mix it through. Add the stock, fish sauce and palm sugar, stir to combine and bring to a simmer. Continue simmering for 15 minutes to thicken up slightly. Taste and season with more fish sauce or just a good pinch of salt. Add the prawns and fish balls and cook for 2–3 minutes, or until the prawns are pink and starting to curl. Turn off the heat.

Cook your rice noodles per the packet instructions and divide among 4 bowls. Pour over the laksa and top with the prawns, fish balls and a nest of bean sprouts. Sprinkle over the red chilli and coriander and serve with a wedge of lime on the side.

RICHARD LONG
—

To create his walking artworks, Richard Long carries Californian dehydrated food which, in his opinion, is 'so much better than the stuff you can get in England.' Despite the sense of romance his work evokes, there's a necessary practicality to it. These aren't just casual strolls in the countryside (most of the time); instead, Long has carried out a 560-mile hike in Spain, walked for six days in the Sahara Desert and built a stone sculpture in Antarctica. He needs a carefully planned menu of food and drink, calculated to sustain him through these arduous tasks.

Ultimately, the length and difficulty of Long's walks depend on the artist's own body, the amount of water he can carry and where he can stop off along the way to rest and refuel – a tapas bar in Spain, for example. He makes work as he walks, often returning to the studio or a gallery to create something there too. It's both wild and tame; a true adventure while carrying sachets of pre-made food. All he needs to do is add water. 'I feel like I'm in a state of grace when I'm on a wilderness walk on my own, with just my rucksack on my back and my camping food', Long said. 'I'm mentally free from the stuff of modern life.'

Away from the cities and supermarkets, every now and then Long finds a foraged morsel. These tasty moments act as landmarks for his journeys and the written works he creates from them, such as 'INDIGO JUICE OF A BLACKBERRY AT 69 MILES', in his piece *WHITE LIGHT WALK* (1987). Food breaks up the rhythm of walking, interrupting what he sees, smells, hears and touches along the way. The plants he forages change according to the seasons, just like the landscape around him. Those blackberries wouldn't have been there had he walked in the spring.

Due to the rise of industrialised farming and supermarkets, many of us now have access to any ingredient we want, whenever we want it. But seasonal and foraged foods are making a comeback among home cooks and chefs alike. Locally and sustainably sourced ingredients are of growing interest to environmentally conscious consumers, while the demand for foraging courses has risen in recent years. There has also been an increase in local produce on restaurant menus, with many chefs changing their dishes to adjust to the ingredients available each season. With the fragility of our food systems exposed by the impacts of both climate change and COVID-19, it seems only right that we should be sourcing food a little closer to home.

Some people are preparing for potential food insecurity by buying freeze-dried produce, stocking up in case of emergency. For Long, freeze-dried food provides warming meals that are light to carry and can be easily prepared by mixing the sachets with water that has been heated over a campfire. The campfire is of vital importance to Long's journeys, providing him with warmth and symbolically marking the end of each day's walking with a just-add-water meal.

Richard Long, *Small White Pebble Circles*, 1987
Marble, 4 × 200 × 200 cm
Tate, London

SPINACH AND FETA SPIRAL PIE

—

This beautiful treat is equally as good hot or cold. Serve it hot with a side of roasted peppers or slice it up cold and pop it in your rucksack for the perfect lunch on the go.

SERVES 4–6

FOR THE FILLING
1 medium onion
3 garlic cloves
1 tablespoon olive oil
Fine salt
1 kg (2½ lb) frozen spinach
   (or 800 g / 1¾ lb fresh)
3 eggs
250 g (8¾ oz) ricotta
   cheese
200 g (7 oz) feta cheese
60 g (2 oz) Parmesan
   cheese, finely grated
1 small handful fresh dill,
   finely chopped
1 unwaxed lemon, zested
1 teaspoon chilli flakes

FOR THE PIE
6 sheets filo pastry
   (thawed, if frozen)
40 g (2½ tablespoons)
   unsalted butter, melted
1 tablespoon white sesame
   seeds
30 g (1 oz) Parmesan
   cheese

Preheat the oven to 190°C / 170°C fan (375°F / 340°F fan).

For the filling, finely chop the onion and crush the garlic. Heat the olive oil in a large sauté pan over medium-high heat, then add the onion, garlic and a pinch of salt and fry for 5–7 minutes, or until softened. Transfer to a bowl and set aside.

Return the pan to the heat and add the spinach. Cook until fully defrosted and most of the water has evaporated – this should take about 10 minutes. Drain the spinach in a fine-mesh sieve or a colander lined with a clean cloth and use the back of a spoon to push out as much of the remaining water as you can. (If using fresh spinach, wilt the leaves in a hot pan with a little water, cool and remove excess water in the same way). Tip it out onto a cutting board and roughly chop the leaves with a sharp knife. Leave to cool for 5 minutes.

In a large bowl, mix together the eggs, ricotta, feta, Parmesan, dill, lemon zest and chilli flakes, along with the cooked onion and garlic. Add the chopped spinach and mix again until evenly combined. Season with a generous sprinkling of salt and stir for a final time.

For the pie, place 1 sheet of filo pastry on a clean work surface with a long edge facing you. Use a pastry brush to gently brush it with a light layer of melted butter to act as a glue and place a second sheet of filo directly on top.

Spoon one-third of the spinach mixture in a line along the long edge of the pastry – the side closest to you – about 2.5 cm (1 in) from the edge. Carefully roll the pastry over the mixture to form a tight cylinder. Keep rolling it over itself until the entire sheet is wrapped around the filling, brushing the pastry with butter as you roll to seal it.

Gently wind the cylinder into a coil and place it on a baking tray lined with parchment paper.

Repeat the process two more times, continuing from the end of the coil you've already made, to create a larger spiral.

Brush the entire pie with the remaining melted butter and sprinkle over the sesame seeds. Bake for 50–60 minutes, or until golden brown and cooked through.

To serve, transfer the pie to a serving plate. Finely grate over the Parmesan and serve at the table before slicing.

HOWARD HODGKIN

Howard Hodgkin was a creature of habit. Each morning started with poached eggs, cooked by his husband Antony. Each evening was marked with a cocktail, mixed by his assistant. After Hodgkin's death, Antony spoke fondly of how the artist would often not drink the cocktail but simply hold and look at the V-shaped glass, enjoying the ritual as a way to mark the end of the working day. Hodgkin was a highly sentimental and emotional person and treasured moments like this – both significant and mundane.

From the kitchen to the studio, Hodgkin's habits were fixed and often slow. In stark contrast to his colourful paintings, he worked in an extremely minimalist studio. The blank white walls were lined with a collection of large empty canvases, which were used not for painting on, but to hide unfinished works from sight until he was ready to continue working on them. Although spontaneous in their appearance, his paintings were completed incredibly slowly; he sometimes left paintings aside for years before returning to them. *Lovers* (1984–1992), with its free and impulsive curves, took eight years to complete.

Ironically, Hodgkin hated what he called 'the horrors of painting'. He never looked forward to the process of creating work but would simply 'feel a painting coming on' and have to start. But despite this dislike and his slow painting style, he was a prolific artist, completing hundreds of works during his lifetime. Through these paintings, Hodgkin takes us through the colourful vortexes of his mind, translating his personal memories and experiences for us to decipher. Only the titles give anything tangible away and often merely suggest the moment immortalised in paint, with many not pointing us in a direction at all. He didn't expand on the titles but said the works should speak for themselves without being read literally.

Due to the abstracted quality of his paintings, Hodgkin is often labelled as an abstract artist. But he pushed against this. For him, the specific memory or feeling behind each artwork grounds the painting, as if he is presenting the moment simply in another format. The sensory magic lies in his dynamic use of colour. Through this mastery, Hodgkin pulls the viewer in to experience the essence of a moment, igniting the senses. This is particularly explicit in his paintings with edible titles: the blue greys of *Dry Martini* (2015/16) beneath a sweep of scarlet red and *Toffee* (2012) with its greens and oranges dragged through a chewy swathe of brown, burst with flavour. But is this what the artist saw?

Since Hodgkin's death, Antony has provided insight into his own thoughts on the moments captured within each of the artist's paintings but even he can't be sure. Hodgkin was such a private painter he didn't even let his husband in on that secret. *Cocktails for Two* (2016/17) – which was created quickly by the artist's standards – with its sweeps of orange and grey and exposed areas of wood, was, in Antony's opinion, not a literal interpretation of the title or a play on words, but more likely Hodgkin's way of capturing the feelings and sensations of his beloved evening ritual – that significant marker between day and night. Through the power of colour, Hodgkin keeps delicious memories fresh in our minds forever.

Howard Hodgkin, *Lovers*, 1984–1992
Oil on Wood, 171.5 × 185.4 cm
Private collection

SHAKSHUKA

—

The word *shakshuka* translates to 'mixture'. Just like the ingredients in this recipe, the lovers suggested in the painting interlace with one another, mixing together, both in colour and form.

SERVES 2

FOR THE SHAKSHUKA
200 g (7 oz) jarred roasted
   red peppers, drained
2 garlic cloves
1 tablespoon olive oil
½ teaspoon cumin seeds
½ teaspoon paprika
400 g (14 oz) tinned
   chopped tomatoes
Fine salt
4 eggs
1 small handful fresh flat-
   leaf parsley leaves
1 small handful fresh
   coriander (cilantro)
   leaves

FOR THE TOAST
1 garlic clove, peeled
4 slices crusty bread
   (page 44) / ciabatta

For the shakshuka, roughly chop the peppers and thinly slice the garlic.

Heat the olive oil in a high-sided frying pan (for which you have a lid) over medium-high heat. Add the cumin seeds and once they start to pop, add the garlic and paprika and fry for 1–2 minutes to make an aromatic oil. Turn off the heat and let the oil cool for 20–30 seconds to stop it spattering when you add the other ingredients.

Add the tomatoes and chopped peppers to the pan and stir. Put over medium heat and simmer for 5–10 minutes, or until the mixture has reduced and thickened, and the oil has come to the surface. Season with salt. Turn down the heat and use a large spoon to create 4 holes in the mixture to house the eggs.

Crack the eggs, one at a time, into ramekins to ensure no shell escapes into the mixture, then tip them into the holes in the sauce. Turn the heat back up to a simmer and place the lid on the pan. Cook for 2–3 minutes, or until the egg whites are firm. (If you don't have a lidded frying pan, you can put the pan under the grill for 1–2 minutes. Make sure the pan handle is ovenproof and check on the eggs regularly to avoid them over cooking – the yolks should be runny.)

Meanwhile, toast the bread slices until golden and crisp. Cut the garlic in half and liberally rub the bread on both sides with the cut sides of the clove.

Finely chop the parsley and coriander.

Once the eggs are cooked but still runny, take the pan off the heat and remove the lid. Pop the yolks with a knife and sprinkle over a small pinch of salt for extra flavour. Scatter over the chopped parsley and coriander.

Serve in the pan with the toast on the side.

JEAN DUBUFFET

—

For Jean Dubuffet there was 'only one healthy diet for artistic creation: permanent revolution.'

Dubuffet often compared the process of making art to cooking. He created 'recipes' for what he called '*hautes pâtes*' – thick pastes made up of a variety of unusual ingredients – which he used to produce unique textures on the canvas. Cement, tar, plaster, glue, varnish, mud, pebbles, sand, twine, branches, pigments, mirror and glass all made their way into his mixes, as he abandoned traditional painting methods to create artworks that exist somewhere between painting and sculpture.

Dubuffet started his professional career as a wine merchant. Although determined to be an artist from an early age and training at the prestigious Académie Julian in Paris, he rejected traditional teaching and put down the paint brushes to follow in his parent's footsteps, opening a wine shop in the city. Although he returned to art full time in 1942, his interest in wine continued, influencing his practice throughout his career, particularly once he progressed into sculpture in the 1950s. *The Soul of Morvan* (1954), for example, is a twisted figure created from grape wood and vines, sourced from the area that inspired the work: the Morvan wine region in France. The artist also frequently used wine bottle shards, regularly including them in his recipes for his *pâtes*, which followed the processes of wine creation by going through stages of fermentation and transformation. We all know that great wine improves as it ages and ferments; it seems Dubuffet believed the same of his art.

The *pâtes* he concocted were so heavy and unstable that they often cracked and fell off the canvas, sometimes before they even reached public view. Some recipes melted when they got too hot, others fractured when they got too cold. But for the artist, it was all part of the process. Coining the term 'Art Brut' (Raw Art) to define his work, Dubuffet's practice was a reaction against conventional ideas of beauty and a rejection of the traditions of art history, shocking his audience into considering art from a different perspective. 'If you serve someone spinach that is cooked the way it should be, no one notices or remembers that they have eaten spinach', Dubuffet explained. 'Whereas', he continued, 'if you burn it, it shocks their taste-buds and they become immediately aware that it is burned spinach and they gain new insights into the characteristics of spinach'.

The artist, who was also a prodigious writer, often used food analogies to explore his practice, using relatable imagery of cooking and the dinner table to communicate his thoughts and processes. The critics often joined him, making a pun of his name, 'du buffet'.

In 1958, the artist posed for a portrait sitting not in his paste-filled studio, but at a dining table wearing a smart suit and tie. In one hand he holds a book, in the other a fork, which spears a lump of what looks like bread or paper-pulp but could, of course, be one of his *pâtes*; a metaphor for his intense consumption of the arts, perhaps. But for Dubuffet, a fork was not just a tool for eating, it was also for creating. He used the tines to scratch the surface of his *pâtes*, creating a sandy, soil-like texture in pieces such as *Will to Power (Volonté de puissance)* (1946) – a mysterious work that invites countless interpretations.

Dubuffet is also famed for a contrasting series of work he made in the mid 1950s: collages created from butterfly wings, including *Jardin Nacré* (1955). Somehow these works have an added rawness to them with an element of aggression, as the artist had captured and killed the butterflies himself. But this was Dubuffet's way of shocking his audience to connect to his work. He said: 'One way of treating art: let the artist's mind, his moods and impressions, be offered raw, with their smells still vivid, just as you eat a herring without cooking it, but right after pulling it from the sea, when it's still dripping.' Art Brut: so raw it's still flapping.

Jean Dubuffet, *Jardin Nacré*, 1955
Mixed media collage with butterfly wings, 21 × 29 cm
Musée des Arts décoratifs, Paris

MOULES MARINIÈRES WITH HERB-SALTED FRENCH FRIES

—

With their butterfly-like shells in a creamy wine sauce, these mussels are best served with a white wine from Le Havre, if you can find it, as a nod to Dubuffet's first job.

SERVES 4

FOR THE FRENCH FRIES
800 g (1 ¾ lb) Maris Piper or King Edward potatoes
Sunflower oil, for deep frying (about 1 L / 4 ½ cups)

FOR THE HERB SALT
2 tablespoons fresh basil
2 tablespoons fresh rosemary
2 tablespoons fresh flat-leaf parsley
2 tablespoons coarse sea salt

FOR THE MUSSELS:
2 kg (4 ½ lb) fresh mussels
1 leek
2 garlic cloves
1 ½ tablespoons unsalted butter
1 teaspoon olive oil
100 ml (⅓ cup plus 1 tablespoon) white wine
60 ml (¼ cup) double cream (heavy cream)
1 small handful chopped fresh flat-leaf parsley leave

For the French fries, cut the potatoes into thin sticks (about 1 cm / ⅜ in thick) and immediately submerge them in a bowl of cold water. Leave them to soak for 1 hour to remove the starch.

For the herb salt, tip the basil, rosemary, parsley and salt into a food processor and pulse until fully combined. Transfer to a small bowl and set aside.

For the mussels, in a bowl of cold water, wash the mussels thoroughly, then debeard them and remove any barnacles with a blunt knife. Discard any mussels that are broken or float. Cover the mussels with fresh, cold water until ready to cook.

Drain the potatoes and pat them dry with a clean tea towel or paper towel. Fill a deep, heavy-bottomed pan one-third of the way up with sunflower oil and heat to 140°C (275°F) or until a tester cube of bread browns in 60 seconds.

Fry the potatoes in batches for 3–4 minutes, moving them around to ensure even cooking. They should be cooked through but not golden. Use a slotted spoon to transfer the potatoes to a baking tray lined with paper towels to drain. Continue frying the potatoes.

Turn up the heat and bring the sunflower oil to 180°C (350°F). Re-fry the potatoes in batches for 1–2 more minutes, or until really crisp. Drain on fresh paper towels, sprinkle immediately with pinches of the herb salt and keep warm.

Cut the leek lengthwise into quarters, then chop into very fine pieces. Crush the garlic.

In a large saucepan (for which you have a lid), combine the butter and olive oil over low heat. Once the butter is melted, add the leek and garlic. Cook, stirring frequently, for 5–10 minutes, or until soft and transparent. Pour in the wine, turn up the heat and bring to a boil. Cook off the alcohol for about 30 seconds.

Drain the mussels, tip them into the pan and cover with the lid. Leave to steam for 2–3 minutes, or until the mussels open. Discard any mussels with unopened shells. Add the double cream and parsley and stir.

Use a ladle to divide the mussels and their liquor into bowls and serve with a generous portion of fries on the side. Don't forget to provide a bowl for the shells and plenty of napkins!

LUCIO FONTANA

—

In 1994, the Italian pasta company Barilla launched the ad campaign '*Pasta Fatta ad Arte*' ('Artfully made pasta'). Inspired by artworks within the Barilla Modern Art Collection, the campaign featured photographs of the famous blue Barilla pasta boxes, each altered to imitate its artistic inspiration, with accompanying recipes. *Farfalle al Taglio di Salmone* (butterfly pasta with cuts of salmon) featured a box of farfalle pasta with two cuts in its front, inspired by the work of Argentine-Italian Spatialist, Lucio Fontana.

Fontana is best known for his '*tagli*' ('cuts') artworks series, which he created over the course of the 1950s and 1960s. Shocking in its dual complexity and simplicity, Fontana pushed the boundaries of the canvas, making careful incisions in the façade to transform it from a two-dimensional plane into a three-dimensional sculpture, seeking out the fourth dimension in the intangible something that lay beyond the canvas.

At a Sotheby's auction in Manhattan in 2015, the celebrated Italian chef Massimo Bottura stood in front of a '*tagli*' work by Fontana and said, 'It's exactly like when you taste *parmigiana* risotto, one simple gesture will tell you everything.' Celebrated for his culinary artistry, Bottura has cooked at many important art events, including the Sotheby's auction, where the work in question, *Concetto spaziale, Attesa (Spatial Concept, Waiting)* (1965), sold for over sixteen million US dollars. But although fascinated by the artwork, Bottura was there to do what he does best: cook. 'Fontana was about breaking tradition, puncturing, making a radical gesture', Lisa Dennison, Sotheby's Chairman of North and South America, said at the event, 'It's precisely what Massimo does with his food.' True to form, the chef served an artistic feast for the collectors inspired by modern and contemporary art; spinning plates of veal with splashes of colourful sauces, after Damien Hirst's iconic spin paintings, and for dessert, *Oops! I dropped the lemon tart*; a dish born from an accident in the kitchen and inspired by Ai Weiwei's performance piece *Dropping the Han Dynasty Urn* (1995).

But despite his interest in other artists, Bottura is regularly drawn back to the work of Fontana. These two visionaries share an ambition for achieving the seemingly impossible. Just as Fontana used a single cut to create an impact, Bottura often works with just one ingredient to blow his diners' minds. At his restaurant

Osteria Francescana in Modena, Bottura serves *Five Ages of Parmigiano Reggiano in Different Textures and Temperatures*. Parmesan cheese is presented at five different stages of ageing, in five different forms: a soufflé, sauce, foam, wafer and an edible cloud.

Other experiments attempt to take food even further. In his book *Never Trust a Skinny Italian Chef*, Bottura serves up a dish entitled *All the Tongues of the World*; a recipe that attempts to reach the fourth dimension. 'Was it too much to ask flavour to travel beyond territorial borders or to push a recipe across space and time?', Bottura asks, 'We could try.' To create this extra-terrestrial dish, sous-vide veal tongue is encased in a black dough of flour, salt, coffee grounds and vegetable carbon before being baked. Like a meteorite with a large slit in the top, the baking vessel closely resembles Fontana's bronze work *Natura* (1959/60). But to serve, the dough is cut open to reveal the tongue – returned, transformed, from its voyage to the fourth dimension – which is then placed in the centre of the plate to be orbited by numerous pools of 'satellite sauces', each from a different culinary tradition.

Fontana's own work often touched on cosmic themes. During the era of space exploration, he created a series entitled *Concetto spaziale, La fine di Dio (Spatial Concept, The End of God)* (1963/64). Like so many artists throughout art history, he was intrigued by eggs. These oval canvases were painted in rich candy colours and glitters and sprinkled with an array of '*tagli*' and '*bucchi*' ('holes'); pierced by a sharp object and widened by the artist's fingers. The pieces were later named 'astral eggs', pointing to the role of eggs as a universal symbol throughout both art history and religion for the creation of life. With Fontana's pierced constellation of holes, they take on the image of the solar system – a cosmos – as translated onto Bottura's plate.

Lucio Fontana, *Spatial Concept, Waiting*, 1965
Waterpainting on canvas
Museo Novecento, Florence

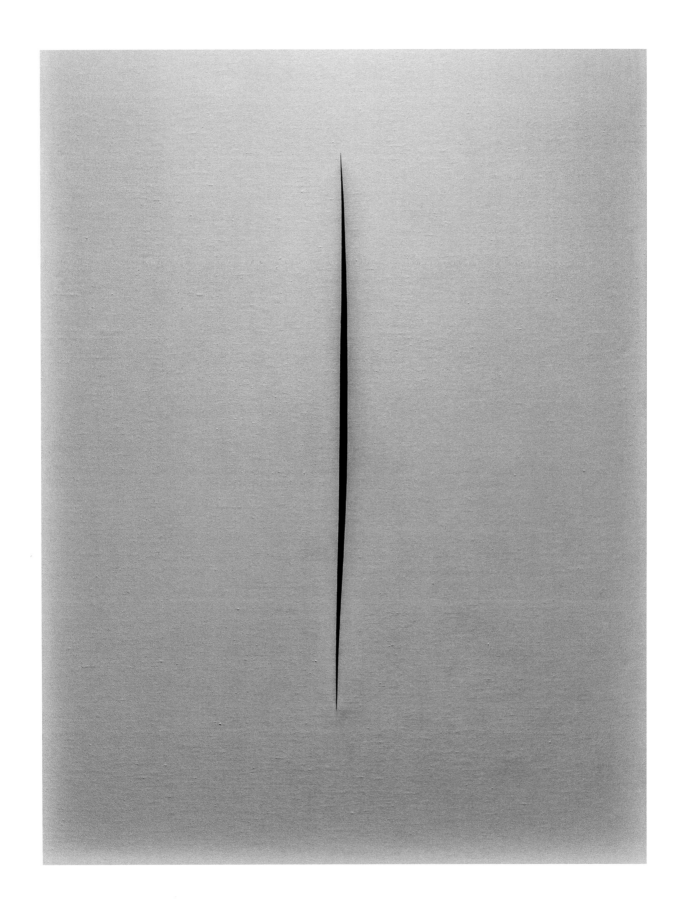

CHARRED CAULIFLOWER CHEESE PIE

—

Finished with a Fontana-style *taglio* (cut), this pie may not transport you to the fourth dimension, but its delicious, nostalgic flavours could take you back in time.

SERVES 4–6

1 large cauliflower (about 900 g / 2 lb)
1 teaspoon dried oregano
1 tablespoon olive oil
700 ml (2 ¾ cup plus 1 tbsp) full fat milk
1 small onion
1 bay leaf
10 whole black peppercorns
50 g (3 ½ tablespoons) unsalted butter
50 g (⅓ cup plus 2 teaspoons) plain flour (all-purpose flour)
150 g (5 oz) mature Cheddar cheese, grated
40 g (1 ½ oz) Parmesan cheese, finely grated
1 teaspoon Dijon mustard
Fine salt
Cracked black pepper
1 sheet puff pastry (thawed, if frozen)
1 egg

Preheat the oven to 220°C / 200°C fan (425°F / 400°F fan).

Break the cauliflower into florets and put them in a 27 × 20 × 5 cm (10.5 × 8 × 2 in) rectangular pie dish or ceramic baking dish. The cauliflower should sit just below the lip to stop the pastry from collapsing into the dish later. Add the oregano and olive oil and toss until the cauliflower is fully coated. Roast for 15 minutes, then stir the cauliflower and roast for 15 more minutes, or until golden brown and slightly charred.

Heat the milk in a small saucepan over medium heat to a low simmer. Peel and halve the onion and add it to the milk with the bay leaf and peppercorns. Turn off the heat and leave to infuse.

Melt the butter in a medium saucepan over medium heat. Add the plain flour and whisk to form a paste. Cook for about 1 minute, whisking constantly.

Strain the aromatics from the milk and gradually pour it into the pan with the flour paste, whisking as you go until smooth and thick. Remove from the heat. Add the Cheddar and Parmesan, a handful at a time and whisking as you go, until fully melted. Stir in the mustard and season with salt and pepper. Pour over the cauliflower in the dish and let cool for 20–30 minutes.

Preheat the oven to 200°C / 180°C fan (400°F / 350°F fan).

Meanwhile, on a lightly floured surface, use a rolling pin to roll out the puff pastry to the size of your baking dish, with a little overhang, and about ½ cm (1/6 in) thick. Lightly whisk the egg and use a pastry brush to brush a thin layer around the lip of the baking dish, to act as a glue. Lay the pastry over the dish and press down on the edges to make a tight seal. Trim off any excess pastry and brush the entire top surface with an even layer of the egg wash.

Use a sharp knife to cut a slit in the centre of the pie à la Fontana and bake for 25–30 minutes, or until golden.

Remove from the oven and serve with a leafy side salad.

GARY HUME
—

Each February, Gary Hume leaves his London studio for his secluded farm in upstate New York, to make maple syrup. He and his wife, fellow artist Georgie Hopton, split their time between both homes, designing their schedule to not only take into account their timetables as artists – with exhibitions to work towards and studios to run – but also the seasonal changes at the farm.

The couple cross the Atlantic to plant the vegetable garden each spring and spend the summer tending to the gardens, before harvesting their crop. With forty acres to play with, they grow an abundance of vegetables, herbs and flowers – squash, tomatoes, sunflowers, dill, asparagus. The rest of the land is kept as part nature reserve, part playground, with a wildflower meadow, three orchards and two ponds, one reserved for the wildlife and the other kept weed-free for swimming. In other words, Paradise.

The two artists create work in both locations and although their practices are very different in style and approach, they each take influence from the gardens. Hopton creates her work using a variety of natural materials. She has fridges in both studios and nature makes its way inside to be used in her diverse work, from collage to wallpaper designs; stamping flowers, vegetables and leaves to create bright, almost geometric compositions. Radishes and carrots are pulled straight from the soil, chopped, coated in paint and pressed onto paper or fabric. She gives in to the unpredictability of nature, allowing her work to be dictated by the natural forms of the vegetables.

In contrast, although Hume also takes inspiration from the garden – depicting flowers, vegetables and birds in his work, as well as more abstracted organic shapes – his plastic-looking, glossy paintings can seem far removed from the natural world. Surrounded by shelves of dripping paint cans and endless stacks of plastic mixing pots, Hume communicates with his paintings, and it takes a lot of both violence and calmness to create each work. The process is a turbulent battle, simultaneously destroying and creating. A surprise, perhaps, when you see his works in a gallery setting, hung boldly on the wall like calm, colourful mirrors.

His choice of medium is another surprise: Dulux Household Gloss Paint – which he pours and brushes over aluminium panels. The high petroleum content can make you feel quite dizzy when working inside but perhaps this is why he craves fresh air so much. But, like the vegetable garden, his paintings change with the days and seasons, reflecting light in a different way depending on the hour of day, connecting it back to nature. *Water Painting* (1999) is created from layers of varying shades of earthy greens, with a topcoat of a brownish hue, which sits somewhere between Dulux *Lichen* and *Pea Soup*. The white lines over the glossy green surface appear to be liquid, as though the whole painting would ripple and move if touched; a surface that you as the viewer also float upon, reflected in the sheen.

Despite their different approaches to creating, Hume and Hopton often work together, both in the studio and in the kitchen. They enjoy cooking and make a variety of recipes from scratch using their own produce, such as homemade cider vinegar from the apple orchards.

Following their first ever joint exhibition *Hurricanes Hardly Ever Happen* in 2020, the couple were invited to contribute a recipe to *Wallpaper** magazine's Artist's Palate series and submitted their vibrant recipe for *Pasta Liguria*. When explaining why they chose this dish, Hopton expressed the pride they feel in their home-grown produce, saying, 'apart from the fact that this dish is utterly delicious and profoundly comforting, we get stupidly excited at the prospect of using our early potatoes, the ever-giving beans and lots of aromatic basil from our vegetable garden'. The artist suggested the readers follow their example and enjoy the dish 'in hot bowls in front of a good film, with a glass of something that shines in the light like wet grass'. Like one of Hume's paintings, perhaps.

Gary Hume, *Water Painting*, 1999
Household paint on aluminium panel, 305 × 244 × 2.1 cm
Tate, London

PEA SOUP WITH HORSERADISH CRÈME FRAÎCHE

—

Inspired by Hume's unique choice of material and application, this soup is smooth and opaque. A vibrant green, it's rich and savoury with a beautiful sheen like that of Hume's paintings. Channel your inner artist as you drizzle over the crème fraîche or invite your guests to create their own masterpieces at the table.

SERVES 4

FOR THE SOUP
3 echalion shallots (banana shallots)
1 large garlic clove
40 g (2 ½ tablespoons) unsalted butter
1 tablespoon olive oil
2 potatoes (about 250 g [8 ¾ oz] total)
1 slice lemon
750 ml (3 cups) vegetable stock
500 g (17 ¾ oz) frozen peas
Fine salt
Cracked black pepper

FOR THE DRIZZLE
3 tablespoons crème fraîche
1 tablespoon horseradish sauce or ½ tablespoon fresh horseradish, finely grated
3 tablespoons full fat milk

TO SERVE
Extra-virgin olive oil

For the soup, finely chop the shallots and garlic.

In a large saucepan, warm the butter and olive oil over medium heat until the butter is melted. Add the shallot and cook, stirring regularly, for 5–7 minutes, or until softened.

Meanwhile, peel and chop the potatoes into 2.5 cm (1 in) cubes.

Once the shallots are softened, add the garlic and lemon slice and fry, stirring to make sure it doesn't catch, for 1–2 minutes. Remove the lemon and set aside. Add the potatoes and vegetable stock. Turn up the heat slightly and bring to a boil. Continue boiling for about 10 minutes, or until the potatoes are soft. Add the peas and return to a boil. Continue boiling for 1 more minute, then taste and season with salt and pepper. If the soup needs a little extra brightness, add the lemon slice back in for a couple of minutes.

Remove the pan from the heat, remove the lemon slice (if used) and let cool for 10–15 minutes.

Transfer the soup to a blender and blitz until smooth.

For the drizzle, in a small bowl, mix the crème fraîche and horseradish, then add the milk to make it pourable – you want the drizzle to be about the thickness of double cream (heavy cream).

Return the soup to the pan and reheat, then divide among bowls. Drizzle 1 tablespoon of the horseradish-crème fraîche on top of each serving or bring the bowl to the table for guests to create their own masterpieces. Finish with a little extra-virgin olive oil.

DANIEL SPOERRI

—

Imagine going for dinner and then buying the dinner table you ate at, exactly as you left it – dirty plates and all – arranged, unintentionally, by you. That's what Daniel Spoerri offered his guests at his temporary restaurant gallery in 1963. For eleven days the artist transformed Gallery J in Paris into a restaurant, serving up a different menu each day for twenty guests. At the end of each meal, the artist glued down everything left on the table in the exact position he found them, trapping the moment in time forever. At the end of the project, the eleven works, known as 'trap-paintings' or 'snare-pictures', were then turned and mounted onto the wall, exhibited and offered for sale to the diners, his collaborators.

These preserved tablescapes were not the result of ordinary meals. Spoerri served up a variety of thematic menus, some inspired by different countries' cuisines, including Hungary, Serbia, Mexico and China. There was also a budget menu called *Menu de Prison (Prison Menu)*, where for 1.5 francs (most menus were 15 francs), the guests ate lean cabbage soup with bread. This basic menu was copied from a nearby prison where dinner was served simultaneously, as if his guests were sharing their meal with the inmates from afar.

At a similar event a few years later, Spoerri served up his *Menu Travesti* ('costumed' or 'disguised' menu). Here, the courses were double-disguised, being served back to front, yet, despite appearances, also in the right order. While the dessert was served first and appetisers last, the 'dessert' turned out to be an appetiser after all – a cigar-shaped grissini with a cup of 'coffee' that was really a savoury consommé – and the 'appetiser' a dessert. On one occasion, what looked like ice cream with chocolate pralines, was in fact mashed potatoes and meatballs.

Perhaps unsurprisingly, there were often bits of food leftover at the end of each meal. These too were preserved, causing some storage issues. After purchasing a trap-painting, one of the artist's first collectors, gallerist Arturo Schwarz, wrote to Spoerri, requesting a replacement of the organic ingredients of the work. Rats had invaded his storage facility and eaten the leftover food off the plates. Spoerri declined, stating that it was part of the work; a piece created by chance, that continually changes and evolves with time and, in this

instance, rats, who had become another of the artist's collaborators.

Over the course of his career, Spoerri has explored 'everything that is edible or seems edible', a concept he later entitled 'Eat Art'. He was one of the founders of the Nouveau Réalisme movement, a group that worked to demonstrate the end of preciousness within art. These artists considered reality to be their primary medium and worked to find art in everyday life and objects. Earlier in his career, he had created the *Grocery Store* exhibition in Copenhagen in 1961, where he handed out eighty freshly baked bread rolls to visitors in place of a catalogue. Each roll was filled with rubbish, broken glass and nails, as a comment on food waste and society's aggressive level of consumption. But Spoerri was an avid consumer in his own way. He collected things, in particular, kitchen items. He created a large and extensive collection which he exhibited, in a similar vein to his trap-paintings and often alongside them (at Galerie J, for example), often focusing on one item in particular. His collection of potato peelers was particularly impressive, consisting of one hundred items, all of which were slightly different. 'It seemed to me that the typically Swiss virtue of thrift was expressed most perfectly and ironically in this invention', he said.

In 1966, Spoerri left his collections to focus his mind on just one task: cooking. He moved from the chaos of Paris, where he had lived for nearly a decade, to Symi, a remote Greek island. Here, Spoerri spent an entire year solely concentrated on cooking, using the limited but beautiful ingredients available to him. His daily notes in the kitchen alongside observations of island life were published in 1967 entitled *Mythology & Meatballs: A Greek Island Diary Cookbook*.

Three years later, Spoerri hosted his *L'ultima Cena* ('The Last Supper') at Restaurant Biffi in Milan's central arcade. Ten years after the birth of the movement, Nouveau Réalisme was coming to an end. And to mark the occasion, Spoerri cooked a dish in honour of each of the group's artists based on their work and methods: seafood set in jelly for Arman, food wrapped in foil for Jeanne-Claude and Christo and an exploding cake for Jean Tinguely. The performance was ultimately completed in and by the stomachs of the artists, marking the end of the movement. But, as Spoerri himself put it: 'If all art forms were to disappear, the noble art of cooking would remain.'

CHEESE FONDUE WITH POTATOES, RADISHES, PICKLED CORNICHONS AND CHICORY

—

This indulgent cheese fondue is the perfect sharing dish for a memorable dinner party. If you're extra committed, why not glue down your leftovers to preserve the moment, Spoerri-style?

**SERVES 4–6,
AS A STARTER OR MAIN**

FOR DIPPING
500 g (17 ¾ oz) baby
   potatoes
400 g (14 oz) radishes
180 g (6 oz) pickled
   cornichons, drained
2 heads red chicory
   (about 150 g / 5 oz)

FOR THE FONDUE
1 tablespoon cornflour
   (cornstarch)
3 tablespoons kirsch
1 garlic clove
300 ml (1 cup plus
   3 tablespoons) dry
   white wine
600 g (21 oz) Gruyère
   cheese, grated
½ teaspoon ground black
   pepper
¼ teaspoon paprika
¼ teaspoon ground nutmeg

For dipping, bring a large pan of salted water to a boil. Add the potatoes and boil for 10 minutes, or until tender. Drain and leave to steam in the colander.

Halve some of the radishes, keeping some whole for variation. Do the same with the cornichons. Chop off the base of the chicory and pull off the leaves. Arrange the potatoes, radishes, cornichons and chicory on a serving platter.

For the fondue, in a jug or small bowl, whisk together the cornflour and kirsch until smooth.

Peel and halve the garlic clove. Rub the inside of a fondue pan or saucepan with the cut sides of garlic and discard. Put the pan over high heat. Add the wine and heat until steaming but not bubbling. Lower the heat slightly, then very gradually add the Gruyère, stirring constantly, and wait until each handful is fully melted and smooth before adding more. Slowly add the cornstarch mixture, whisking quickly as you go. Add the black pepper, paprika and nutmeg and stir until thick and bubbling.

Place the pan over a fondue burner in the middle of the table or onto a heat-proof mat – if you don't have a fondue burner, you may need to reheat the fondue on the stove a few times.

Serve with the plate of dipping ingredients.

JÓZSEF RIPPL-RÓNAI
—

In 1896, József Rippl-Rónai created one of the first Art Nouveau rooms in Hungary. Commissioned by his patron, Count Tivadar Andrássy, Rippl-Rónai decorated the dining room of the Count's grand town house in Budapest, designing every last detail: the furniture, the intricate tapestries (which were painstakingly executed by his wife, Lazarine), and a vast porcelain dinner service of 300 pieces.

Like many of the artists of the time, Rippl-Rónai was heavily influenced by Japanese art, patterns and textiles with their bold, flat planes of colour and defined outlines. Highly contemporary in style, many of his designs could have been created today, with sophisticated colour combinations and nature-inspired patterns bordering on the abstract. Sadly, the dining room was destroyed during World War II, with no surviving inventory. However, numerous sample pieces from the collection remain, preserving the fluid, floral style of Rippl-Rónai's designs – though we can't be certain which (if any) of them were used in the final dinner set.

Rippl-Rónai worked during the era of the Austro-Hungarian Empire, a time of great cultural change. As these two nations came together, Austrian and Hungarian cultures mixed to create new innovations, including in their cuisine. Pastry shops and coffee houses were popular in the two great capital cities of Budapest and Vienna, offering important social spots for artists and writers. French culinary skills and methods were introduced via Austria, whilst preserving the traditional flavours of Hungary. Paprika was used increasingly and became the distinctive flavour of Hungarian food. Originally brought over from Turkey in the fifteenth century, it is most famously used in the traditional dish *guylas* (pronounced goo-lash), a meat stew dating back to the medieval period and still eaten regularly today.

During this period, the Tokaj region rose to fame across Europe for its sweet wines, and Budapest became revered for its delicious and highly technical cakes and pastries. New dishes were often named after famous people or places in the nineteenth century. On Christmas day of the year of Rippl-Rónai's commission, the American socialite Clara Ward abandoned her Hungarian prince husband and ran away with the handsome violinist Rigó Jancsi (who was also married). In response to the scandal, the cake *Rigójancsi* was invented. A layered chocolate sponge cake with apricot jam, chocolate cream and a chocolate glaze, it's a rich combination of contrasting flavours, in honour of their forbidden, fairytale love.

In addition to ceramics, Rippl-Rónai was a painter. His style changed dramatically throughout his oeuvre, progressing from a soft, intimate style in his Nabis works, such as *Woman with Birdcage* (1892), to an almost pop-art style of painting known as 'corn' style (in Hungarian, *'kukoricásnak'*) in works such as *Interior* (1909). Rippl-Rónai's 'corn' technique was similar to that of Pointillism and Divisionism, with shapes made up of small dabs of colour – like pieces of corn – a technique that is unique to Rippl-Rónai and arguably brought about modern painting in Hungary. His own culinary innovation through the medium of art.

József Rippl-Rónai, *Woman and Bird Cage*, 1892
Oil on canvas, 185.5 × 130 cm
Hungarian National Gallery, Budapest

ROASTED AUBERGINE WITH BLUE CHEESE SAUCE AND A PARSLEY DRESSING

—

This dish is for serious blue-cheese lovers. Serve it as a main course with potatoes and salad, or as a side dish to steak or roast chicken, for a truly decadent meal.

**SERVES 4–6,
AS MAIN OR SIDE**

FOR THE AUBERGINES
2 medium aubergines
  (eggplant)

FOR THE CHEESE SAUCE
60 g (4 tablespoons)
  unsalted butter
2 echalion shallots (banana
  shallots), very finely
  chopped
1 large garlic clove, finely
  chopped
60 ml (¼ cup) white
  vermouth (or white wine)
150 ml (½ cup plus
  2 tablespoons) double
  cream (heavy cream)
150 g (5 oz) creamy blue
  cheese (such as Saint
  Agur)

FOR THE DRESSING
1 small handful fresh
  flat-leaf parsley leaves,
  finely chopped
2 tablespoons extra-virgin
  olive oil
3 tablespoons lemon juice
¼ teaspoon fine salt

Preheat the oven to 180°C / 160°F fan (350°F / 320°F fan).

For the aubergines, use a fork to prick the aubergines all over, then put them in a large ovenproof dish. Bake for 25 minutes, then flip the aubergine and continue baking for 25 more minutes, or until soft through. Remove from the oven and make crosswise cuts, about 2.5 cm (1 in) apart, into the flesh of the softened aubergines without cutting all the way through.

Meanwhile, for the cheese sauce, in a medium frying pan, melt the butter over medium heat. Add the shallots and sauté for 5 minutes, or until softened and starting to brown – don't be afraid of them browning, this gives the sauce that gorgeous ochre shade. Add the chopped garlic and fry for 1 more minute. Add the vermouth and let it boil off for 20 seconds. Turn down the heat slightly and pour in the double cream. Crumble in 120 g (4 oz) of the blue cheese, reserving the rest for serving, and stir until melted. Transfer to a blender or food processor and blitz until smooth.

For the dressing, in a small bowl, whisk together the parsley, olive oil, lemon juice and salt.

To serve, pour the cheese sauce onto a warmed serving plate. Arrange the aubergines on top, spoon over the dressing and crumble over the remaining blue cheese.

JACOB LAWRENCE

—

From 1910 to 1970, six million Black Americans left their homes in the Southern States to move north and west, in search of a better life. With white men drafted to war – despite the 2.5 million Black American men who registered for the draft, they were often passed over by the all-white draft boards – factory jobs opened up in the big cities, like Chicago and New York, drawing Black communities away from the poor farms of the South, with hopes of safety from the threat of lynching and more prosperity. The Great Migration saw the movement not only of people, but of cultural and culinary traditions as well, transforming American cuisine forever.

Jacob Lawrence and his family were part of this mass movement, ending up in Harlem, New York; the largest Black urban community in the country at the time. Harlem was an exciting place to live, full of creativity and innovation, particularly during the 1920s and 1930s – a period known as the Harlem Renaissance. Fascinated by his local area, Lawrence captured the hustle and bustle of the city from a young age, depicting the experience of Black life in America. He had a particular interest in the consequences of The Great Migration and researched the movement, reading about Black history and listening to stories from his parents and neighbours. His resulting work *The Migration Series* features sixty images that communicate the experiences of the community: a faceless crowd waiting patiently at a train station; an exhausted family carrying their heavy belongings; an impoverished mother slicing bacon for her thin child.

Wherever they settled, migrants brought a taste of home with them. Many transported seeds to continue their culinary traditions by growing staple ingredients, such as black-eyed peas and corn, making the most of the tiny plots of land available in the cities. Food shops and eateries started to pop up, starting with carts, before vendors made enough money to open bricks-and-mortar shops and restaurants. The queen of soul food, Pamela Strobel (also known as Princess Pamela), was among these entrepreneurs, opening The Little Kitchen in New York in 1965. As a live jazz band played each night, Strobel served dishes to guests including celebrities Andy Warhol, Gloria Steinem and Diana Ross.

In the street food scene, fried chicken, fried fish and barbecue became wildly popular – dishes which make up a huge proportion of American cuisine today. Barbecue was particularly fashionable, not only because of its flavours but also because it was a cheap venture to start up. Pit masters could work from their own backyards and were able to scale up the quantity of food they produced to any number, provided they had enough space and enough meat. True barbecue refers to a whole hog, which has been cooked and smoked for many hours over hardwood coals, traditionally set in a pit dug in the ground. But variations on the tradition started to emerge all over America where the migrants settled, using local ingredients to flavour different, often smaller, cuts of meat, which take less time to cook.

Pork is essential to both Southern and Soul Food (a description coined by the Black Power movement of the 1960s), and is used not only as the main event, in comforting dishes such as smothered pork chops, but as a flavouring for many nostalgic dishes, including the beloved slow-cooked collard greens. For years, slaves had limited access to meat and had to make do with poorer cuts, such as the ribs and feet, which were given to them in their weekly rations. The best cuts were reserved for the white property owners. But from a few simple ingredients a whole culture of food was established, full of delicious dishes that now grace tables all over the USA and beyond; think cornbread, fried chicken, mac and cheese, biscuits and gravy, and gumbo, to name but a few. Dishes that both commemorate the hardships of the Black migrant experience and celebrate the resilience and resourcefulness of the community, just as Jacob Lawrence did through his work.

Jacob Lawrence, *From Every Southern Town Migrants Left by the Hundreds to Travel North*, 1940–1941
Casein tempera on hardboard, 30.5 × 45.7 cm
The Phillips Collection, Washington D.C.

SMOTHERED PORK CHOPS WITH OKRA AND TOMATO SALSA

—

This dish is adapted from Sheila Ferguson's recipe for Smothered Pork Chops in her book *Soul Food: Classic Cuisine from the Deep South*. It's comforting and delicious, with an added freshness from the zingy salsa.

SERVES 4

FOR THE SALSA
180 g (6 oz) okra
2 tomatoes
1 small handful fresh
    coriander (cilantro)
    leaves, finely chopped
2 tablespoons finely
    chopped pickled
    jalapeño slices
1 tablespoon white wine
    vinegar

FOR THE PORK CHOPS
100 g (3 ½ oz) plain flour
    (all-purpose flour)
1 teaspoon smoked paprika
1 teaspoon dried oregano
Fine salt
4 bone-in pork chops
2 medium onions
3 tablespoons olive oil
40 g (2 ½ tablespoons)
    unsalted butter
500 ml (2 cups) chicken
    stock
100 ml (⅓ cup plus
    1 tablespoon) double
    cream (heavy cream)

For the salsa, prepare the okra by cutting off the stems. Bring a medium pan of salted water to a boil. Tip in the okra and boil, stirring occasionally, for 3 minutes, or until cooked but still have crunch. Drain and tip into a bowl of ice water to cool and stop the cooking.

Cut each tomato into 8 wedges.

Once the okra is cool, cut it crosswise into 2–3 cm (about 1 in) thick rounds and put in a medium bowl. Add the coriander, jalapeños and white wine vinegar. Mix and set aside.

For the pork chops, in a shallow dish, combine the plain flour, paprika, oregano and a generous pinch of salt. Coat each pork chop in the flour mixture and shake off any excess. Keep the leftover flour to one side.

Peel and halve the onions, then cut them into thin half-moons.

In a large frying pan or skillet, warm the olive oil over high heat. Add the pork chops and cook, flipping once, for 3 minutes per side, or until browned. Transfer the browned pork chops to a plate and set aside. Use a spoon to remove and discard all but 1 tablespoon of the fat in the pan.

Put the pan over low heat, add the butter and let melt. Add the onions and a generous pinch of salt and cook, stirring constantly, for 15 minutes, or until the onions are soft and caramelised. Sprinkle in 2 tablespoons of the reserved flour mixture and cook, stirring occasionally, for 5 more minutes. Add the stock and bring to a boil, using a wooden spoon to scrape up any caramelised bits off the bottom of the pan for extra flavour. Add the double cream and continue cooking, stirring frequently to prevent lumps, for 2–3 minutes, or until slightly thickened. Return the pork chops to the pan and cook for 8–10 more minutes, or until fully cooked through.

Serve in the pan with the salsa scattered on top.

ALISON KNOWLES
—

In 2008, Alison Knowles stood on the bridge of the Turbine Hall of Tate Modern in London, throwing vast handfuls of salad onto a tarpaulin below. Accompanied by live music, a team of chefs chopped the ingredients to the beat, with microphones amplifying the sound of their work. Knowles then dramatically dropped the leaves and vegetables from a height, before mixing them with a rake and serving the prepared salad to the audience. Just as her friend John Cage turned silence into music, Knowles turned making a salad into a concert.

Knowles is associated with Fluxus, an artistic group who predominantly worked in the 1960s and 1970s in America. Founded by George Maciunas, Fluxus artists created art from overlooked activities of everyday life and recontextualised them as performance. As they stated in their 1963 manifesto, their aim was to 'promote NON ART REALITY.' In doing so, they challenged the traditions of art and art venues, working with unusual materials in unusual locations. Fluxus artists often created performance instructions, known as 'Propositions' or 'Event Scores', keeping the detail to a minimum to allow for individual interpretation and chance. In 1965, Knowles released a pamphlet of Event Scores, including *#2 Proposition* (1962) the instructions of which were simply 'Make a salad.'

Fluxus artists often used food as a material for art, drawn to the temporary, perishable nature of food and the possibility of producing endless variations of the same work. The group would often host 'Fluxmeals' for New Year, where each artist would contribute a dish invented for the meal, some edible, some not so edible. 'Monomeals' were a common theme; meals of just one colour such as red or white, or based around one ingredient such as potatoes or fish. The Fluxus 'Fishmeal' dinner featured a variety of unusual fish-based dishes, including a fish fizzy drink, fish candy and fish ice cream.

For the New Year's banquet in 1969, Knowles contributed *Shit Porridge*. The ingredients were not revealed, so the only way of knowing what the dish was really made of was to eat it. Fortunately for those brave tasters, it was made of beans, not excrement – an ingredient that Knowles has used frequently throughout her career.

Every cuisine uses beans in some capacity; they're cheap (another important consideration for many Fluxus artists) and when dried they make a great sound. Knowles utilises this aspect in some of her sound pieces, such as *Giant Bean Turner.* First performed in 1995, she created a musical instrument from a human-sized paper sack filled with dried beans, which she turned to make the sound of roaring waves as the beans fell.

The source of Knowles' ideas for performance come from her own daily life – including her meals – and in 1969, she created one of her most celebrated works, *The Identical Lunch*. The proposition: 'A tunafish sandwich on wheat toast, with lettuce and butter, no mayo and a cup of soup or a glass of buttermilk.' Knowles realised that she had been eating the same lunch every day and in doing so, she had inadvertently produced a piece of performance art. She therefore invited a few guests to join her for lunch each day. Despite being nominally the same, each sandwich was unique and each eater's reaction to it was also individual. Like any Fluxus artwork, *The Identical Lunch* can be performed by anyone and the Fluxus founder Maciunas decided to make his own version of Knowles' lunch, but with a devious twist. He prepared the sandwich and glass of buttermilk as instructed, before putting the whole thing into a blender. The resulting cold fishy soup (which would have fit in well at the Fishmeal) was then distributed to the audience in little cups; according to Knowles, it was surprisingly delicious. Since then, she has gone on to perform both interpretations of *The Identical Lunch* all over the world.

So, next time you have a tuna sandwich, pay close attention to the process of both making and eating it. And of course, make sure to wash it down with a cup of soup, or a glass of buttermilk. (Blend at your own risk.)

Alison Knowles, *Make a Salad*, 2008
Performance, 180 minutes
Tate, London

GREEN ORZO SALAD

—

Chop the ingredients to a beat and drop them into the bowl from a height to really *Make a Salad*.

**SERVES 4–8,
AS A MAIN OR SIDE**

FOR THE SALAD
1 large red onion
2 teaspoons olive oil
1 broccoli head (about
    400 g / 14 oz)
180 g (6 oz) orzo
50 g (1¾ oz) fresh spinach
    leaves
1 tablespoon capers

FOR THE DRESSING
1 avocado
1 handful fresh basil leaves
1 small handful fresh
    flat-leaf parsley leaves
1 small garlic clove, peeled
100 ml (⅓ cup plus
    1 tablespoon) extra-
    virgin olive oil
2 tablespoons sherry
    vinegar
½ lemon, juiced
½ teaspoon fine salt

Preheat the oven to 200°C / 180°C fan (400°F / 350°F fan).

For the salad, halve the red onion and cut it into 1 cm (⅜ in) thick half-moons. Put in a large baking dish, drizzle with 1 teaspoon of the olive oil and toss to coat. Roast for 10 minutes.

Meanwhile, cut the broccoli into small, bite-size florets and chop the stem into similar sized pieces. Sprinkle on top of the onion, drizzle with the remaining 1 teaspoon of olive oil and stir to coat in the oil and combine with the onion. Roast for 25 minutes, or until slightly softened and browned.

In a small saucepan, cook the orzo according to the packet instructions until al dente. Drain and set aside.

For the dressing, in a blender or food processor, combine the avocado, basil, parsley, garlic, olive oil, sherry vinegar, lemon juice and salt and blitz until smooth. If the dressing is too thick, blend in a little water to thin it. The dressing should taste pretty strong and vinegary, so that it doesn't get lost when stirred through – orzo sucks up a lot of flavour.

Roughly chop the spinach and put it in a large serving bowl. Add the broccoli, onion, orzo and all but 2 tablespoons of the dressing. Stir to combine.

Drizzle over the reserved dressing, sprinkle with the capers and serve warm.

PABLO PICASSO

—

Pablo Picasso didn't like to talk during meals. According to his lover Fernande Olivier, 'sometimes he would not utter a word from beginning to end'.

The artist was an unusual character and is known to have conducted every aspect of his life with a similar level of intensity, particularly his art practice. He was an obsessive creator and is estimated to have made over 50,000 artworks over the course of his career. To do this, he prioritised his art over everything else and, once he moved to Paris, he developed a very strict routine to ensure he dedicated as many hours as possible to creating work. Picasso would start his day late, waking up at 11 a.m. to have breakfast, before spending a few hours with friends, who clearly worked around his timetable. From 2 p.m., he would go to his studio, where he would work until about 3 a.m., only breaking to eat dinner from 10 p.m. to 11 p.m., before getting his eight hours of sleep and starting all over again.

He may have only eaten two meals per day, but food was an essential part of Picasso's practice. He painted still lifes, worked with ceramics and held his first two solo exhibitions at Els Quatre Gats (The Four Cats), his local restaurant when he lived in Barcelona as a young man. He would go there daily to both eat and draw, auctioning off his creations at the end of the night to pay for his meal. As he aged, he considered food to play an essential role in his creative output. And once he reached his fifties, he kept himself on a very strict and simple diet which he hoped would help keep his health from deteriorating and enable him to maintain his level of productivity. Encouraged by his doctor, he ate simple fish and vegetable dishes, grapes and rice pudding with mineral water or milk. There are many wonderful photographs taken by David Douglas Duncan of the artist enjoying his fish supper. The photographer said of his visit, 'Picasso had just filleted a sole meunière with almost surgical precision when he picked up the bones

to finish off the last stray morsels … Picasso then put down the skeleton, disappeared – and returned with a slab of moist potter's clay. He'd eaten the sole, now its skeleton was to be immortalised.' It's possible that this became part of his famous ceramic work *Bullfight and Fish* (1957); a hand-painted plate with the imprinted slab sitting precariously on top.

Picasso started to work with ceramics after the war. It's said he made the shift because working in clay meant he could work on a smaller scale, which was less demanding than his paintings. But, being Picasso, this didn't mean he worked with any less enthusiasm. In fact, he produced about 3,500 ceramic works in total. He was aware of the links between his work and the kitchen; ceramics are not only used for cooking and serving food but when they are created, they are baked in the oven like bread to harden. His painting style also changed after the war; and his diet is reflected in his still lifes of the time, including *Still Life, Fish and Frying Pan; Nature morte, Poissons et poêle* (1936). Pieces like this, produced after 1935, are not categorised into certain styles from various points of the artist's career such as his Blue Period or Cubism, as they each incorporate different elements of his past periods into a new, fluid and all-encompassing style that Picasso continued to explore throughout his later years.

Ultimately, it seems his strict diet and intensive routine worked as Picasso intended. The artist lived until the age of ninety-one and it's said he was creating work with the same enthusiasm until just three hours before his death. An artist through and through.

Pablo Picasso, *Still Life, Fish and Frying Pan*, 1936
Oil on canvas, 28 × 41 cm
Private collection

WHOLE ROASTED SEA BREAM WITH SPANISH PISTO

—

This recipe is a nod to Pablo Picasso's diet. The base is a Spanish pisto, a dish which differs slightly depending on which region of Spain it's cooked in. This particular pisto is a variation on a traditional recipe from Andalusia, the region where Picasso was born, in Malaga. Often referred to as Spanish ratatouille, it is both healthy and hearty.

If you want to go all out, after the meal, why not take inspiration from Picasso and create your own artwork by imprinting the fish bones in clay?

SERVES 2–4

FOR THE PISTO
1 large onion
3 garlic cloves
1 teaspoon fresh thyme
    leaves
2 tablespoons olive oil
30 g (2 tablespoons) butter
1 medium aubergine
    (eggplant)
Fine salt
1 yellow bell pepper
1 medium courgette
    (zucchini)
400 g (14 oz) tinned
    chopped tomatoes
250 ml (1 cup) passata

FOR THE FISH
1 small fennel bulb
2 small whole sea bream,
    scaled, gutted and
    cleaned, with the fins
    removed (approx. 250 g /
    9 oz each)
Fine salt
2 tablespoons olive oil
½ lemon, thinly sliced

For the pisto, finely chop the onion, garlic and thyme.

In a large saucepan, warm the olive oil and butter over medium heat until the butter is melted. Add the onion and cook, stirring frequently, for 8–12 minutes, or until translucent. About 2 minutes before the onion is done, add the garlic and thyme to the pan.

As the onion cooks, cut the aubergine into 2.5 cm (1 in) cubes and arrange on a plate in a single layer. Sprinkle with 2 teaspoons of salt and set aside for 5 minutes to draw out some of the water.

Meanwhile, cut the yellow bell pepper and courgette into bite-size pieces.

Pat the aubergine dry with paper towels or a clean tea towel and tip them into the pan, along with the pepper and courgette. Cook, stirring frequently, for 5 minutes, or until slightly softened. Add the chopped tomatoes and passata and bring to a simmer. Cook for 15–20 minutes, or until the sauce is slightly reduced and the oil rises to the top. Season with salt.

Preheat the oven to 180°C / 160°C fan (350°F / 320°F fan).

For the fish, remove any fronds from the fennel and reserve for garnish. Cut the bulb lengthwise into ½ cm (⅙ in) thick slices.

In a large dry frying pan (with an ovenproof handle) over high heat, cook the fennel for 1–2 minutes on each side, or until slightly charred.

On a clean chopping board, carefully score the fish on both sides with a sharp knife and season each cut with a tiny pinch of salt. Drizzle ½ tablespoon of olive oil over each fish and rub the skin to coat both sides of the fish. Season the cavity with salt and stuff it with the lemon slices and half of the fennel. Stir the rest of the fennel into the pisto.

Put the frying pan over medium-high heat and warm 1 tablespoon of olive oil. Add the fish and fry, flipping once, for 1–2 minutes on each side, or until crispy. Remove the fish from the pan.

Once the pisto has thickened, transfer it into the frying pan. Place the fish on top and roast in the oven for 15–20 minutes, or until the fish is cooked through – the flesh should easily flake off the bone with a fork.

Scatter the fish with the reserved fennel fronds and serve it in the pan.

GABRIEL OROZCO

—

Gabriel Orozco was on a regular trip to the supermarket when he realised that if an item was moved to a different place within the perfectly ordered store, it generated chaos. Thus, his series *Cinco Problemas (Five Problems)* (1992) was born; photographs that, for anyone who likes to keep things neat, are torturous to look at. Tins of cat food balance on watermelons; potatoes sit in the stationery aisle; a single can disrupts the lines of a perfectly stacked shelf; Orozco's photographs transform the familiar into the absurd by disrupting our notion of how things should be.

Twenty-five years later, Orozco created his very own supermarket, installing a fully functioning OXXO store (a chain in Latin America) in Kurimanzutto Gallery in Mexico City. On entering the gallery, playfully titled *OROXXO*, visitors were given an 'OROXXO' dollar, which they could 'spend' on certain items in the store – affordable products that would be available in any OXXO shop (crisps, drinks and so on). But there were other items that this dollar could not buy. Three hundred selected products had been branded with a red, gold and blue logo, setting them apart from their unbranded fellows and instantly transforming them into works of art. As an added twist, the value of these chosen products was ultimately decided by whichever buyer was willing to purchase the first pieces. Prices started at an eye-watering $30,000, for items such as a bag of crisps that would usually cost less than $2. The items then dropped in price by 50 per cent after the sale of each edition, turning the usual progression of the art market on its head. Here, Orozco was making a comment on both the art market and general consumer culture; he was not only making a joke of the sale of his own work, but also of buyers' willingness to purchase pieces, knowing that the next buyer would pay half the price.

As in the case of these artworks, price is often determined by exclusivity. Food – even outside the context of an art gallery – is no exception: think wagyu beef, Beluga caviar and bluefin tuna. These rare foods reach extraordinary prices simply for the exclusive luxury of eating them, after which, their value is entirely lost. Wagyu beef reaches prices of $3,200 per steak, while just one kilogram (2.2 lbs) of Beluga Caviar can set you back over $20,000. In 2019, Japanese sushi tycoon

Kiyoshi Kimura bought the world's most expensive (and endangered) fish, forking out $3.1 million for a 278-kilogram (612 lb) bluefin tuna. A staggering price that would nevertheless buy you less than 144th of the most expensive painting ever sold. *Salvator Mundi* (c.1499–1510) by Leonardo Da Vinci sold for $450.3 million in 2017.

But it's not only luxury ingredients that can achieve that 'exclusive' label. Retailers artificially introduce this idea into affordable, everyday products by releasing limited edition versions. Brands such as McDonald's, Walkers and Magnum have mastered the art of making the ordinary extraordinary by introducing unusual (and sometimes controversial) variations on their products for a limited number or period of time. Whether it comes in the form of one-off packaging or a weird new flavour, exclusivity both entices new customers and keeps the interest of existing clientele. Ultimately, it increases sales.

Orozco's work breaks down these ideas. His work both adds value to cheap commercial items and strips value from works of art, whilst retaining exclusivity. Anything outside the familiar can, in theory, have interest, and therefore potentially infinite monetary value. Perhaps we should all look at the supermarket shelves a little differently in the future.

Gabriel Orozco, *Sleeping Leaves*, 1991
Photograph, azo dye print (Ilfochrome), 31.7 × 47.7 cm
National Gallery of Canada, Ottawa

SPINACH PANCAKES WITH EGGS AND FETA

—

This is a colourful and spicy twist on a classic brunch dish. I recommend serving the chilli oil at the table for your guests to decide how spicy they like it!

SERVES 4–8

FOR THE PANCAKES
150 g (5 oz) fresh spinach leaves
120 g (¾ cup plus 1½ tablespoons) plain flour (all-purpose flour)
270 ml (1 cup plus 1 tablespoon) full fat milk
1 egg
½ teaspoon fine salt
Vegetable oil, for frying

FOR THE FILLING
8 eggs
60 g (2 oz) fresh baby spinach leaves
160 g (5½ oz) feta cheese
2 tablespoons chilli oil (see page 36)

For the pancakes, in a blender, combine the spinach, plain flour, milk, egg and salt and blend until smooth.

Place a large nonstick frying pan (for which you have a lid) over medium heat. Add ½ teaspoon of the vegetable oil, swirling the pan to coat it in oil. Add a ladle of batter, swirling the pan to create a thin, even layer. Cook for 1–2 minutes on the first side, or until fully set, then flip the pancake and cook for another minute. Tip the pancake out onto a warm plate and keep warm. Repeat until all the batter is used, adding more oil as needed – you should get 8 pancakes.

For the filling, put the same pan over high heat and once hot, crack in the eggs. Cover the pan and fry the eggs for 1–2 minutes, or until the whites are cooked but the yolks are still runny.

To serve, place the pancakes flat on plates. Add a few spinach leaves and a fried egg to one half of each pancake. Crumble over the feta and add a drizzle of chilli oil. Fold the pancakes over to put the spinach leaves to sleep and serve with more chilli oil.

DESSERTS

VICTOR VASARELY

—

According to his son Yvaral, Victor Vasarely was a chaotic cook. 'My father, normally so precise and organised, transformed the kitchen into a real mess', he said. This is certainly a contrast to the artist's usual style of working. Heavily influenced by the Bauhaus movement as well as Cubism, Dada and Futurism, Vasarely created what were perhaps the first kinetic artworks that did not move, founding the Op art movement. Incredibly precise in their construction, he worked in a variety of mediums, using a minimal number of geometric shapes, to suggest motion within static forms.

A graphic artist working initially for advertising agencies, Vasarely strived to create artwork that was accessible to the masses. He had experimented with Op art aesthetics as far back as the 1930s, but his work became widely known in the 1950s. The optical illusions of Op art greatly influenced popular culture and this new art form inspired the design, advertising, music and fashion of the time. Food soon followed suit. During the 1950s and 1960s food in Europe and beyond became more colourful and more unnatural, in shape, colour and ingredients. Canned and jellied food reigned, and dishes were served in bright, tempting patterns, particularly once rationing ended after the war. Pâtés topped with bacon or anchovy crosses, devilled eggs and pineapple upside down cakes with glacé cherries became popular alongside the revival of geometric Battenberg cakes. Unfortunately, dishes such as Jello Salad also began to appear, particularly in America. Fruits or vegetables were set in a flavoured jelly or aspic with mayonnaise and/or whipped cream, served on a bed of lettuce leaves.

But some more tempting dishes also appeared on the table. Once flour, butter and sugar were no longer rationed, people started to bake again, especially in the patisseries of France where Vasarely had settled before World War II. The artist enjoyed cooking and baking and he often made Hungarian foods from his childhood, singing Hungarian folk songs as he cooked. His favourite dish was sugared plum dumplings: fresh plums or pitted prunes surrounded with a mashed potato dough and coated in cinnamon breadcrumbs. He couldn't return

home because of the Communist regime and cooking helped him to connect to his roots from afar. Yvaral often joined his father in the kitchen and the pair created a variety of traditional dishes. 'Our specialties were the goulas [goulash], the toltott paprika [paprika cabbage], the korozott [feta cheese spread], and of course the szilva gombac [sugared plum dumplings].'

The father-son duo also collaborated outside the kitchen. In 1972, they designed the dining room for the Deutsche Bundesbank Central Office in Frankfurt. A psychedelic installation of 582 coloured disks made of plastic and aluminium lined the walls in shades of yellow, gold, grey and silver. A pulsating artwork in a liveable space, Vasarely wanted to incorporate his approach to design into everyday life, including the spaces where people ate. The shapes move under the viewer's gaze, playing with perception. Thirteen floors up with a wall-to-wall window overlooking the city on one side, it must have been quite an experience to eat there.

Victor Vasarely's designs are well known to many of us as a part of daily life, often without realising it. The 1972 Munich Olympics symbol, the diamond shaped Renault logo and the cover of David Bowie's second album *Space Oddity* were all designed by him. In addition, many artists have taken inspiration from the Op art movement, particularly during the counterculture of the 1960s, when psychedelic designs reigned. And some artists continue the legacy of Op art today. So, next time you see a psychedelic pattern or a Renault car driving by, think of Vasarely – the father of precise design – and his very messy kitchen.

Victor Vasarely, *Saman N° 3313*, 1984
Acrylic on canvas, 78 × 78 cm
Private collection

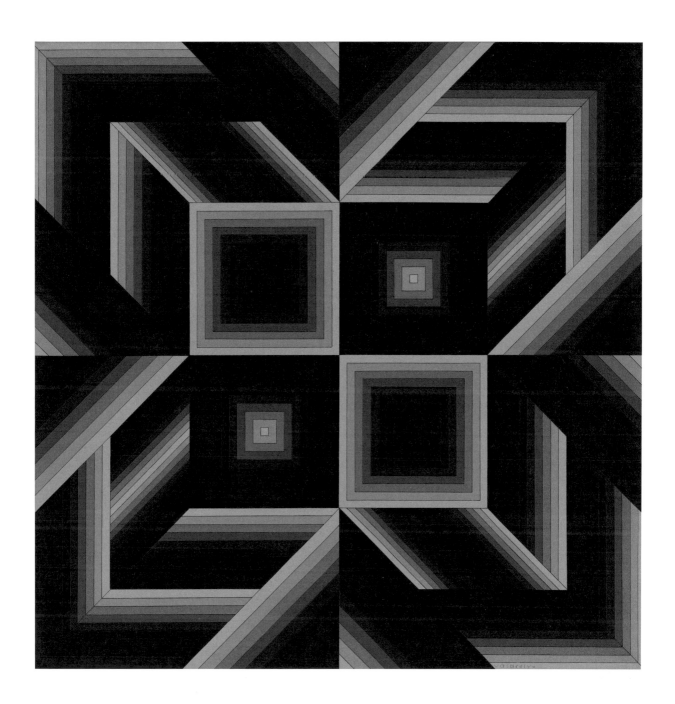

RHUBARB FRANGIPANE TART WITH CARDAMOM GLAZE

—

There's something very satisfying about the precision of baking, but if you're anything like me, the process can still be quite messy. Personally, I'm not shy about throwing flour around and neither was Victor Vasarely. So, feel free to follow the Op artist's example for this recipe. And don't worry, the end result is a clean, geometric tart-work that's so beautiful your guests will never suspect the chaos that created it.

**MAKES 1 TART-WORK
SERVES 6–8**

FOR THE PASTRY
200 g (1¼ cups plus
    2 tablespoons) plain flour
    (all-purpose flour)
2 tablespoons icing sugar
    (confectioners' sugar)
Fine salt
100 g (7 tablespoons)
    unsalted butter, chilled
1 egg yolk
Cold water, as needed

FOR THE FILLING
120 g (½ cup) unsalted
    butter, softened
125 g (½ cup plus
    2 tablespoons) caster
    sugar (superfine sugar)
1 egg
125 g (1¼ cups) ground
    almonds
250 g (9 oz) pink rhubarb

FOR THE GLAZE
2 tablespoons caster sugar
    (superfine sugar)
3 cardamom pods

TO SERVE
Crème fraîche

For the pastry, in a large bowl, combine the plain flour, icing sugar and a pinch of salt. Cut the butter into small cubes and use your fingertips to rub it into the flour mixture until it resembles fine breadcrumbs. Add the egg yolk and use your hands to bring the mixture together into a smooth dough, adding a little cold water, as needed, until the dough leaves the sides of the bowl clean. Wrap the pastry dough in cling film and put it in the refrigerator to chill for 30 minutes.

On a lightly floured surface, use a rolling pin to roll out the chilled pastry dough until about 3 mm (⅛ in) thick. Carefully lift the pastry and lay it over a 23 cm (9 in) fluted, loose-bottomed round tart tin. Use your knuckles to press the pastry into the edges of the tin to create a sealed lining. Don't worry if the pastry crumbles. If it is too difficult to lift as one piece, take small pieces and push them into place, making sure there are no holes. Trim off any excess. Put the pastry shell in the refrigerator to chill for 30 minutes. Don't skip this step – it ensures the pastry holds its shape and has a crisp bottom.

Preheat the oven to 180°C / 160°C fan (350°F / 320°F fan).

Meanwhile, for the frangipane, in a large bowl combine the butter and caster sugar and use a wooden spoon to beat until creamy. Add the egg and beat to incorporate, then fold in the ground almonds until fully combined.

Cut the rhubarb crosswise at a 45° angle to create lozenge shapes, each about 4 cm (1½ in) long. Chop half of the stems with the cuts going left to right, and half going right to left to create variety within your geometric pattern. Plan your pattern in advance as you will need to work quickly. The flat sides will be facing up for the final design.

Once the pastry shell is chilled, set the tin on a baking tray to make it easier to lift. Line the bottom of the pastry shell with parchment paper, pour in baking beans or rice and blind bake for 15 minutes. Remove the beans and paper and bake for 10 more minutes, or until the pastry is lightly golden. Let cool for 5 minutes.

Spread the frangipane in the slightly cooled tart shell. Quickly add the rhubarb to create your geometric pattern, gently pushing the pieces into the filling, so that only the flat side of the rhubarb is showing. Bake for 35–45 minutes, or until the frangipane is set and golden brown. Set on a wire rack to cool.

Meanwhile, for the glaze, in a small saucepan, dissolve the caster sugar in 75 ml (5 tablespoons) of water. Lightly crush the cardamom pods with the back of a spoon and add the pods to the pan. Bring to a simmer over medium-low heat and cook until the liquid reduces slightly into a syrup. Using a pastry brush, gently dab the frangipane and rhubarb with the syrup to glaze them. The frangipane will soak up some of the liquid, so keep dabbing until all the syrup is used up.

Once the tart is completely cool, remove it from its tin by placing it onto a can and gently pulling down on the sides of the tin. Carefully slide the tart off the base onto a serving plate and serve with crème fraîche.

DAVID NASH

—

On Christmas Day 1971, David Nash created his first artworks using charred wood: 'They were like two little Christmas puddings', he said. Little did he know that those two puddings would spark the beginning of a vast series of work that Nash is still exploring today. He is fascinated by wood and the way charring transforms it. 'You're changing the experience from a vegetable experience, wood is vegetable, to a mineral experience,' Nash says, 'because you're actually coating, you're creating a layer of carbon.'

Charring has long been used as a method of transformation, particularly in the world of food. Cooking over flames could date back as far as one million years BC and is used in cultures and cuisines across the world. In recent years, some chefs have refined this basic cooking technique, using fire to intentionally char food in a fine dining environment to create a variety of textures and flavours. It's the art of charred versus burnt.

Charring is the partial burning of an ingredient to blacken its surface. Cooking at a high temperature starts the Maillard reaction: sugar and protein molecules bond and mix, resulting in caramelisation, browning the surface and unlocking new and enticing aromas and flavours. Charring takes this process a step further, to the point of blackening the outside, rather than browning it. Think smoky baba ganoush, charred pepper salsa and burnt Basque cheesecake.

Many chefs have used charring as a method to enhance the flavour of their food, and none more so than Francis Mallmann, the Argentinian chef who cooks almost exclusively over fire, exploring unusual barbeque techniques on his private island in Patagonia. Mallmann, who for many years was known for cooking exquisite cuts of meat as the main event of his meals, has recently turned his attention to fruits and vegetables. He builds elaborate structures to give the ingredients access to the right amount of heat, suspending whole pineapples and cabbages over the wood fires from a bespoke iron dome, taller than himself.

But burning food can, of course, be an accident – humans have been mistakenly incinerating meals for a million years. Although this makes food inedible, burned food from fires past can help us better understand our own history. Scientists and archaeologists seeking to learn more about the development of human diets can use new microscope technology to unlock information, performing detailed analysis of food that has been preserved through burning. In an Iron Age site in Southern India, for example, archaeologists came across charred lumps of food which they discovered were the remains of a batter or stew made of legumes and pulses, as well as millet flat bread – a food that is still eaten in the area today, nearly 3,000 years later. Now it's possible to determine not only the ingredients our ancestors ate, but the methods in which they prepared them. Burnt food can open up all kinds of opportunities. Just like Nash's two little Christmas puddings.

David Nash, *Pyramid, Sphere, Cube*, 1997–1998
Oak, 320 × 450 × 350 cm
Tate, London

CHOCOLATE TRUFFLES WITH COCOA POWDER AND SMOKED SUGAR

—

These truffles are moreish but sophisticated, especially with the unexpected addition of smoked sugar. Why not serve the bowl of set chocolate at the table and invite your guests to create their own truffles? I recommend serving truffles with a glass of dessert wine for a truly luxurious experience.

MAKES 24 TRUFFLES

150 g (5 oz) high-quality dark chocolate, 70% cocoa
2 tablespoons unsalted butter
150 ml (½ cup plus 2 tablespoons) double cream (heavy cream)
Fine salt
Cocoa powder (about 25 g / ⅓ cup), for coating
Smoked sugar (about 3 tablespoons), for coating

Use a sharp knife to cut the chocolate into small crumb-size pieces. Put it into a large heatproof bowl.

Melt the butter in a small saucepan over medium heat. Add the double cream, stir and bring to a simmer. Remove the pan from the heat and slowly pour the mixture over the chocolate, stirring as you pour, until smooth and glossy. Add a pinch of salt and stir again. Let the mixture cool for 20–30 minutes, then put it in the refrigerator to chill and set for at least 3 hours.

When ready to make the truffles, put the cocoa powder and smoked sugar into separate small bowls.

To form the truffles, dip a teaspoon or melon baller briefly into a cup of hot water, shake it dry, then use it to scoop up bite-size balls of the mixture. Quickly form the mixture into truffles, rolling the chocolate between your palms to form balls and using your fingers and a butter knife to create cubes and pyramids. This is quite a messy process, so keep cooling your hands in cold water and drying them between each truffle to keep the chocolate from melting too much.

Once each truffle is formed, immediately drop it into the cocoa powder or smoked sugar, shaking the bowls to ensure an even coating. Use a toothpick or spoon to transfer the truffles onto a baking tray or plate lined with parchment paper.

Once all the truffles have been formed and coated, put them in the refrigerator to firm up for 20 minutes, or until ready to serve.

For the perfect texture, remove the truffles from the refrigerator 10 minutes before serving.

PAUL CÉZANNE

—

Paul Cézanne loved anchovies. So much so that each morning he would head out for his studio carrying a picnic of rolled aubergine slices, covered with anchovy spread, to sustain him for his day of painting.

He didn't make them himself but had a housekeeper, Madame Brémond, who made every meal for him, just as his mother had done before her. Cézanne loved strong, simple flavours and she would cook Provençal dishes that celebrated local ingredients, including his favourite meal *Pommes de terres à l'huile*, a simple dish of potatoes cooked in olive oil with garlic. Other favourites included goat's cheese with honey and almonds, oven-baked tomatoes, garlic soup and pears poached in honey – all bursting with flavour.

During his time in Paris, Cézanne had lived very frugally. He went to very cheap restaurants, and, like a true Provençal, he often ate bread soaked in olive oil, which he brought with him from home. But the artist soon left the city and returned to his birthplace Aix-en-Provence, not only because of his failure to gain the recognition and respect of critics, but because he knew he could live a much more comfortable life in the south where, most importantly, he could eat better. This culinary improvement is also reflected in his artwork. Cézanne is arguably most famous for his still-life paintings and Provence provided an abundance of beautiful produce to work from; even potatoes looked better in the countryside light. And although critics at the time considered him to be a poor draughtsman, as he used unrealistic perspectives and scales, he is now celebrated for flouting these norms as it enabled him to create paintings of his subjects as he experienced them, rather than how they actually looked.

Over the next two decades, Cézanne developed his painting style and created hundreds of still lifes, revisiting the same subjects and scenes over and over to perfect his craft. Twenty-five years after leaving, he returned to the capital to hold his first solo show, saying 'with an apple I will astonish Paris'. True to his word – though admittedly more so with pears than apples – his work did cause a stir. *Three Pears* (c. 1888–1890) was particularly well received. So well in fact, that his friends and fellow artists Pierre-Auguste Renoir and Edgar Degas argued over who would buy it. Degas won. And from then on, Cézanne's work finally began to gain some recognition, although it was still not embraced by the masses. But his life became that bit more comfortable, especially as he inherited a substantial sum from his father, and Madame Brémond fed him to his heart's content.

Cézanne was a very enthusiastic eater and was a regular guest and host of dinner parties with friends such as Claude Monet. The American painter Mary Cassatt who met Cézanne at a dinner party, wrote of how she had been surprised by the Frenchman's table manners: 'He scraped his soup bowl and then lifted it and poured the last drops of soup into his spoon. He then picked up a chop and pulled the meat off the bone with his fingers. He ate with his knife, emphasised his speech with it, never once putting it down from the beginning of the meal to the end.' Unfortunately for Cézanne, his body couldn't quite keep up with this enthusiasm. He developed mild diabetes and had to be more careful about what he ate. Ever sensitive to the artist's needs, Madame Brémond created appropriate meals which were low in fat and sugar but still always packed with flavour. The Provençal French have a saying *'L'aigo boulido sauvo la vido'* ('garlic broth saves lives'). Clearly Brémond agreed and Cézanne ate garlic soup even more regularly from then on, which must have suited him very nicely.

Paul Cézanne, *Three Pears*, c. 1888–1890
Watercolour, gouache and graphite
on cream laid paper, 24.2 × 31 cm
Princeton University Art Museum, Princeton

SAFFRON AND CARDAMOM POACHED PEARS

—

In the style of Paul Cézanne, this recipe celebrates pears in their perfect simplicity. Although often associated with Middle Eastern and Iranian cuisine, saffron was an abundant trade in France in the seventeenth and eighteenth centuries and is therefore a key ingredient in many traditional French recipes, including the Provençal fish stew *bouillabaisse*. One of the highest producing regions of saffron was Provence, where Cézanne created some of his most iconic paintings, including *Three Pears* (1888–1890). The saffron lends a beautiful but very subtle perfume that brings out the pear's delicate flavour. Not keen on white sugar? Substitute about 80 ml (⅓ cup) of honey – à la Madame Brémond.

This recipe can be made up to three days in advance and stored in an airtight container in the refrigerator. Just make sure the pears are fully submerged in their syrup to stop them from turning brown.

SERVES 8

240 g (1 cup plus 3 tablespoons) caster sugar (superfine sugar)
6 cardamom pods
Pinch of saffron threads
8 ripe pears, preferably Williams (Bartlett) or Rocha

TO SERVE
Whipped cream or ice cream (optional)

Fill a saucepan large enough to fit the pears in a single layer with 1½ L (6 cups) of water and place over medium-high heat. Add the caster sugar and stir until dissolved. Lightly crush the cardamom pods with the back of a spoon to split them open, then add them, along with the saffron, to the water and bring to a gentle simmer.

Meanwhile, peel the pears. Keep the stems intact and use a small, sharp knife to cut out the bottom part of the core. If you would rather halve them, reduce the cooking time by a third. Place the pears in the pan, adding more water as needed to completely cover the flesh of the pears. Gently simmer, occasionally spooning the syrup over the pears if they float, for 30–35 minutes, or until the pears are softened but still have bite.

Remove the pears and put them in a bowl or airtight container if making in advance. Simmer the syrup for another 10–15 minutes, or until reduced by about one-quarter – it will still be thin.

Pour the syrup over the pears – they should be fully submerged. Cover and refrigerate for 2 hours, or until chilled.

Serve the pears, arranged on a serving plate in a pool of the aromatic syrup, with whipped cream or ice cream on the side, if desired.

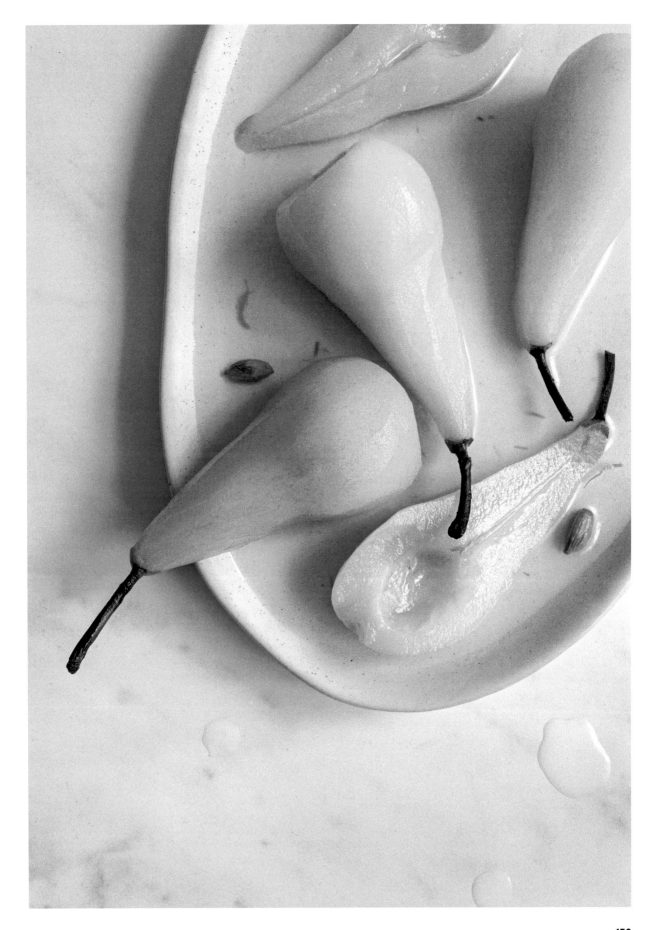

CLAUDE MONET

—

Claude Monet ate lunch at 11.30 a.m. sharp – no sooner, no later. He lived by a rigid timetable, which he also expected everyone around him to follow, including his guests. If anything wasn't up to his standard, he'd go into a rage; a common occurrence, particularly if his painting wasn't going well. In 1908, he famously destroyed fifteen water-lily canvases he'd been working on for three years, right before they were set to be exhibited. He constantly strived for perfection in his art and in his daily life – and even in his food.

Monet ate lunch early because he got up at dawn. He'd look at the mountains to check the weather conditions, bathe, and sit down for breakfast with his stepdaughter Blanche. She was also an artist and often worked as Monet's assistant, setting up easels and canvases wherever he chose to work that day. They ate eggs, bacon, sausages, cheese, omelette and toast with homemade preserves – customs Monet had picked up during his travels around Europe – before heading into the garden or to his boat studio, to paint until lunch.

Guests were welcomed for lunch rather than dinner as Monet didn't enjoy painting in the harsh midday light and went to bed early to maintain his routine. Artists Pissarro, Renoir, Sisley and Cézanne were regular visitors, while collectors, such as the Kuroki family, were particularly special guests. The meal was served either formally in the bright-yellow dining room on Limoges porcelain of the artist's own design, or informally as a picnic out in the garden – *en plein air* – if the weather allowed. A picnic was particularly welcome if Monet had successfully foraged *cèpes*, his favourite mushroom.

The artist collected recipes throughout his life, carefully recording meals of note during his travels, but his recipe for *cèpes* is argued to be the only one in his collection that he could really claim to be his own. He may have dictated what was on the menu, but he never did the cooking: 'I have two skills only', Monet said, 'horticulture and painting'. Many of the recipes in Monet's collection are by his chef Marguerite, or else from friends and guests: salt cod soup (*bouillabaisse de morue*) from Paul Cézanne, a recipe for chanterelles (*recette de girolles*) by Stéphane Mallarmé and a copy of the original recipe for tarte Tatin, taken directly from its inventors, the Tatin sisters.

As per the artist's precise instructions, dinner was also served early, always starting with soup, then an egg or cheese souffle, followed by a poultry or gratin main with a salad. Monet was even particular about his salad and would insist on making his own dressing at the table, which contained so much black pepper no-one else could stomach it. The salad leaves were grown in the gardens, as were many of the ingredients that reached the dinner table. His famous home Maison du Pressoir, now known as Maison du Monet, had large decorative gardens by the house as well as a walled kitchen garden on the other side of the village, which Monet and his staff meticulously attended to. The artist took great care in sourcing and purchasing the seeds for the flower and vegetable gardens and in choosing the breeds of the poultry he raised. Everything was done to Monet's specifications and the gardens were carefully managed to keep him happy – a tomato picked even slightly too early could set him off.

Just as they affected the gardens, the seasons also influenced Monet's work; he sensitively captured the changes in his countless paintings of water lilies and year-long series of haystack studies. The seasons also heavily influenced what his family ate throughout the year. Many of his lesser-known works reflect the changing seasons within his home. Still lifes of perfectly ripe melons and sunny picnic scenes in the glorious gardens give us a glimpse of the dreamy summer months, while paintings of game from his family's hunting expeditions show us what the family enjoyed during the winter. With his life and practice so intertwined, Monet mastered the art of living, curating his surroundings to form an enviably picturesque life. As long as it was done his way, of course.

Claude Monet, *Wheatstacks, Snow Effect, Morning*, 1891
Oil on canvas, 64.8 × 100.3 cm
Getty Center, Los Angeles

FRENCH BREAKFAST MUFFINS WITH HONEY AND THYME BUTTER

—

The texture of these muffins is similar to scones and perfect for lathering with the delicious butter at breakfast or as part of an afternoon tea. Serve them outside *en plein air* to really embrace Claude Monet's way of life.

MAKES 12 MUFFINS

FOR THE HONEY AND THYME BUTTER
2 teaspoons fresh thyme leaves
80 g (5½ tablespoons) unsalted butter, softened
4 teaspoons runny honey
1 teaspoon fine salt

FOR THE MUFFINS
100 g (7 tablespoons) unsalted butter, melted
280 g (2 cups) plain flour (all-purpose flour)
2 teaspoons baking powder
125 g (½ cup plus 2 tablespoons) caster sugar (superfine sugar)
1 teaspoon fine salt
½ teaspoon ground nutmeg
150 ml (½ cup plus 2 tablespoons) full fat milk
2 eggs
1 teaspoon vanilla bean paste

FOR THE TOPPING
50 g (1¾ oz) caster sugar (superfine sugar)
1 teaspoon ground cinnamon
70 g (5 tablespoons) unsalted butter, melted

For the honey and thyme butter, use the back of a wooden spoon to crush the thyme leaves and release their aroma, then finely chop them.

In a medium-sized bowl, use a wooden spoon to beat the butter until light and fluffy. Add the thyme leaves, honey and salt and mix to combine. Tip onto a piece of parchment paper and form the butter into a log or rectangle. Wrap the parchment paper around the butter and refrigerate. Remove from the refrigerator 10 minutes before ready to serve to allow it to soften slightly.

Preheat the oven to 180°C / 160°C fan (350°F / 320°F fan). Brush a 12-cup muffin tin with 1 teaspoon of the melted butter.

For the muffins, sift the plain flour and baking powder into a large bowl, then stir in the caster sugar, salt and nutmeg. Make a well in the centre, then add the milk, eggs, vanilla bean paste and the remaining melted butter and mix until combined.

Divide the batter evenly among the muffin cups – they should be quite full. Bake for 25 minutes, or until the tops are golden and a skewer inserted in the middle of a muffin comes out clean. Let cool for 5 minutes.

For the topping, in a small bowl, mix together the caster sugar and cinnamon. Pour the melted butter into a separate small bowl.

Remove the muffins from the tin and dip the tops into the melted butter one at a time. Shake off any excess, then immediately roll the muffin tops in the cinnamon sugar.

Serve the muffins warm with the honey and thyme butter on the side.

VINCENT VAN GOGH

—

Vincent van Gogh lived a colourful existence, fuelled predominantly by absinthe, with an occasional bit of bread and cheese on the side. He may have been intoxicated by the 'green fairy' but for a while, he saw nothing but yellow. Whether this was an actual symptom of jaundice caused by his drinking or simply an obsession has been debated by doctors and art historians alike. But what is clear is that the artist was in love with the colour yellow; so in love, that the vibrant hue was the dominant colour in almost all of his paintings after he moved to Arles in 1888.

Van Gogh was a Post-Impressionist painter who worked with unexpected colour palettes to create vibrant works that expressed the world as he perceived it. The development of this movement, and the previous era of Impressionism, correlated with significant chemical advances, making higher-quality, more intensely pigmented paint widely accessible. John Rand's invention of collapsible tin tubes to hold premixed oil paints in 1841 meant that artists no longer had to create their own paint from scratch and had instant access to rich colour that they could take beyond the confines of the studio. One of these colours was chrome yellow, Van Gogh's yellow of choice.

The artist's infatuation with this bold shade intensified as his health weakened. His doctor regularly banned him from entering his studio as he was known to drink turpentine when he ran out of (or couldn't afford) absinthe. But this was not the only danger his studio posed. Van Gogh also ate the yellow paint he worked with. He associated the colour with happiness and according to rumours, he thought eating the paint would bring that happiness inside him. But the medical notes of his doctor contradict this, stating that at the height of his 'madness' the artist ate the paint with the clear intention of poisoning himself. Van Gogh wrote to his brother Theo saying, 'It appears that I pick up filthy things and eat them, although my memories of these bad moments are vague.' Either way, the artist struggled from psychotic episodes and illusions, famously cutting off part of his own ear in 1888; the same year the sunflowers burst into bloom under his brush.

For Van Gogh, painting was the only thing that mattered. Food was not important – though being poor probably didn't help – and his lack of popularity and respect among art critics was undoubtedly an added challenge. But despite his clear struggle with alcoholism and poor mental health, he's celebrated for producing what are arguably the most vibrant and happiness-inducing paintings of all time. A true testament to the extraordinary power of colour.

Vincent van Gogh, *Sunflowers*, 1889
Oil on canvas, 95 × 75 cm
Van Gogh Museum, Amsterdam

ORANGE CUSTARD TART

—

There's no doubt that Vincent van Gogh would have approved of the colour of this tart-work. A burst of sunshine, it's a decadent and cheerful treat.

**MAKES 1 TART-WORK
SERVES 6–8**

FOR THE PASTRY
200 g (1½ cups) plain flour
(all-purpose flour)
2 tablespoons icing sugar
(confectioners' sugar)
Fine salt
100 g (7 tablespoons)
unsalted butter, chilled
1 egg yolk
Cold water, as needed

FOR THE TOPPING
175 g (¾ cup plus
2 tablespoons) caster
sugar (superfine sugar)
1 orange

FOR THE FILLING
3 eggs
200 g (1 cup) caster sugar
(superfine sugar)
Fine salt
3 oranges, zested and
juiced (about 200 ml / ¾
cup plus 1 tablespoon
juice)
200 ml (¾ cup plus
1 tablespoon) double
cream (heavy cream)

For the pastry, in a large bowl, combine the plain flour, icing sugar and a pinch of salt. Cut the butter into small cubes and use your fingertips to rub it into the flour mixture until it resembles fine breadcrumbs. Add the egg yolk and use your hands to bring the mixture together into a smooth dough, adding a little cold water, as needed, until the dough leaves the sides of the bowl clean. Wrap the pastry dough in cling film and put it in the refrigerator to chill for 30 minutes.

Meanwhile, for the topping, in a large frying pan, dissolve the caster sugar in 500 ml (2 cups) of water and bring to a simmer. Cut the orange across its equator into roughly ½ cm (⅙ in) thick slices, then add the slices to the pan in a single layer. Simmer for 20 minutes, then flip the orange slices and continue simmering for another 20 minutes, or until the skins are soft. You may need to add a little water as the orange slices simmer to keep them from catching but don't drown them – you want the slices to end up coated in a thick syrup. Remove from the heat, then use tongs to transfer the individual orange slices onto a sheet of parchment paper and let cool completely. Discard the syrup.

On a lightly floured surface, use a rolling pin to roll out the chilled pastry dough until about 3 mm (⅛ in) thick. Carefully lift the pastry and lay it over a fluted loose-bottomed 23 cm (9 in) round tart tin. Use your knuckles to press the pastry into the edges and corners of the tin to create a sealed lining. Don't worry if the pastry crumbles. If it is too difficult to lift as one piece, just take small pieces and push them into place, making sure there are no holes. Trim off any excess by pushing a rolling pin over the dish. Put the pastry shell in the refrigerator to chill for another 30 minutes. Don't skip this step – it ensures the pastry holds its shape and has a perfectly crisp bottom.

Preheat the oven to 180°C / 160°C fan (350°F / 320°F fan).

For the filling, in a large bowl, whisk together the eggs, caster sugar and a pinch of salt. Add all but 1 teaspoon of the orange zest and all of the orange juice and whisk again. Pour in the double cream and whisk again until smooth. Pour the filling into a medium saucepan, put over low heat and cook, whisking constantly, for about 5 minutes, or until thickened slightly into a custard. Transfer to a clean bowl and set aside to cool.

Once the pastry shell is chilled, set the tin on a baking tray to make it easier to lift. Line the bottom of the pastry shell with parchment paper, pour in baking beans or rice and blind bake for 15 minutes. Remove the beans and paper and blind bake for 10 more minutes, or until the pastry is lightly golden. If the base puffs up at all, remove from the oven and wait a couple of minutes for it to deflate before adding the custard.

Pour the filling into the tart shell. Lower the oven temperature to 160°C / 140°C fan (320°F / 275°F fan) and bake for 30–40 minutes, or until the filling is set, with a slight wobble. If the top starts to brown at all, cover the tart loosely with a piece of parchment paper. Remove the tart from the oven and set it, still in its tin, on a wire rack to cool completely, then chill in the refrigerator until ready to serve.

To serve, remove the tart from its tin by placing it onto a can and gently pulling down on the sides of the tin. The high butter content of this pastry should make it easy to slip off. Carefully slide the tart off the base onto a serving plate.

Top the tart with the orange slices, mimicking the composition of the sunflowers, and sprinkle over the reserved orange zest. Slice and serve it at the table.

GEORGIA O'KEEFFE
—

Georgia O'Keeffe wanted her food to be as nutritious as possible. So much so, that she would only pick corn from her garden once the water was already boiling to make sure there was a minimal loss of vitamins.

The artist was very conscious of what she ate as she believed food powered her creative mind. Because of this, she ate an organic diet, using only the highest quality ingredients and once she moved to New Mexico, she got many of her supplies from farms owned by friends and family within just a few miles of her home, as well as from her own abundant garden. She grew a variety of fruits and vegetables, including plenty of garlic (her favourite super food) and a large crop of berries to make antioxidant-rich juices and smoothies, which she would offer to friends. Her gardener was the most regular recipient of these concoctions and O'Keeffe would almost force them on him, insisting they would help him live longer.

O'Keeffe's belief in the power of food was likely influenced by her upbringing. Her family had a dairy farm where they also grew organic fruit and vegetables, and O'Keeffe learnt the importance of high-quality food, as well as how to cook nutritious meals and bake bread, from an early age. Bread making became a daily ritual for the artist as an adult. She would freshly grind her own wheat each morning, using a countertop mill – a serious slog for the sake of some extra vitamins – and she continued this dedication in the kitchen for many decades.

But once she reached her nineties, she was joined in her home by her assistant Margaret Wood, who cooked for her and relieved the artist of heavy jobs such as canning and preserving. 'Food served in the O'Keeffe household was always nutritious, tasty and simply but beautifully presented', Margaret said in her cookbook, *A Painter's Kitchen: Recipes from the Kitchen of Georgia O'Keeffe*. Published after the artist's death, the book features a collection of seventy recipes they had made together, including O'Keeffe's homemade yoghurt and rare indulgent treats, such as vanilla ice cream. Simplest of all is the recipe for wild asparagus, which explains in just three sentences how to prep the stalks for steaming or sauteing (your choice) to serve with butter. Aware of her enviable lifestyle, O'Keeffe once asked Margaret, 'Do you think other people eat as well as we do?'

The artist's love of the landscape of New Mexico extended beyond the kitchen, into her studio, where she created works equally as rich in colour as the food on her plate. She approached nature in a unique way, seeking out essential abstract forms within the world around her to express her feelings and emotions in response to nature and place, primarily studying the mountainous landscape as well as the flowers and bones she found within it. *Red Hill and White Shell* (1938) captures her love of the American Southwest; the colours, use of light and space evoking her emotional connection to the location. Her work was widely celebrated by critics, who labelled her as the best female painter. But, a defiant feminist, O'Keeffe rejected what she considered to be a sexist label, famously saying, 'the men liked to put me down as the best woman painter. I think I'm one of the best painters.'

Her wholesome lifestyle in such a beautiful setting was clearly the only medicine the artist needed, and O'Keeffe did live in almost perfect health, until she began to lose her sight in the late 1960s. As a painter, she understandably struggled with the loss but not one to be put down for long, she adapted. She shifted her practice to work in clay and created ceramic works from touch, living (and creating) to the grand age of ninety-eight. Now, as we look back on her incredible life, she is not only celebrated as one of the forerunners of the feminist art movement but considered to be a pioneer of the local organic food movement. A label she would likely have been very proud of.

Georgia O'Keeffe, *Red Hill and White Shell*, 1938
Oil on canvas, 76.2 × 92.7 cm
Museum of Fine Arts, Houston

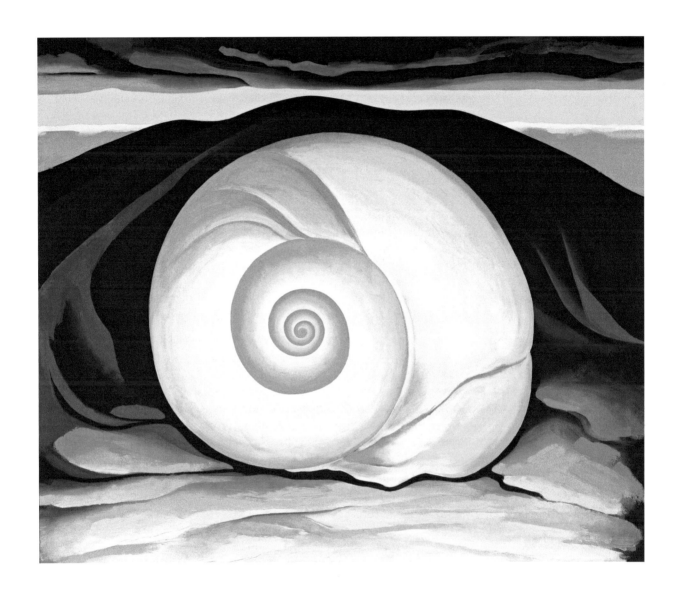

LEMON CURD AND RASPBERRY TRIFLE

—

Although she may not have approved of the sugar content of this recipe, this dish reflects the sense of nostalgia Georgia O'Keeffe captured in her landscape paintings – a nostalgia that can also be found in food. The smell and taste of a dish, or even just one ingredient, can immediately spark a memory of a place, or transport us back to specific moments in time – just as the shapes and colours of O'Keeffe's paintings encapsulate memories of her favourite place, the American Southwest. This recipe features lemon curd, a favourite of my dad's and which I bought for him whenever I came across a special jar. The taste and smell transport me back to some very happy memories.

SERVES 8

FOR THE LEMON CURD
3 large unwaxed lemons
3 eggs plus 1 egg yolk
Fine salt
120 g (½ cup) unsalted
   butter
200 g (1 cup) caster sugar
   (superfine sugar)

FOR THE CUSTARD
400 ml (1½ cups plus
   2 tablespoons) full fat
   milk
1 teaspoon vanilla bean
   paste
3 egg yolks
2 tablespoons caster sugar
   (superfine sugar)
1 tablespoon cornflour
   (cornstarch)

**FOR THE RASPBERRY
COULIS**
200 g (7 oz) fresh
   raspberries
2 tablespoons icing sugar
   (confectioners' sugar)
1 heaped teaspoon
   cornflour (cornstarch)

TO ASSEMBLE
70 g (⅔ cup) sliced
   almonds
300 g (10 oz) shortbread
   biscuits
300 ml (1 cup plus
   3 tablespoons) double
   cream (heavy cream)
300 g (10 oz) fresh
   raspberries

For the lemon curd, zest and juice the lemons into a medium bowl. Add the eggs, egg yolk and a pinch of salt and whisk well to combine.

In a medium saucepan, combine the butter and caster sugar over low heat. Once the butter is melted, quickly whisk in the lemony egg mixture until fully combined. Continue cooking over low heat, stirring constantly to prevent the eggs from curdling, for 10–15 minutes, or until it has a custard-like texture and coats the back of a spoon – it will get a little thicker as it cools. (If you do have any white pieces of egg in the curd, pass it through a fine-mesh sieve to remove them). Remove from the heat and let cool slightly, then transfer the lemon curd to a small bowl and put it in the refrigerator to chill until ready to assemble the trifles.

For the custard, in a small saucepan, warm the milk and vanilla over medium heat until just boiling. Remove from the heat and let cool for 1–2 minutes.

In a large bowl, whisk together the egg yolks, caster sugar and cornflour until pale and creamy. Gradually pour in the warm milk, continuously whisking as you go. Pour the mixture back into the pan and cook over low heat, whisking constantly and not allowing it to bubble, for 10–15 minutes, or until thickened. Transfer the custard to a small bowl and let cool completely. Lay a piece of cling film directly on the surface of the custard to stop a skin from forming, then put it in the refrigerator to chill for 1–2 hours.

For the raspberry coulis, in a small saucepan, combine the raspberries, icing sugar and 2 tablespoons of water over medium heat. Cook, stirring occasionally, for 2–3 minutes, or until the raspberries turn to mush. Push the mixture through a fine-mesh sieve to remove the seeds, then pour it back into the pan.

In a small glass, whisk together the cornflour and 2 tablespoons of water.

Put the pan with the raspberry mixture back over medium heat, stir in the cornflour mixture and cook for about 1 minute, or until thickened. Transfer the raspberry coulis to a small bowl and put it in the refrigerator to chill until ready to serve.

In a small dry frying pan over medium heat, toast the sliced almonds, stirring constantly, for 1–2 minutes, or until golden and smelling intensely nutty. Transfer to a small bowl and let cool.

Fill a resealable plastic bag with the shortbread biscuits and use a rolling pin to bash them into fine sand-like crumbs.

Once all the other elements are cool or chilled, in a large bowl, whip the double cream until it forms soft peaks.

To assemble, tip the shortbread crumbs into the bottom of a clear trifle dish and press down to form an even layer. Add a layer of fresh raspberries, with their points facing upwards, and pour over the coulis. Sprinkle over the almonds, then pour over the lemon curd, followed by the custard.

Pour the whipped cream on top in a large shell-like swirl and serve.

ROY LICHTENSTEIN

—

When asked to contribute to *The Museum of Modern Art Artist's Cookbook* in 1977, Roy Lichtenstein submitted his favourite recipe, *Primordial Soup*: 'the atmosphere that may have generated life on earth'. A blended combination of hydrogen, ammonia, methane, water vapor, nitrogen and carbon monoxide, the 'soup' is heated slowly in a pan so that 'soon, in geological time, amino acids will synthesise, become protein, and begin self replications'. The artist suggests finishing the dish with a garnish of parsley and lemon slices on the side.

Perhaps unsurprisingly, this great Pop artist didn't spend much time cooking. That task was left to his wife, Dorothy, who contributed three recipes of her own to the cookbook. Roy himself admitted that when left to his own devices, he'd 'heat up a can of soup and eat a peanut butter and jelly sandwich', often choosing granola with bananas for lunch. Dorothy made more refined meals; nothing fancy and, more importantly, nothing rich. The family's diet was very considered, and Dorothy served them macrobiotic, low-fat meals. 'I think he had a really visceral idea that eating clotted cream was going immediately to his arteries', Dorothy said of Roy. She adapted many recipes accordingly, including her recipe for *Vitello Tonnato* – her specialty dish of cold veal topped with a creamy tuna and caper sauce – to exclude any cream or mayonnaise. 'I am now working on a way to eliminate the veal as well', she said.

In the studio, food played a prominent role for Lichtenstein. He revisited the subject throughout his oeuvre, painting fruit bowls, cups of coffee and many iconic American foods, such as hot dogs and cherry pie (foods he wouldn't eat himself). He used the traditional subject matter of still life as a foundation for experimentation, playing with form, texture and surfaces, from transparent bowls to solid tables, flowing fabrics and soft fruits, adapting shading to Ben-Day dots and lines, with planes of colour in reduced tones. The resulting paintings are flat while still giving the illusion of depth and form, much like comic-book images. In response to criticism of his techniques, the Pop artist simply replied, 'I don't care what, say, a cup of coffee looks like, I only care how it's drawn.'

In the 1960s, Lichtenstein transitioned into ceramics and transformed those coffee cup drawings into mind-bending sculptures, creating a series of small towers of connected cups. They served no function and although they were three dimensional, they were shaded with Ben-Day dots and lines as if they were flat. A comment on contemporary culture, the consumerist boom and the resulting new diner culture, Lichtenstein had taken the icon of a coffee cup used to signpost diners and re-dimensionalised it, if you will, back into three dimensions, while retaining some of its two dimensionality and symbolic status. He went on to create sets of functional dinner plates and tea sets with the same Ben-Day shading, as well as a series of screen-printed paper plates.

Lichtenstein and fellow artists provoked many debates about what could be considered art, particularly with the opening of the 1964 exhibition *The American Supermarket* at Bianchini Gallery. A collaboration between Lichtenstein, Andy Warhol, Claes Oldenburg and others, the artists transformed the New York gallery into a functioning supermarket, with aisles selling items such as eggs, fresh fruit, frozen food and canned goods. The items' likenesses were also up for sale, created by a participating artist (Warhol sold autographed Campbell Soup cans for $18 alongside his paintings of them for $1,500) all of which could be taken home in a $12 paper shopping bag with a screen print of Lichtenstein's iconic image of a roast turkey on the front. A bargain.

Roy Lichtenstein, *Brushstroke*, 1965
Screenprint on paper, 56.5 × 72.4 cm
Tate, London

CHURROS WITH CINNAMON SUGAR AND CHOCOLATE SAUCE

—

This recipe would probably grip Roy Lichtenstein with fear.

Get creative when piping the churros to create a variety of brushstrokes, or invite your guests to create their own shapes for an interactive dessert. You can prepare the batter a couple of hours in advance for ease.

SERVES 4–8

FOR THE CHURROS
50 g (3½ tablespoons)
  unsalted butter, melted
300 ml (1 cup plus
  3 tablespoons) just-
  boiled water
1 teaspoon vanilla extract
Fine salt
250 g (1¾ cups) plain flour
  (all-purpose flour)
1 teaspoon baking powder
Sunflower oil, for deep
  frying (about 750 ml / 3
  cups)
75 g (6 tablespoons) caster
  sugar (superfine sugar)
2 teaspoons ground
  cinnamon

FOR THE SAUCE
100 g (3½ oz) dark
  chocolate, 70% cocoa
1 tablespoon golden syrup
½ teaspoon vanilla extract
100 ml (⅓ cup plus
  1 tablespoon) double
  cream (heavy cream)

For the churros, combine the melted butter, just-boiled water, vanilla and a pinch of salt in a heatproof jug and stir.

Sift the plain flour and baking powder into a large bowl. Make a well in the centre and pour in the butter mixture, stirring quickly with a wooden spoon until fully combined and smooth. Let rest for 15 minutes.

For the sauce, in a heatproof bowl set over a pan of simmering water, melt the chocolate. Remove from the heat, add the golden syrup and vanilla and stir to combine. Pour in the double cream, stirring until smooth. Keep warm while you fry the churros.

Fill a large, deep-sided saucepan with enough oil to come about one-third of the way up the sides. Heat the oil to 180°C (350°F), or until a cube of bread browns within 1 minute.

Cover a baking tray with two layers of paper towel. Add the caster sugar and cinnamon to another tray and stir to combine.

Fill a piping bag fitted with a small closed star-shape nozzle with the churro dough. Working in batches, carefully pipe the dough into the hot oil, aiming for lengths about 10–15 cm (4–6 in) and snipping off the ends with a pair of scissors. Create different loops and wiggles for variety. Fry the churros, turning them over in the oil, for 2–3 minutes, or until golden all over. Keep checking the oil temperature and adjust the heat accordingly – it should stay between 170°C and 190°C (340°F and 375°F). Use a slotted spoon to remove the churros and transfer them to the paper-lined tray to drain off the excess oil for a couple of minutes.

While the churros are still hot, roll them in the cinnamon sugar. Arrange the churros on a serving plate and serve with a bowl of the warm chocolate dipping sauce on the side.

MARKUS PERNHART
—

Markus Pernhart climbed Grossglockner, Austria's highest mountain, multiple times, frequenting its summit which stands at 3,800 metres (12,467 feet). The mountaineering artist would sit in the snow and ice for hours on end, using a pan of hot coals to heat his frozen hands and defrost his paints, all to create topographically accurate representations of the landscape he loved.

Mountains have been a source of inspiration throughout art history, with many artists working to capture the magnificence of nature around them. The Alps have regularly featured in European art and this mountain range took a particular hold of the nineteenth-century artists, known as the Romantics, who glorified the grandeur of nature. The Romantics worked to capture the emotions that the landscape instilled within them through the dramatisation of the scenery, often painting wild scenes with cataclysmic storms that verged on the mystical. Pernhart was among this group, but he had a much more realistic approach to his depiction of the landscape, keen to capture the mountains as they actually looked rather than the Romantic idea of them from afar. He achieved this by climbing them to get the most dramatic views and show the world what they really looked like from the top.

The Alps have also influenced European food. In Alpine cuisine, preserved meats and melty cheeses reign, with plenty of filling carbohydrates on the side – no doubt what Pernhart ate to fuel his challenging climbs. But more decadent and refined Alpine-inspired dishes also emerged in the cities. *Salzburger Nockerl*, is a dramatic dessert inspired by the mountains near Salzburg. Large peaks of meringue soufflé are served golden from the oven and dusted with a generous sprinkling of icing sugar to resemble the mountains in the first snow.

Sugar had been considered a luxury in Europe until the early nineteenth century. But increased farming of sugar beet made refined white sugar more widely available, lowering the price and enabling sweet foods to become more accessible to people of all classes. At the top of the food chain, Emperor Franz Joseph and Empress Elisabeth of Austria had a particularly sweet tooth and a dish similar to *Salzburger Nockerl* was created in their honour by their court chef Leopold. *Kaiserschmarrn* – meaning *Emperor's mess* – is said to have been named when the Empress Elisabeth, who was worried about maintaining her wasp waist, left the dish untouched, so the emperor took her plate supposedly saying, 'Now let me see what "*Schmarrn*" (nonsense) our chef has cooked up'. Sitting somewhere between a pancake and a waffle, sweet batter is part-baked in the oven, stirred roughly with a fork and baked again, resulting in little lumps of caramelised dough that are often served with a plum sauce and sprinkled with a flurry of sugary snow. Like *Salzburger Nockerl*, *Kaiserschmarren* is so hefty that it's sometimes served as a main course.

The sugar-loving emperor and empress celebrated all things Austrian. The empress in particular had an eye for beautiful things and recognised the skill of Pernhart's artwork, collecting thirty-one drawings from his album of 198 popular sights of Carinthia, as well as a painting of Grossglockner Mountain for her own personal collection. During his lifetime, Pernhart created over 1,200 paintings, drawings and engravings of the local landscape and kept numerous sketchbooks during his climbing adventures that preserve his love of the mountains – battling the elements to provide a sweet view for those less adventurous than himself.

Markus Pernhart, *View of the 'Grossglockner' Mountain (The Great Bellringer)*, 1857
Oil on canvas, 44.9 × 36.2 cm
Kärntner Landesgalerie, Klagenfurt am Wörthersee

CHOCOLATE-DIPPED MERINGUES WITH A SALTED PECAN AND ROSEMARY CRUMB

—

These mini mountains are a delight. Although perfect for satisfying your sweet tooth, the addition of dark chocolate and a salted nut and herb crumb keeps them from being overly sugary. I recommend serving these tiny peaks with espresso as a sophisticated end to a dinner party.

MAKES 40–50 MERINGUES

FOR THE MERINGUES
3 egg whites
150 g (¾ cup) caster sugar (superfine sugar)

FOR THE COATING
100 g (3½ oz) dark chocolate, 70% cocoa
60 g (2 oz) milk chocolate
100 g (3½ oz) pecans
2 teaspoons fresh rosemary needles
1½ teaspoons flaky sea salt

Preheat the oven to 160°C / 140°C fan (320°F / 275°F fan).

For the meringues, in the bowl of a stand mixer fitted with the whisk attachment or in a large bowl if using a handheld mixer, whip the egg whites until they triple in volume and form stiff peaks. Sprinkle in the caster sugar, 1 tablespoon at a time, and whip thoroughly between each spoonful until the sugar has been incorporated. Repeat until all the sugar has been added. The meringue should be super smooth and glossy.

Spoon the meringue into a piping bag fitted with a round nozzle attachment (or DIY by cutting off the corner of a resealable plastic bag). Pipe the mixture into bite-sized mountains, each about 4 cm (1½ in) wide, onto a baking tray lined with parchment paper or a silicone baking mat. Squeeze out the meringue gently, then lift up and quickly release your grip to create the perfect peak. The meringues won't expand much in the oven so you can pack them in quite tightly, leaving about 1.25 cm (½ in) between.

Put the meringues in the oven and immediately lower the oven temperature to 100°C / 80°C fan (210°F / 175°F fan). This will ensure they cook quickly, then slowly, resulting in a fluffy, marshmallow-like centre with a crisp outer shell that remains as white as snow. Bake for 60 minutes.

Remove the meringues from the oven and very carefully slide them (still attached to the parchment paper) onto a wire rack and let cool for 20–30 minutes.

For the coating, snap the chocolate into bite-size pieces and put it in a heatproof bowl set over a pan of simmering water. Stir the chocolate until it's fully melted, then remove from the heat and set aside to cool slightly.

In a small dry pan over high heat, toast the pecans, stirring to keep them from burning, for 2–3 minutes, or until they smell intensely nutty. Transfer the pecans to a food processor.

Use the back of a wooden spoon to bash the rosemary to release its aroma, then add it to the food processor. Blitz in bursts until the mixture is finely ground, then transfer to a shallow bowl, add the salt and stir to incorporate.

Once the meringues are completely cool, very carefully hold them in the middle to remove them from the parchment paper, then dip the bases into the melted chocolate to coat the bottoms, coming just a little bit up the sides. Shake off any excess chocolate and immediately dip the chocolate-covered part of the meringues into the pecan thyme crumb, very gently rolling them around to cover the chocolate.

Put the meringues onto a clean sheet of parchment paper to set for 20–30 minutes. Serve as a petit-four with an espresso.

Note: If you have any nut mixture left over, save it to sprinkle over fresh pasta, with a grating of Parmesan.

JEAN-MICHEL BASQUIAT

—

Before blasting into fame in the early 1980s, Jean-Michel Basquiat spent periods of time homeless in New York City, not knowing when or what his next meal would be. After he made his mark on the New York art scene, the transformation was extreme. 'We went from stealing bread on the way home from the Mudd Club and eating pasta to buying groceries at Dean & DeLuca', said Suzanne Mallouk, Basquiat's girlfriend and muse. 'The fridge was full of pastries and caviar, we were drinking Cristal champagne. We were 21 years old.'

When not indulging at home, Basquiat would join his great friend Andy Warhol at the restaurant of the moment, Mr Chow, where they first met in 1981. Mr Chow (Michael Chow – AKA Zhōu Yīnghuá), who has recently embarked on a career as an artist himself, has a particular skill for identifying upcoming talent. According to his own estimation, of all the artists he approached, '90 per cent became established and famous'. Basquiat was no exception and Chow commissioned a portrait of himself from the young artist, just as he did from Warhol, David Hockney, Jonas Wood and Peter Blake.

But Basquiat didn't let just anyone buy his work. If he didn't like a collector, he would simply refuse their sale, sometimes violently: 'If somebody said "I want a painting with shades of red in it to match my couch", he would become absolutely furious', said Mallouk. 'He would throw them out. He would often pour food on their heads from outside the window, like cereal or water or milk as they were leaving.' On one such occasion, the visiting collectors had brought the artist a bucket of Kentucky Fried Chicken. Basquiat was so insulted by the gesture that he chased them out, throwing the chicken at them as they ran. He faced racial slurs and injustice throughout his short life, and he worked to both portray his own experiences of racism and celebrate his heritage through his art.

Basquiat celebrated important Black figures such as athletes and musicians in his paintings, such as his painting *Max Roach* (1984), while also capturing moments of injustice. This was often illustrated through the inclusion of food, an important symbol of culture, family and community. Many of these works are titled in Spanish, after his mother's Puerto Rican heritage, such as *Untitled (Pollo Frito)* (fried chicken) (1982), which he created during his most productive and iconic year of work. This painting could be, in part, a response to the collector's offensive gesture: a statement on racism, through the stereotyped associations of fried chicken.

The racist stigma surrounding fried chicken is complex and begins with the emancipation of slaves in 1863. Though freed from slavery, Black Americans were still not entitled to many freedoms enjoyed by white Americans. They were not allowed to own anything classified as livestock (such as pigs and cows), but they were allowed to raise chickens. Many ran chicken farms and opened butcher shops, while Black women often sold fried chicken to support their families, using recipes developed by their enslaved ancestors.

Fried chicken is eaten with the fingers, not with a knife and fork. The dominant white culture used this as an excuse to label Black people as uncivilised and animalistic, creating a set of stereotypes and stigmas that still hold sway; to this day, many Black Americans will not eat fried chicken in public. In 1980s New York, Basquiat was waging his own war against such stigmas through the medium of his dynamic, and now priceless, work. As his girlfriend Suzanne Mallouk put it, 'Everything he did was an attack on racism and I loved him for this.'

Jean-Michel Basquiat, *Max Roach*, 1984
Acrylic and oil chalk on canvas, 152.5 × 152.5 cm
Private collection

BERRY COBBLER

—

The ultimate easy comfort food. Consider the recipe a blank canvas, ready for your own artistic interpretation. Add in fresh plums for a summery cobbler, or sliced apples with a little cinnamon for a more autumnal feel. Most fruits work well; just adjust the sugar depending on the sweetness of the filling.

SERVES 6–8

FOR THE FRUIT FILLING
800 g (1¾ lb) frozen mixed
  berries
50 g (¼ cup) caster sugar
  (superfine sugar)
2 tablespoons cornflour
  (cornstarch)
1 small unwaxed lemon,
  zested
1 teaspoon lemon juice
½ teaspoon vanilla extract

**FOR THE BISCUIT
TOPPING**
200 g (1½ cups) plain flour
  (all-purpose flour)
35 g (6 tablespoons)
  ground almonds
3 tablespoons caster sugar
  (superfine sugar)
1½ teaspoons baking
  powder
½ teaspoon fine salt
80 g (5½ tablespoons)
  unsalted butter, chilled
100 g (¼ cup plus
  3 tablespoons) natural
  (regular) yoghurt
2 tablespoons full fat milk
1 tablespoon Demerara
  sugar

TO SERVE
Vanilla ice cream

Preheat the oven to 180°C / 160°C fan (350°F / 320°F fan).

For the fruit filling, in a large bowl, combine the berries, caster sugar, cornflour, lemon zest and juice and the vanilla and stir to coat the berries evenly. Spread in an even layer in a large rectangular baking dish that measures about 27 × 20 × 5 cm (10.5 × 8 × 2 in).

For the biscuit topping, in a large bowl, whisk together the plain flour, ground almonds, caster sugar, baking powder and salt. Cut the butter into small cubes and use your fingertips to rub it into the flour mixture until it resembles fine breadcrumbs. Add the yoghurt and stir until you create a sticky dough. Add some of the milk, as needed, to make the dough more malleable.

Take handfuls of the dough and flatten it out between your palms until about 1 cm (⅜ in) thick. Place each piece of dough over the berries, leaving gaps for the fruit to peek through. Brush the top of the dough with the remaining milk and sprinkle over the Demerara sugar. Bake for 40–50 minutes, or until the topping is golden brown and cooked through – a skewer inserted in the centre of a biscuit should come out clean.

Let cool for 5 minutes before serving with scoops of vanilla ice cream – it melts beautifully into the fruit to make it creamy and rich.

SALVADOR DALÍ
—

At the age of six, Salvador Dalí dreamed of becoming a chef. He didn't follow through on this ambition; as an adult, he never cooked for himself. Nevertheless, in 1973, the sixty-nine-year-old artist released what is arguably one of his greatest masterpieces, *Les Diners de Gala,* an almost absurdly opulent cookbook full of fantastical, edible works of art, all following the rules of what he called 'Dalinian gastro esthetics.'

Dalí considered the jaw to be 'our best tool to grasp philosophical knowledge'; food was always important to him, both at the dinner table and in the studio. In fact, the more you look, the more food seems to pop up in unexpected places throughout Dalí's oeuvre: fried eggs hang suspended over plates in dream-like deserts; still lifes explode above pristine white tablecloths; a telephone earpiece is replaced with a cooked lobster. Even *The Persistence of Memory* (1931) was supposedly inspired by an oozing, half-eaten cheese, the limp clocks depicting 'the camembert of time'.

Gala, to whom the book is dedicated, was Dalí's wife and muse, and co-host of his legendary dinner parties. Each dinner was a spectacle, attended by the artists and celebrities of the day, dressed in elaborate costumes. Gala once famously acquired a huge unicorn headdress, which she wore as she reclined on a red velvet throne, while her guests were entertained by lions, monkeys and Babou (Dalí's pet ocelot). At one meal, diners were shocked when live frogs began to leap out of the platters and dishes.

But despite the drama and distractions, the dinners were ultimately about the food, which Dalí preserved within his cookbook. *Les Diners de Gala* is written for food-lovers after the artist's own heart: 'If you are a disciple of one of those calorie-counters who turns the joys of eating into a form of punishment,' Dalí writes in the introduction, 'close this book at once; it is too lively, too aggressive and far too impertinent for you.' The 136 'impertinent' recipes in the book are not only fascinating, comical and often stomach-churning, but sensationally captured through dazzling 1970s food photography, recreating the Dalinian presentation from those fantastical parties.

Created or inspired by the best Parisian chefs of the day, with a Dalí twist, most of the recipes are not achievable for the home cook, but many sound so unappetizing that it doesn't really matter. *Peacock a l'Imperiale dressed and surrounded by its court*, for example, consists of a bright blue, feathered peacock sitting on a plate of nine glazed quails, while a recipe for cabbage and pigeon requires the meat to be served alongside several fully feathered dead birds in a macabre display. To make the simply named *Cauliflower with Roquefort* involves balancing cauliflower florets around a silver Cinderella slipper which stands on a curiously shaped concoction of eggs, flour, cheese and rice. Dalí loved cauliflower, particularly Romanesco broccoli, which he found aesthetically and philosophically appealing because of its fractal form. In fact, he loved the brassica so much that he once filled his white Rolls Royce Phantom II with 500 kilograms (1,102 lbs) of it and drove to Paris from Spain to give a lecture, telling the audience 'everything ends up in the cauliflower!'

But this was not Dalí's only food obsession. The artist was also fascinated by shellfish, which he intriguingly pairs with eggs in chapter two, 'Les Cannibalismes de L'Automne' ('Autumn Cannibalism') because, according to the Dalinian thought process, they both have outer shells: 'I only like to eat what has a clear and intelligible form …' Dalí said, '… if I hate that detestable degrading vegetable called spinach it is because it is shapeless, like liberty. The opposite of spinach is armor. I love eating suits of arms. In fact I love all shellfish … food that only a battle to peel makes it vulnerable to the conquest of our palate.' Eggs, peeled and unpeeled, cracked and fried, crop up time and time again in his work as a symbol for birth, sexuality, reproduction and the cycle of life. But it's the shellfish that really steals the show in his book. The *pièce de résistance* has to be *Bush of crayfish in Viking herbs*, a show-stopping, cone-shaped tower of brilliant red crayfish, studded with curly parsley. Although there isn't an actual recipe for this creation as the chef decided not to divulge it, Dalí provides some vague guidelines for particularly brave readers.

Salvador Dalí, *The Persistence of Memory*, 1931
Oil on canvas, 24.1 × 33 cm
Museum of Modern Art, New York

For Dalí, eating bordered on a religious experience. In the artist's Surrealistic world view, food had a power greater than its calories or its taste. It was symbolically wrapped up with sexuality, faith, society and death:

'The bread and the wine of the Last Supper are mystical to everyone,' he wrote. 'They are Eucharistic symbols. Cannibalism is also a symbol. The praying mantis mates and then eats its mate. That is my last word on food.'

GOAT'S CHEESE ICE CREAM

—

This recipe is a real conversation starter. Although goat's cheese may not sound like an obvious ice cream flavour, it's surprisingly delicious. Serve it as a dessert with honey and sea salt, or as a savoury palate cleanser with a side of beetroot, and your guests will talk about it forever. I first tasted this surprising combination many years ago, at a dinner hosted by my very talented friend Sam, and it's stuck with me ever since. I think it would be right at home at any of Dalí's wild parties.

This recipe can be made with or without an ice cream maker.

**MAKES 750 ML
ICE CREAM**

350 ml (1¼ cups) full fat
    milk
300 ml (1 cup plus
    3 tablespoons) double
    cream (heavy cream)
6 egg yolks
1 tablespoon runny honey,
    plus more to serve
    (if serving as a sweet
    dessert)
Fine salt
125 g (4¼ oz) soft, rindless
    goat's cheese
Flaky sea salt
Cooked beetroot, to serve
    (if serving as a savoury
    palate cleanser)

If using an ice cream machine, freeze the bowl in advance, following the manufacturer's instructions.

In a medium saucepan, bring the milk and double cream to a boil.

Meanwhile, in a large heatproof bowl, whisk together the egg yolks, honey and a small pinch of salt until glossy.

Once the double cream and milk start bubbling, gradually pour the mixture into the egg mixture in a slow, steady stream, whisking constantly to prevent the eggs from curdling, until fully combined. (If you do have any white pieces of egg in the mixture, pass it through a fine-mesh sieve to remove them). Tip the mixture back into the saucepan and crumble in the goat's cheese. Put the pan over low heat and cook gently, whisking continuously and not allowing to boil, for about 10 minutes, or until the cheese is incorporated and the mixture thickens enough to coat the back of a spoon. Transfer to a clean large bowl and let cool completely, then put the custard in the refrigerator to chill for 30 minutes.

If using an ice cream machine, turn it on and slowly pour in the cooled custard. Churn for 15–30 minutes (this will vary depending on your machine – refer back to your manufacturer's instructions.) Transfer the ice cream to an airtight container and freeze for at least 2 hours, or until firm.

If not using an ice cream machine, pour the cooled custard into a large, resealable plastic bag. Squeeze out any air and seal the bag. Arrange the bag so it lays flat in the freezer and freeze for at least 5 hours or overnight – massage the bag every now and then to stop large ice crystals forming.

Once the ice cream is frozen, use a sharp knife to break it up into small chunks and place them in a food processor or powerful blender. Pulse until smooth, then transfer the ice cream to an airtight container and freeze for another 2 hours, or until firm.

When ready to serve, remove the ice cream from the freezer and let it soften slightly for 5–10 minutes. I recommend presenting it in glass tumblers so you can watch it melt like one of Dalí's clocks.

For a sweet dessert, finish with a drizzle of honey and a pinch of salt, or simply enjoy the ice cream on its own.

For a savoury palate cleanser, finish with a pinch of salt and serve it with a side of cooked beetroot, to bring out the ice cream's earthy notes. Trust me: It's weird but wonderful.

BRIDGET RILEY

—

Bridget Riley rose to fame in the Swinging Sixties for her mind-bending paintings which went on to define the entire era. But she soon fell out of favour again and faced a period of struggling; while fashion houses were profiting off her black and white designs, Riley said she was 'eating paper'. But two decades later, she returned to the spotlight, where she has firmly remained ever since, and her ground-breaking work has reached over $5 million at auction. Clearly, she was ahead of her time.

Riley's work creates optical illusions through repetitive, geometric patterns, in ways that often induce feelings of dizziness or seasickness in the viewer. It's interesting then that a number of her works are housed in restaurant collections, to be enjoyed by diners tucking into their meal. Her work hangs proudly on the wall of Core, a London restaurant run by prestigious chef Clare Smyth, and until recently was displayed at The Ivy in London, an establishment well-known for its enviable art collection. *The Ivy Painting*, commissioned by the restaurant in 1998, is typical of the colourful series Riley began in the eighties, with a rainbow of zigzag shapes. It recently sold for £413,000 – more than $600,000 dollars.

For art-collecting restaurateurs, the worlds of cooking and fine art are very much intertwined, where art restaurants exhibit the talents of both chefs and artists under one roof. Chef and restaurateur Mark Hix is particularly renowned for bringing these two worlds together, famously opening the restaurant The Pharmacy with Damien Hirst in 1998 (and Pharmacy 2 in 2016), and until the sector-crippling year of 2020, housed his own extraordinary art collection in his group of restaurants spread across the UK. Hix believes that more people view art in a restaurant than in a gallery; the busy dining experience makes the art more comfortable and approachable than a silent white gallery space.

Bridget Riley is a firm favourite with Hix, whose work he believes connects to his own culinary practice: 'I remember many years ago doing a talk with Bridget Riley and Michael Craig-Martin, who likened his work to how I cook', said Hix. 'I have a hard and fast rule that there should be no more than three ingredients on a plate. And if you look at Michael's work, there are never more than three colours. Bridget Riley is a bit like that too.' Hix's first ever art purchases were two pieces by Riley, which he bought directly from the artist. This makes them extra special; he claims that they would be the artworks he would save from a fire.

Eating great dishes surrounded by great art – or 'Aesthetic Dining', as art restaurant writer Christina Makris calls it – ultimately alters the experience of the food. 'These establishments provide an experience for diners to exercise their aesthetic capabilities', Makris says. 'In the presence of art, we are never passive observers, we contemplate, reflect, appreciate.' Displaying fine art shifts the diner's attitude, encouraging visitors to consider what they're eating as they would contemplate an artwork in a gallery. And perhaps Riley's work is the perfect choice. Its immersive quality reminds viewers of their own body and almost forces a reaction, just like a good plate of food does.

Bridget Riley, *Blaze 1*, 1964
Screenprint on paper, 53 × 52.1 cm
Tate, London

ROASTED PINEAPPLE MERINGUE PIE

—

This recipe allows you to create a different tart-work each time you make it, depending on how you pipe out the meringue. Don't worry about creating the perfect pattern; use creative license to make your own Bridget Riley-inspired design.

**MAKES 1 TART-WORK
SERVES 6–8**

FOR THE FILLING
1 (435 g [15¼ oz]) can
   pineapple chunks in juice
2 tablespoons unsalted
   butter
3 egg yolks (reserve
   the egg whites for the
   meringue)
3 tablespoons cornflour
   (cornstarch)
Fine salt

FOR THE PASTRY
200 g (1¼ cups plus
   2 tablespoons) plain
   flour (all-purpose flour)
20 g (2 tablespoons) icing
   sugar (confectioners'
   sugar)
Fine salt
100 g (7 tablespoons)
   unsalted butter, chilled
1 egg yolk (reserve the egg
   white for the meringue)
Cold water, as needed

FOR THE MERINGUE
4 egg whites
200 g (1 cup) caster sugar
   (superfine sugar)

Preheat the oven to 180°C / 160°C fan (350°F / 320°F fan).

For the filling, drain the pineapple, reserving the juice, and spread the chunks in a medium baking dish. Cut the butter into cubes and scatter around the dish. Bake for 25 minutes.

For the pastry, in a large bowl, combine the plain flour, icing sugar and a pinch of salt. Cut the butter into small cubes and use your fingertips to rub it into the flour mixture until it resembles fine breadcrumbs. Add the egg yolk and use your hands to bring the mixture together into a smooth dough, adding a little cold water, as needed, until it leaves the sides of the bowl clean. Wrap the dough in cling film and chill in the refrigerator for 30 minutes.

Remove the pineapple from the oven and pour in 200 ml (¾ cup plus 1 tablespoon) of the reserved pineapple juice from the can (top up with water if needed). Use a wooden spoon to scrape any caramelised bits off the bottom of the dish and set it aside to cool.

On a lightly floured surface, use a rolling pin to roll out the chilled pastry dough until about 3 mm (⅛ in) thick. Carefully lift the pastry and lay it over a fluted loose-bottomed 23 cm (9 in) round tart tin. Use your knuckles to press the pastry into the tin to create a sealed lining. Don't worry if the pastry crumbles. If it is too difficult to lift as one piece, take small pieces and push them into place. Trim off any excess. Put the pastry shell in the refrigerator to chill for another 30 minutes.

Preheat the oven to 180°C / 160°C fan (350°F / 320°F fan).

Once chilled, set the tin on a baking tray to make it easier to lift. Line the bottom of the pastry shell with parchment paper, pour in baking beans or rice and blind bake for 15 minutes. Remove the beans and paper and bake for 10 more minutes, or until the pastry is lightly golden. If the base puffs up at all, remove from the oven and wait for it to deflate before adding the filling.

Transfer the pineapple and caramelised juices to a blender or food processor and blitz until smooth. Tip into a small nonstick saucepan and bring to a simmer over medium heat.

In a small bowl, whisk together the cornflour, egg yolks and a pinch of salt. Once the pineapple is simmering, lower the heat and scoop 2 tablespoons of the pineapple mixture into the egg mixture, whisking constantly to prevent the eggs from curdling, until fully incorporated. Tip the mixture back into the saucepan and continue whisking for 1–2 minutes, or until thickened to a custard-like consistency and the whisk lines hold their shape. (If you have any white pieces of egg, pass it through a fine-mesh sieve to remove them).

Pour the filling into the pastry shell and put it in the refrigerator to chill for at least 1 hour.

For the meringue, in the bowl of a stand mixer fitted with the whisk attachment or in a large bowl if using a handheld mixer, whip the egg whites until they triple in volume and form stiff peaks. Sprinkle in the caster sugar, 1 tablespoon at a time, and whip thoroughly between each spoonful until incorporated. Repeat until all the sugar has been added.

Spoon the meringue into a piping bag fitted with a star nozzle attachment. Remove the tart from the refrigerator and pipe out an even layer of meringue across the top as your base. Pipe a second layer with a zigzag design in 3 rings, working from the outside in.

Use a blowtorch to brown the meringue and bring out the design. Or place the tart under a hot grill (broiler) for 30–60 seconds, watching it constantly to make sure it doesn't burn.

To serve, remove the tart from its tin by placing it onto a can and gently pulling down on the sides of the tin. Slide the tart off the base onto a serving plate and slice at the table.

RENÉ MAGRITTE

—

In 1972, Audrey Hepburn attended the legendary Surrealist Ball at Baroness Marie-Hélène de Rothschild's chateau on the outskirts of Paris, wearing a birdcage hat inspired by the work of René Magritte. The dress code was 'black tie with a Surrealist headdress' and the guests went all out; one attendee wore an apple in front of her face all night, after Matisse's iconic self-portrait *The Son of Man*, 1946. This dinner party has gone down in history as one of the most lavish social events of all time. The Surrealists didn't do anything by half: footmen dressed as cats directed guests through a maze into the dining room, where the plates were furred and the tables were decorated with taxidermy turtles and deconstructed plastic dolls. The food was served not on the plates but on a naked mannequin lying on a bed of roses, offering surreal concoctions such as *Sir-loin*, and *Goat's Cheese Roasted in Post-Coital Sadness*.

The Surrealists had a deep fascination with food and Magritte was no exception. He was particularly interested in apples. Captivated by the idea of mystery, Magritte repeatedly used the motif of an apple to create a sense of the inexplicable within his work: 'Those of my pictures that show very familiar objects, an apple, for example, pose questions. We no longer understand when we look at an apple; its mysterious quality has thus been evoked.' In Magritte's world, apples wear masks (*Prêtre Marie*, 1961), fill entire rooms (*The Listening Room*, 1952), and float in the sky like opaque, green suns (*The Postcard*, 1960). They're no longer apples at all.

Taken out of its usual context, the apple takes on a completely different and mysterious power; the same goes for all of the food items captured in the artist's Surreal world. The apple in *C'est n'est pas une pomme* (*This is not an apple*) (1964) is declared to not be an apple, yet it is. Conversely, *This is a Piece of Cheese* (*Ceci est un morceau de fromage*) (1936 or 1937) is declared to be cheese, yet it isn't. Elsewhere, a bottle transforms into a carrot (*L'Explication*, 1962) and baguettes float in the sky like clouds (*The Golden Legend*, 1958). The images are both funny and serious, inviting and uncomfortable, mysteries that can't be explained; making the ordinary extraordinary, and challenging the viewer's perception of reality.

But although Magritte created such Surreal and mystical worlds in his artwork, he lived an exceptionally ordinary life. He lived in a nice house in the suburbs of Brussels with his wife Georgette and their Pomeranian, where he painted in the dining room in his slippers. He wore a suit and tie with a bowler hat, like many bankers at the time (as seen in his self-portraits) and enjoyed simple pleasures in life, such as walking his dog, seeing friends and cooking. In the kitchen, his food had little mystery: he followed simple recipes, treating his guests to cheese fondue and chocolate mousse – nothing Surreal in sight.

The simplicity of the food he ate was deeply important to Magritte. In 1937, the artist spent five weeks away from home in London to complete a commission of three large paintings for Edward James, a poet, art collector and patron. It seems Magritte did not enjoy his stay and deeply missed home cooking. He grew tired of English cuisine and in advance of his return to Brussels, he sent his wife Georgette a letter requesting a homecoming dinner. Enclosed was an intricately detailed three-course menu, with the precise measurements and a few preparation methods for his wife to follow: 'First course: 4 hard-boiled eggs with anchovies (anchovies in round bottles); 200 grams of prawns peeled by you, around the eggs, with a sliced tomato; 50 grams of green olives, cut in half (the stones removed); half a grated carrot; 2 or 3 lettuce leaves; and mayonnaise. Second course: 2 kilograms of roast beef; chicory; French fries or croquettes. Dessert: cake with sponge fingers; coffee'. No flying apples here.

René Magritte, *The Scale of Fire*, 1934–1935
Oil on canvas, 54 × 73 cm
Private collection

FLAMBÉ APPLE PANCAKES

—

These apples may not fly, wear masks or fill entire rooms as they do in the world of René Magritte – but they certainly are delicious. Flambé the brandy at the table to give your guests something to remember.

SERVES 4

FOR THE PANCAKES
200 g (1¼ cups) plain flour (all-purpose flour)
Fine salt
4 eggs
600 ml (2¼ cups plus 2 tablespoons) full fat milk
2 tablespoons sunflower oil
Unsalted butter, for frying

FOR THE CARAMELISED APPLES
3 apples
40 g (2½ tablespoons) unsalted butter
3 tablespoons brown sugar
Fine salt
90 ml (6 tablespoons) brandy

Arrange a rack in the middle of the oven and preheat the oven to 50°C (120°F). Put a heatproof plate on the middle rack to keep the pancakes warm.

For the pancakes, in a large bowl, whisk together the plain flour and a pinch of salt. Make a well in the centre, add the eggs and start whisking. Gradually pour in the milk, whisking as you go, then add the sunflower oil and whisk until smooth. Let sit for 10 minutes.

In a medium nonstick frying pan, melt a small knob of butter over medium heat, swirling the pan to coat the surface in butter. Pour a ladle-full of the pancake batter into the pan and swirl the pan to create an even layer. Cook, flipping once, for about 1 minute on each side, or until golden and speckled. Transfer the cooked pancake to the heated plate in the oven and continue cooking the rest of the pancake batter, adding more butter as needed – you should get 12 pancakes.

For the caramelised apples, peel and core the apples and cut them each into 8 segments.

Put the same medium nonstick frying pan over medium heat and melt the butter. Add the apples and cook, stirring regularly, for 5–7 minutes, or until the apples are slightly softened but still have some bite. Add the brown sugar with a pinch of salt and cook, stirring constantly, for 1–2 more minutes. The apples should be coated in caramel.

Arrange 3 pancakes on each of 4 plates. Top each with 6 apple pieces and drizzle with the delicious caramel.

To serve, in a small saucepan, heat the brandy over high heat until steaming. Use a blow torch or a long match to light the brandy in the pan on fire, then carefully pour it over the pancakes in front of your guests. Turn down the lights for added drama.

DIETER ROTH
—

'Morality is an injection of chocolate into the veins of all men', declared the 1918 *Dada Manifesto*.

The Dadaists were sickened by the sweetness of chocolate, a sweetness that they claimed 'determined charity and pity', about which there is 'nothing good'. Ultimately, the Dadaists rejected logic, reason and anything to do with the modern capitalist society they found themselves in. Their work was the antithesis of these ideas, and they used a vast variety of mediums – from traditional painting and collage to large scale installations, performance and poetry – to ask difficult questions about society.

Chocolate was an important medium for the Dada movement, particularly in the art of Dieter Roth whose work is considered to be Neo-Dada. Roth created work that questioned the fundamental properties of art and the methods of displaying it. He considered chocolate to be closely linked to the cycle of life; it ages and decays, cracking and changing with time. But he also saw its connection with disgust, through its visual link to excrement. He enjoyed the irony that in certain forms, chocolate could quite easily be mistaken for something repulsive – something bodies excrete and discard – despite being so widely considered as delicious. His work *Rabbit Dropping Rabbit (Karnickelköttelkarnickel)* (1972), for example, explored the cycle of life and death through the visual of a chocolate Easter bunny made of rabbit poo.

Like human lives, chocolate doesn't last forever. In 1968, Roth created a self-portrait of himself as an older man from chocolate and birdseed. Following his belief in the importance of the impermanence of all things, even art, *P.O.TH.A.A.VFB (Portrait of the Artist as Vogelfutterbüste [Birdseed Bust])* was intended to be placed outside to be consumed by birds and eroded by the rain. It was never created to last. But the museum insisted on preserving and displaying the sculpture, which posed some significant issues in storage. The chocolate attracted lice. Roth probably wouldn't have minded the lice. Disgust was, after all, of great interest to the Dadaists, and Roth created some truly stomach-churning pieces in his time. These works questioned everything we know and think about art and the context of the art gallery and included some pests of his own. In 1970, he unveiled his installation *Staple Cheese (A Race)* at Eugenia Butler Gallery in Los Angeles. Thirty-seven suitcases filled with different cheeses were arranged around the gallery space and then left for several months, over a Californian summer. The work evolved and changed with time, with far from palatable consequences. What was once edible, soon became inedible. The resulting decay created an unbearable stench that visitors could smell long before they laid eyes on the work, transforming the usually aesthetic and pleasant experience of visiting a gallery into a multi-sensory and repulsive one. Huge quantities of larvae swarmed over the cheese, creating an environment so disgusting that the US health authorities tried to shut the exhibition down. The gallery resisted; it was part of the work.

In addition to creating art from food, Roth also created 'food' from art. His series of *Literaturwürste (Literature Sausages)* worked to make pieces of literature he considered to be unpalatable, more digestible – yet, still inedible. Each sausage was cooked following a traditional recipe but with a twist: the meat was substituted for paper. Pages from books, articles and essays that disgusted the artist were shredded, before being cooked with garlic, fennel and salt and stuffed into a sausage casing. The book's title was stuck to the outside of each sausage, which was hung up like meat in a butcher's shop. But this library of meat was not designed to last long. The timeless medium of literature is made mortal through the natural ingredients, a reminder of impermanence with the ever-present undertone of disgust. Roth must have had a very strong stomach.

Dieter Roth, *Literaturwurst (Martin Walser: Halbzeit)
[Literature Sausage (Martin Walser: Halbzeit)]*, 1967
Minced book, gelatin, lard and spices,
cut and pressed into sausage skin
Dieter Roth Foundation, Hamburg

CHOCOLATE SALAMI

—

You'll be delighted to know that unlike Dieter Roth's artwork, this meat-free salami is also paper-free – and quite possibly the antithesis of disgusting. A delicious accompaniment to coffee or dessert wine to round off a dinner party.

SERVES 6–10

200 g (7 oz) dark chocolate, 70% cocoa
2 tablespoons Marsala wine
100 g (7 tablespoons) unsalted butter, softened
100 g (½ cup) caster sugar (superfine sugar)
150 g (5 oz) amaretti biscuits
70 g (2 ¼ oz) crystalised ginger
2 tablespoons icing sugar (confectioners' sugar)

Cut or break the chocolate into small pieces and put it in a large heatproof bowl set over a pan of simmering water. Stir until melted, then remove from the heat and set aside to cool for a few minutes. Add the Marsala, stir and watch the magic happen – the chocolate should immediately thicken.

In a second, larger bowl, beat together the butter and caster sugar. Stir in the melted chocolate.

Use your fingers to break the amaretti biscuits into small chunks and roughly chop the ginger into ½ cm (⅙ in) pieces. Add both to the chocolate mixture and fold until evenly distributed.

Lay a piece of parchment paper on a work surface. Tip out the chocolate mixture into the centre, then fold the paper over the top and use your hands to form it into a thick sausage shape. Twist the ends to seal the paper, then put the salami in the refrigerator to chill for at least 4 hours.

Once firm, remove the salami from the refrigerator and dust it with icing sugar. Use your hands or a pastry brush to lightly rub the icing sugar into the surface to make it look like a real salami – you can tie it up and hang it like a real sausage if you wish.

To serve, use a very sharp knife to cut the salami into thin slices, then arrange on a serving plate.

Store the salami in the fridge, wrapped in parchment paper. It will keep for 1 month.

JACKSON POLLOCK

—

Jackson Pollock was a keen baker. He and his wife Lee Krasner were a culinary team who enjoyed hosting dinner parties for their friends and collectors, keeping to their assigned roles in the kitchen. 'He loved to bake...' said Krasner, 'I did the cooking, but he did the baking ... He was very fastidious about his baking – marvellous bread, cake, and apple pies.'

The couple moved from New York to East Hampton in 1945 where they adapted to rural life. They bought the house via a loan from Pollock's patron, the famous gallery-owner Peggy Gugenheim, and were so poor for the first few years that Pollock resorted to giving the local grocer one of his 'drip paintings' to settle an overdue bill. An enviable deal for the shopkeeper in retrospect. A few years later, Pollock's reputation grew – along with his bank account – and his revolutionary 'drip technique' was recognised for highlighting the quality of paint in a way that had never been seen before. The splatters may appear random in application, but Pollock said he knew exactly where each drip would fall and that he worked with great precision to form his compositions. Perhaps this helps to explain why he was so drawn to the accuracy of baking.

The artist first learnt how to bake from his mother Stella, who was a fantastic cook. His father was a fruit and vegetable farmer and Stella never failed to cook exciting food for her husband and five sons, even during the war and Depression years. She specialised in desserts; frozen apple snow and Italian chocolate pudding were often on the menu. Once he and Krasner moved to the Hamptons, Pollock started baking regularly and gained a reputation for his own culinary talents. He was particularly skilled at pastry and won first prize in the local county fair numerous times for his apple pie, which he adapted from one of his mother's recipes. But it wasn't only baking that excited him about their move to the countryside. Influenced by his upbringing, Pollock enjoyed growing and harvesting home grown produce, foraging for wild ingredients in the surrounding countryside and fishing and clamming in the river.

The artists' home is now open to the public and visitors can step into Pollock's studio to see the paint splattered floor before wandering through the vegetable garden to the main house to explore the kitchen. Among the possessions on display is a large collection of recipes hand-written by the couple as well as a selection of Stella's recipes, which provide further insight into their diet and way of life. Included are details of a very restrictive diet prescribed to Pollock with the aim to cure his alcoholism. The artist struggled with drinking throughout his adult life but remained sober during the first five years in their new home, creating some of his most accomplished paintings, including *Autumn Rhythm (Number 30)* in 1950. The diet, which his doctor hoped would cure his addiction, focused heavily on fresh vegetables and juices. Unfortunately for Pollock, sugars and cereals were banned, which must have really hindered his baking. But ultimately, the diet wasn't a cure. The artist returned to drinking and created a series of aggressive black paintings before his tragic death in 1956, aged just forty-four.

Jackson Pollock was a turbulent character who found solace in the comforts of food and nature. An unexpected twist in the story of an artist so often labelled as a drunk, who, as it turns out, had a more wholesome side to him after all.

Jackson Pollock, *Autumn Rhythm (Number 30)*, 1950
Enamel on canvas, 266.7 × 525.8 cm
The Metropolitan Museum of Art, New York

CHOCOLATE BROWNIES

—

When it comes to the work of Jackson Pollock, more is more – but with control. This is exactly how I think cooking with chocolate should be. These brownies are oh-so-chocolatey, but they're just dark enough to stop them from being too sweet. Inspired by the techniques of Pollock, the drizzled top is the finishing touch to this decadent treat.

MAKES 12 BROWNIES

FOR THE BROWNIES
100 g (3½ oz) dark
   chocolate, 70% cocoa
185 g (¾ cup plus
   1 tablespoon) unsalted
   butter
3 eggs
275 g (1¼ cups plus
   2 tablespoons) caster
   sugar (superfine sugar)
1 tablespoon olive oil
Fine salt
85 g (½ cup plus
   2 tablespoons) plain flour
   (all-purpose flour)
40 g (½ cup) cocoa powder

FOR THE DRIZZLE
50 g (1¾ oz) milk
   chocolate
50 g (1¾ oz) white
   chocolate

Preheat oven to 180°C / 160°C fan (350°F / 320°F fan). Line a 20 cm (8 in) square baking tin with parchment paper, leaving some overhang to make the brownies easier to remove from the tin once cooked.

For the brownies, cut or break the chocolate into small pieces and put it in a large heatproof bowl set over a pan of simmering water. Add the butter and stir until the chocolate and butter are both fully melted. Remove from the heat and set aside to cool for a few minutes.

In a large bowl, whisk together the eggs and caster sugar for 2 minutes, or until thick and much paler in colour – I promise, it's worth it for that creamy texture. Add the cooled chocolate mixture, along with the olive oil and a pinch of salt and stir until combined. Sift in the plain flour and cocoa powder and use a spoon to gently fold it in.

Pour the brownie batter into the parchment-lined baking tin and bake for 25 minutes, or until set. To check, shake the tin. If the middle wiggles, pop it back in the oven for a few more minutes.

Set on a wire rack to cool completely.

Meanwhile, for the drizzle, break the milk and white chocolates into small pieces and put in separate small heatproof bowls set over pans of simmering water. Stir until melted.

Use the parchment paper to carefully remove the brownies from the tin, then use a spoon to drizzle over the melted chocolate, alternating between the two colours – in the style of Jackson Pollock.

Let the chocolate set for at least 20 minutes, then cut into 12 brownies and serve.

RIRKRIT TIRAVANIJA
—

In 1990, Rirkrit Tiravanija served Pad Thai at Paula Allen Gallery in New York. Unknown to many of the visitors, this was not a catering service: it was the artwork. For over three decades, Tiravanija has been transforming meals into art. But it's not only the food that is the art, it's the act of serving it and of eating it. The artist and the audience are part of the work too, engaging in the social act of eating together. As Tiravanija puts it, 'The distance between the artist, and the art and the audience gets a bit blurred.'

This series of works started when Tiravanija participated in a group show at Scott Hanson Gallery in New York in 1989. After seeing collections of Asian ceramics sitting behind glass in museum displays, he felt the items were being shown to hold more value as lifeless objects than for their function and the people who used them. Through his work, he wanted to revivify these inanimate objects. His resulting work *untitled 1989 ( )*, (1989) showed a curry in the process of being cooked, with a cooking pot, empty cans and half-used sauce bottles displayed on pedestals. Despite being a success, Tiravanija felt that crafting an interactive experience with the objects would be even more impactful. The following year, he made *untitled 1990 (pad thai)* (1990).

Although it is now known and loved by many cultures across the world, the dish Pad Thai has only been in existence since the late 1930s. Thailand (then Siam) was a diverse nation with many regions, but Prime Minister Plaek Phibunsongkhram (known as Phibun) worried that without a monarchy, there was little sense of national identity. So, he changed the country's name to Thailand and held a cooking competition to create a dish to encourage unity within the newly named nation and thus Pad Thai was born. Phibun pushed the consumption of the dish even harder during World War II. Rice was running short and by processing it to make noodles, around half the quantity of rice was needed than if it was eaten boiled, steamed or fried. The propaganda campaign 'Noodle is Your Lunch' was launched, encouraging Thai people to help the war effort by changing their diet, establishing Pad Thai firmly within Thai cuisine.

By using this dish as a springboard, Tiravanija's work has gone on to change the way art is viewed. His works break down the wall between the contexts of normal life and art and blur the distinction between in-process and finished artworks. This opens a wider definition of art to include not only food, but the exploration of human and social contexts. In turn, his work also questions the relationship between recipes and cultural identities. Tiravanija is Argentinian born with Thai roots, and he has lived in Canada, the USA and Europe, all of which have influenced him and his identity. He often adapts Thai recipes to honour his work's location and question its relationship to identity. For example, he served two Thai curries with rice for his work *untitled (free)* at 303 Gallery in New York in 1992; one an 'authentic version', the other with New York influences.

A decade later, Tiravanija tried a different approach, creating *untitled 2003 (social pudding)* (2003) with Danish art collective Superflex. In contrast to previous events, visitors were not served pre-made food but instead given a branded orange box containing coconut and orange pudding mix. Inspired by mass-produced food, the audience created their own individual servings of pudding, in individual pots; a far cry from the communal curries of previous works. But ultimately, the result was the same. Despite acting alone, visitors created the same dessert, which they then exchanged with one another and ate together. Again, the experiment really came down to the bonding experience of food – an art we can all connect over, no matter where we are or where we come from.

Rirkrit Tiravanija, *untitled 2019 (five easy pieces)*, 2019
5 plastic food sweets, chrome plate, 30 × 18 × 3 cm
Gallery Side 2, Tokyo

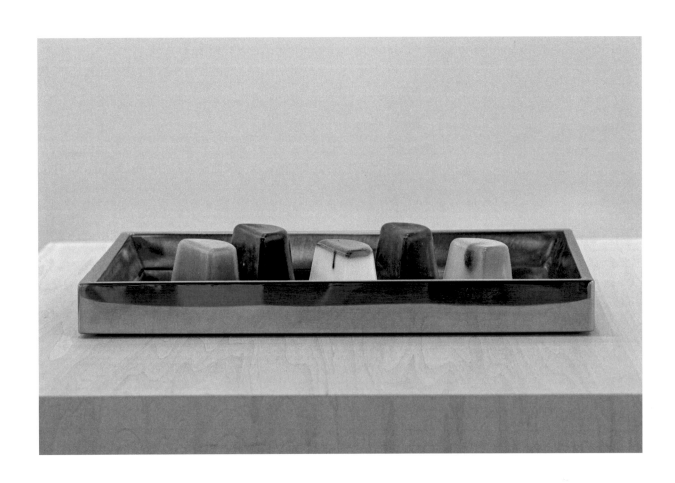

COCONUT CRÈME CARAMEL

—

These individual puddings are smooth and creamy, with the added richness of coconut. Why not make, exchange and eat them with friends to echo the social aspects of Tiravanija's practice?

MAKES 6 SERVINGS

FOR THE CARAMEL
100 g (½ cup) caster sugar
   (superfine sugar)

FOR THE CUSTARD
3 eggs plus 3 egg yolks
100 g (½ cup) caster sugar
   (superfine sugar)
1 teaspoon vanilla extract
Fine salt
400 ml (1½ cups plus
   2 tablespoons) full fat
   coconut milk
100 ml (⅓ cup plus 1
   tablespoon) full fat milk

Set a rack in the middle of the oven and preheat the oven to 160°C / 140°C fan (320°F / 275°F fan).

For the caramel, put a small saucepan over a low heat. Add the caster sugar and 60 ml (¼ cup) of water and stir until the sugar is mostly dissolved. Increase the heat and bring to a boil. Once the mixture starts bubbling, stop stirring and let cook for about 3 minutes, swirling the pan regularly to stop the caramel from burning. If any sugar sticks to the sides of the pan, use a pastry brush dipped in water to brush it off. Once the sugar turns an amber colour, turn off the heat and pour it into the bottoms of six 125 ml (½ cup) pudding moulds.

For the custard, in a large bowl, whisk together the eggs, egg yolks, caster sugar, vanilla and a pinch of salt.

In a small saucepan, bring the coconut milk and milk to a boil over medium-high heat. Once bubbling, immediately remove from the heat and gradually pour it into the egg mixture in a thin, steady stream, whisking as you go, until fully combined. Pour equal amounts into each pudding mould, on top of the caramel.

Place the pudding moulds in a deep baking dish and set the baking dish on the middle rack of the oven. Pour hot water into the baking dish to come halfway up the sides of the puddings. Bake for 30–35 minutes, or until set. Carefully remove the puddings from the baking dish and let cool to room temperature, then refrigerate for at least 4 hours or overnight.

Run a butter knife around the edge of each crème caramel to loosen it, then pop it out onto a plate and serve.

EDWARD BURNE-JONES

—

In 1988, The Victoria & Albert Museum in London released an ad campaign, encouraging the public to visit what they called 'an ace caff with quite a nice museum attached'. Although it's odd to consider food you have to pay for to be more enticing than a free, internationally renowned museum collection, the dining spaces at the V&A do hold their own significant place in history. Plus, as the poster says, 'where else do they give you £100,000,000 worth of *objects d'art* free with every egg salad?'

In 1868, the V&A (known then as the South Kensington Museum) opened three new dining rooms: the Gamble Room, the Poynter Room and the Morris Room. Although they may not sound all that exciting, these rooms were ground-breaking as, together, they formed the world's first museum restaurant. The museum's director Henry Cole wanted to encourage people to stay longer and enjoy a full cultural experience during their visit. And he had found from his time managing the Great Exhibition in 1851 that providing visitors with food and drink was the most effective approach. Everything's better on a full stomach, or so says the inscription from Ecclesiastes painted on the wall of the Gamble Room: 'There is nothing better for a man than that he should eat and drink, and make his soul enjoy the good of his labour'. Despite its success, most other museums didn't open their own restaurants until the early twentieth century.

The design of the Morris Room, also known as the Green Dining Room, was a collaborative project between Arts and Crafts designer William Morris and his life-long friends, architect Philip Webb and painter Edward Burne-Jones. Burne-Jones created designs for the stained-glass windows and a series of small paintings to sit within the green panelling below, both complementing Morris' now internationally renowned wallpaper and glass designs. He took inspiration from two sources for his creations: the signs of the zodiac and historical images of medieval women doing domestic tasks. The end result: twelve panels of his characteristic, melancholic figures holding symbols of the zodiac, interspersed with panels of fruits and berries with goddess-like figures in glass above. Although they were Burne-Jones' designs, Morris employed a group of artisans to paint them. As a result, the finish was so inconsistent that he had all twelve immediately redone

by another Pre-Raphaelite artist, Charles Fairfax Murray. Once complete, the creators used the room to meet with fellow artists and designers; however, despite his connection to the room, Burne-Jones preferred to eat in the Poynter Room. Also known as the grill room, the Poynter Room had a large open grill where diners could watch the chefs grilling meats to order – a new phenomenon for most.

The British diet underwent huge changes in the Victorian era. Railways made food distribution easier and innovations in long-life products such as dried soups, bottled sauces and condensed milk made food storage simpler. Meat became more widely available in the late 1880s with the invention of the refrigerator and was eaten more regularly by people of all classes. The era also saw the introduction of numerous dining courses and the V&A restaurant served different menus with multiple dishes to cater for different social classes. The first-class menu included jugged hare, steak pudding and sweet tarts, while the second-class menu offered veal cutlets, poached egg and spinach and baked buns.

Once a luxurious commodity, sugar also became more widely available at this time which, in turn, made jam more affordable. The British tradition of afternoon tea was started and by the late 1800s, the sugar-loving Victorians (predominantly the working class) were starting their day with jam on toast. Burne-Jones was no exception. In a letter to his pen pal Katie Lewis, the young daughter of his close friends George and Elizabeth Lewis, he specified his breakfast requests for an upcoming stay with the family: 'on Tuesday morning I should like eggs and bacon for breakfast – and coffee and dry toast – finishing with toast, butter and jam – (apricot if possible but don't disarrange the house on my account). I take no sugar with my coffee – but with my tea always.' A surprising and practical request for a man whose artworks are so ethereal and otherworldly.

Edward Burne-Jones, *Sidonia von Bork 1560*, 1860
Watercolour and gouache on paper, 33.3 × 17.1 cm
Tate, London

TIRAMISU WITH CARAMELISED PECANS AND CHOCOLATE LACE LIDS

—

These individual desserts are rich and indulgent. It's a traditional tiramisu recipe, made even more satisfying with the addition of chewy pecans and a snappable chocolate lid.

SERVES 4

FOR THE CARAMELISED PECANS
120 g (1 cup) pecans
3 tablespoons brown sugar

FOR THE TIRAMISU
225 ml (¾ cup plus
  3 tablespoons) hot
  espresso
3 tablespoons Marsala
  wine
2 eggs
50 g (¼ cup) caster sugar
  (superfine sugar)
240 g (1 cup) mascarpone
210 g (7¼ oz) lady fingers
  (about 24)

FOR THE CHOCOLATE LACE
75 g (2½ oz) dark
  chocolate, 70% cocoa
2 teaspoons cocoa powder

For the caramelised pecans, in small dry pan, toast the pecans over medium heat, stirring to make sure they don't burn, for 2–3 minutes, or until they smell intensely nutty. Add the brown sugar and 3 tablespoons of water and stir to fully coat the pecans. Cook, stirring constantly, for about 1 minute, or until most of the water has evaporated and the caramel is thick and glossy.

Tip the pecans onto a piece of parchment paper and spread them out into a single layer. Let cool completely, then roughly chop.

For the tiramisu, in a shallow bowl, combine the espresso and marsala. Set aside to cool.

Separate the egg whites and yolks into 2 large bowls. Whip the whites until stiff peaks form.

Add the caster sugar to the egg yolks and whisk until pale and smooth. Add the mascarpone and mix to combine.

Carefully fold in the egg whites, keeping as much air in the mixture as possible. Fill a piping bag fitted with a medium-sized round tip with the mascarpone mixture (or DIY by cutting off the corner of a resealable plastic bag) – this helps keep the layers neat.

Before you start assembling your tiramisus, tear off a large piece of parchment paper and use a pencil to draw around the rim of the serving glasses. These are your templates for the chocolate lace lids.

Submerge the lady fingers, one at a time, in the espresso mixture sugar-side up for just a second, then shake off any excess. Place 3 fingers, sugar-side up, in a single layer at the bottom of a serving glass. Cover the fingers with ½ tablespoon of chopped pecans, followed by a layer of the mascarpone mixture. Repeat once to fill the glass. Do the same for the other 3 servings.

Put it in the refrigerator to chill for at least 2–3 hours, or up to a day in advance of serving.

For the chocolate lace, roughly chop the chocolate and put 50 g (1¾ oz) of it in a medium heatproof bowl set over a pan of simmering water. Stir until the chocolate melts and reaches 45°C (115°F). Remove the bowl from the heat. Add the remaining chocolate and stir until cooled to 31°C (90°F).

Pour the chocolate into a piping bag and snip off about ½ cm (1/6 in) from the end to make a small opening. Squeeze out the chocolate in a continuous flow over the templates you made earlier, swirling it around to create lace patterns. Make each lid slightly larger than the circles so that they'll sit comfortably on the rim of the serving glasses.

Leave at room temperature for 1–2 hours to set completely.

When ready to serve, carefully peel the lace off the paper. Sieve the cocoa powder over the chocolate lace and carefully place one on top of each glass of tiramisu.

DRINKS

YVES KLEIN
—

In 1958, Yves Klein opened the doors of his exhibition *The Specialization of Sensibility in the Raw Material State of Stabilized Pictorial Sensibility* (or *The Void* for short) at Galerie Iris Clert, in Paris. Accustomed to his iconic monochromatic blue artworks, the 2,500 attendees, who were funnelled in just ten at a time, were shocked to discover on entry that the gallery was not only completely white but totally empty. It seemed there was no artwork to be found, only drinks in the form of blue martinis. But these were more than just refreshments. Made of Cointreau, gin and methylene blue, the artist had secretly controlled not only how the visitors came into the space but what, in turn, came out of them; the cocktails turned their urine blue. The artist made his audience the artwork, continuing the show beyond the confines of the white cube, into the gallery goers' own bodies and homes.

Klein created his first monochromatic work in 1947. With the help of the paint supplier Edouard Adam and chemical company Rhône-Poulenc, he concocted his recipe for the perfect shade of blue. IKB (International Klein Blue) is the ultimate ultramarine; a recipe that combines pigments with resin to create a multi-dimensional finish which, in Klein's opinion, was far superior to the other blues on the market. The artist patented the recipe in 1960, but fortunately for us, the Yves Klein Archives partnered with Ressource paints in 2018 to make this iconic shade available to everyone. Marking what would have been Klein's ninetieth birthday, the release made it possible for art lovers to fill their homes with this electric shade – or perhaps even make their own Klein-inspired artworks.

Also known as Klein Blue, the artist used IKB across a huge variety of media during his short life – from paintings to sculptures and sea sponges to coffee tables. The ANT series (or the *Anthropométries*) is arguably one of Klein's most celebrated and controversial. Dubbed 'living brushes', naked women covered in IKB paint pressed themselves onto the canvas or paper, leaving bodily impressions. The concept for this iconic series was crafted at a dinner party, at the home of Robert Godet in June 1958. Klein created the very first work as an informal performance piece for the other guests, where a painted woman moved her body around on a piece of paper laid on the floor until it was entirely blue.

Blue is one of the rarest colours in the natural world. It's a challenge to create a true IKB-style shade from artificial sources, let alone natural ones. This is particularly difficult in the food world, often resulting in more purple tones, similar to that of blueberries and blue potatoes. Food just isn't often truly blue. Human evolution has taught us to avoid anything truly blue, as it might be poisonous and generally we aren't tempted to eat it. No one wanted to eat Bridget Jones' soup when she accidentally turned it blue. And Alfred Hitchcock's guests struggled through his entirely blue dinner party menu, where blue soup was made even less appetising by an accompanying blue bread roll, followed by dishes of blue trout, blue chicken and blue ice cream.

But it seems there is now a market for such inventions – especially the ice cream. Until recently, truly blue food has been impossible to achieve without resorting to artificial means, such as the E133 brilliant blue colouring agent that tints so many products, including the spirit Curaçao, the liqueur designed to make your cocktail look like the clear blue waters of a tropical island. But natural dyes have been making their way into the market and blue food has seen a significant rise in popularity, with many blue matcha drinks and ice creams gracing our social media feeds. The blue sources in these concoctions are now not only safe to ingest, but widely considered to be superfoods. The two most common dyes are blue spirulina – a dehydrated algae – and butterfly pea flower, a tropical plant native to parts of Indonesia and Malaysia. Both render food a blue Yves Klein would have been proud of. Let's just hope they don't turn anything else blue.

Yves Klein, *Blue Sponge*, c. 1961
Dry pigment and synthetic resin
on natural sponge and metal base,
10.5 × 6 × 4 cm
Private collection

BLUE MARTINI

—

Don't let the colour put you off. This martini is extremely sophisticated, with fragrant orange notes, and is an exciting and unexpected way to kick off a dinner party.

(And don't worry – it won't turn anything blue!)

MAKES 1 COCKTAIL

60 ml (2 fl oz) vodka (or gin, if preferred)
15 ml (½ fl oz) blue Curaçao
15 ml (½ fl oz) vermouth
2 dashes orange bitters
Ice cubes

In a cocktail shaker or mixing glass, combine the vodka, blue Curaçao, vermouth and orange bitters. Fill the shaker with ice cubes and use a spoon to stir until very cold.

Strain into a chilled martini glass and serve.

HENRI MATISSE

—

Henri Matisse ate just one large meal a day to fuel his creativity. He followed a disciplined routine, waking up early to row on the river, then he would play the violin to limber up his fingers to be ready to work until midday, at which point he'd sit down to eat. Then came a luxurious, lengthy siesta before he returned to work until the evening.

It's interesting then that food was so often on Matisse's creative mind and ran as a recurring theme throughout the various eras of his oeuvre; from his earliest Impressionist-style painting, *The Dinner Table* (1897) which he reimagined in the Fauvist style in *The Dessert: Harmony in Red* in 1908, to his almost abstracted paper cut-outs, such as *Végétaux (Vegetables)*, which the artist created from the confines of his wheelchair in 1952. But one item in particular crops up time and again, marking the various stages of his stylistic journey: the chocolate pot.

Matisse's chocolate pot is the most painted object in his collection. Given to him by fellow Fauvist Albert Marquet as a wedding gift in 1898, the curved, metal pot appears in dozens of his works, both as the main subject and as a part of interior scenes. *Still Life with Chocolate Pot*, (1900–1902), hints at the beginnings of Fauvism, with its bold colours and intense brushwork. Matisse soon plunged fully into the Fauvist style, for example in *Interior with Young Girl Reading* (1905/06), which features the chocolate pot as an accent to this composition of planes of opposing, complimentary colours. *Still Life with Blue Tablecloth* (1909) brings the pot back to centre stage in an Expressionist-style painting, showcasing it in a trinity of objects on top of one of the artist's treasured Islamic textile pieces. The pot then disappears from Matisse's work for three decades, poignantly re-emerging into the spotlight shortly after the artist's divorce in *Still Life with a Shell* (1940), a dynamic still life with bold, black outlines. The study for this intriguing work shows the beginnings of Matisse's famous cut-out style; each object is roughly cut from coloured paper to allow him to play with the composition.

Although he collected many pieces like the chocolate pot, Matisse also created numerous vessels of his own, some of which make appearances within his paintings, such as the blue-and-white plate in the bottom left-hand corner of *L'Atelier rouge* (1911). Like his contemporary Picasso, Matisse created ceramics, perhaps inspired by his mother Anna, who worked as a porcelain painter. Among many things, Anna educated Matisse about food. Located in north-eastern France, their hometown of Bohain-en-Vermandois is known for its quality cheeses as well as several types of onion soup, which his mother often made. She created simple and delicious dishes, as well as homemade remedies from the herb and vegetable garden, many of which the artist continued to use throughout his life. He even invented some of his own, including many unusual cures for insomnia. His personal favourite: beer and chips.

After leaving home for Paris, Matisse often struggled financially in the early stages of his career and lived solely on rice when necessary, saving up to buy fruit and vegetables – to paint, not eat. But, as his bank account improved, so did his diet, and he developed a taste for rich and varied dishes, with a particular fondness for *soup de poisson* (fish soup), the recipe for which he wrote down in a letter to French writer Marie Dormoy in 1938. A mix of traditional French flavours and Italian ingredients, his recipe contains a variety of beautiful *fruits de mer* with pappardelle-style pasta in a broth flavoured with fennel seeds, saffron and orange peel.

But as he aged, Matisse's palate changed again. He grew nostalgic for the foods of his youth and once confined to his wheelchair, he asked his assistant Jacqueline Duheme to cook some of his mother's dishes. Duheme obliged and prepared meals such as *flamiche aux poireaux* (leek tart with cream), which was his mother's specialty, and *brandade de morue*: pureed dried salt cod which has been soaked in fresh water for a day, then simmered in milk. Another remedy, perhaps.

Henri Matisse, *L'Atelier rouge*, 1911
Oil on canvas, 181 × 219.1 cm
Museum of Modern Art, New York

DILL-INFUSED BLOODY MARY

—

This Bloody Mary celebrates garnishes – the more, the merrier. Get creative with a variety of colours, textures and shapes to echo Matisse's vibrant style, or set out a selection of garnishes for your guests to create their own masterpieces.

MAKES 1 L (4 CUPS)

FOR THE DILL-INFUSED VODKA
250 ml (1 cup) vodka
1 small bunch fresh dill, plus more for garnish

TO SERVE
750 ml (3 cups) tomato juice
12 dashes Worcestershire sauce
10 dashes Tabasco
4 teaspoon cracked black pepper
Fine salt
Ice cubes

TO GARNISH
Fresh dill fronds
Pickled red cabbage
Small cucumbers
Pickled onions
Olives
Lemon slices
Celery and celery leaves
Gherkins

Prepare the vodka at least 4 hours before you want to use it.

For the vodka, in a medium glass jar, combine the vodka and dill, pushing down the dill to fully submerge it in the vodka. Screw on the lid and put the vodka in the refrigerator to infuse for 4–8 hours, shaking it every now and then to intensify the flavour. Strain before use.

When ready to serve, in a large jug, combine the dill-infused vodka, tomato juice, Worcestershire sauce, Tabasco, black pepper and a pinch of salt. Add lots of ice cubes and stir until very cold.

Fill serving glasses with fresh ice cubes and pour over the Bloody Mary mix, holding back the ice from the jug with a spoon.

Garnish each glass with young celery leaves, dill fronds, lemon wedges and all the pickled items you desire, stacking them up on cocktail sticks for height and variation. Serve immediately.

ADÉLAÏDE LABILLE-GUIARD
—

Adélaïde Labille-Guiard was lucky to have survived the French Revolution. Before the revolt, she was a frequent portraitist for King Louis XVI's aunts and one of the only women to have been admitted to the Académie Royale after a fortuitous intervention by Queen Marie Antoinette herself. With such royal connections, some revolutionaries questioned if she could be trusted. But Labille-Guiard was no royalist. She had welcomed the formation of the National Assembly, the group that represented the voice of the common people, painting portraits of politicians and donating financially to their cause to ensure her safety.

The King's mismanagement of the financial crisis had fuelled the hunger for a revolution. Food played a vital role. Bread and salt were at the heart of it all. Bread was the main source of calories for the population and ensuring a consistent supply had previously helped avoid rioting. The bakers were heavily policed to ensure the supply continued and controlled how many loaves people could buy. Any baker seen to be selling underweight loaves or tampering with their bread with bulking ingredients such as wood chips was severely punished. Competition for bread was high due to a growing population, while poor wheat harvests from severe weather in the late 1780s added to the misery, resulting in severe food shortages and widespread famine. To add a further complication, the bread needed salt and salt was heavily taxed. A huge burden on the poor (and on the bread bakers), the tax varied in different regions. Smuggling and corruption led to severe inflation, with violent treatment of those too poor to pay. Bread was soon costing the average worker over 80 per cent of their income and the riots began.

After the storming of Bastille in 1789, there was no bread. But when the queen was told that her people were starving, it's famously said that she laughed and replied, 'let them eat cake'. This is most likely not true, but she certainly didn't have much sympathy for those suffering. However, there's a common misconception that Marie Antoinette had spent her life eating cake and drinking champagne. She certainly enjoyed her sugary biscuits, crystallised fruit and hot chocolate, but for lunch and dinner she often ate plain boiled poultry or bone broth – far from the elaborately decorated cakes seen in the Sofia Coppola film. She enjoyed an indulgent orange juice; she rarely drank alcohol and often refused to eat altogether when with company. How else could she have maintained such a slim waistline?

Despite her unpopularity, Marie Antoinette was responsible for introducing potatoes into the French diet; a move that saved the lives of many once the wheat harvests failed. Although formerly only fed to pigs and feared to be inedible for humans, the nutritional chemist Antoine-Augustin Parmentier began his mission to bring the crop to the poor of France. He had been fed potatoes by the Prussians when captured during the Seven Years' War, which had kept him in good health. Parmentier persuaded the royal couple to take an interest in the crop and as a result, the queen planted some in the palace gardens. The fashion icon then went on to make this boring tuber a trend, wearing potato blossoms in her hair. Many wealthy women followed in her footsteps, and the humble potato became popular across all levels of society, and a staple in the French diet. Unfortunately for the royal family, this was not enough and, in return for the mismanaged revolt, King Louis XVI, the queen and their son were marched at gunpoint to the Bastille in Paris as the crowd chanted, 'The baker, the baker's wife and the baker's boy'. The queen was beheaded shortly after, following a final meal of vermicelli soup.

The storming of the Bastille led to the Reign of Terror, during which thousands more were executed. Because of her royal history, Labille-Guiard was greatly at risk and she was forced to flee Paris. Incredibly, she survived, and her story was, in time, a happy one. Despite her battles, she eventually returned to the city and established her atelier, dedicating her life to training women artists behind her, working towards equal rights in the world of art.

Adélaïde Labille-Guiard,
Élisabeth Philippine Marie Hélène de Bourbon, dite Madame Elisabeth, 1788
Oil on canvas, 80.7 × 64.2 cm (oval)
Musée de l'Histoire de France, Versailles

PEAR AND GINGER CHAMPAGNE COCKTAIL

—

This pear and ginger combination makes for a sweet and spicy cocktail with an herbal finish. Swap out the Champagne for prosecco, if you prefer – it's a little sweeter but just as delicious.

MAKES 8 COCKTAILS

FOR THE PEAR AND GINGER SYRUP
2 small pears, cored and finely chopped
150 g (¾ cup) caster sugar (superfine sugar)
1 teaspoon ground ginger or 1 (2.5 cm [1 in]) piece fresh ginger, very finely chopped
Fine salt

TO SERVE
1 small pear, cut into 8 thin slices
16 fresh rosemary sprigs
1 L (4 cups) chilled Champagne

For the pear and ginger syrup, in a small pan, bring the pears, caster sugar, ginger, a pinch of salt and 100 ml (⅓ cup plus 1 tablespoon) of water to a boil over medium-high heat. Continue boiling, stirring occasionally, for 10 minutes, or until the pear has fully softened. Remove from the heat and strain through a fine-mesh sieve into a bowl, using a spoon to push through as much liquid and flavour as possible. It should be a beautiful amber colour. Put it in the refrigerator and let cool completely.

When ready to serve, pour 1 tablespoon of the pear and ginger syrup into the bottom of each Champagne flute. Pop in a slice of pear and 2 rosemary sprigs, bending the stems slightly to make them curved. Top up with Champagne and serve.

GORDON MATTA-CLARK
—

In 1971, Gordon Matta-Clark opened Food in SoHo, New York. Part restaurant, part performance, the space was created in collaboration with dancer and photographer Caroline Goodden to provide struggling artists with a good meal (and even part-time jobs), as well as being an arts venue engaged in the performative act of cooking.

Food quickly became a popular gathering place for artists, both emerging and successful, which, in turn, brought in an array of other people, all keen to see the likes of Robert Rauschenberg, Donald Judd and John Cage tucking into their dinners. The meals were special; Food served up a huge variety of dishes, including many that weren't mainstream yet, such as sushi, or dishes using Japanese ingredients, such as wasabi, sake and soy. It was also one of the first restaurants in New York to serve fully vegetarian menus on some days, including dishes such as acorn squash with mint, creamed sorrel, and yams baked in honey butter.

Sunday nights were extra special, because an artist would be invited to take up the role of head chef and serve a menu of their choice. Matta-Clark often stepped into this role himself, serving up unusual dishes that caused both intrigue and horror among his diners. At one meal, titled *Alive*, he hid live brine shrimp within hard boiled eggs. At another, he encased an entire sea bass within a three-foot-long block of aspic, which he wobbled dramatically at the table as if the fish were swimming. Perhaps unsurprisingly, nobody was quite brave enough to eat it. At his famous *Bone Meal*, guests tucked into a feast of oxtail soup, roasted bone marrow, and frog legs, before leaving the restaurant adorned with bone necklaces created from their leftovers.

To showcase the chef of the day and their unique culinary creations, Food was designed to be open plan, so that diners could observe the chaos of the kitchen as the meal was prepared. This too was a new concept in the restaurant sphere. To achieve this, a piece of the kitchen wall had to be removed, and Matta-Clark decided to do the honours himself. As Goodden put it, 'Gordon decided to cut himself a wall sandwich…he cut a horizontal

section through the wall and door and fell in love with it.' This act marked the start of Matta-Clark's renowned series of cut buildings, also known as *Anarchitecture*, where the artist used power tools to cut in half, or cut vast holes in, buildings awaiting demolition.

Food always remained a part of Matta-Clark's practice. 'To Gordon, I think everything in life was an art event', said Goodden. He explored methods of cooking through his work, outside of the traditional kitchen setting: he deep fried photographs; roasted a whole pig under the Brooklyn Bridge as a performance; and experimented with growing sheets of mould as a method of cooking. In 1970, he exhibited the work *Museum* at the Bykert gallery, a display of bacterial substances at varying stages of growth. In different sized vessels, he combined agar (a gelatinous substance extracted from seaweed) and water with a variety of foods, such as sugar, juice, stock, vegetable scraps, chocolate, sperm-oil, yeast and even half-eaten sandwiches, and observed the subsequent microbial growth. The organic material was consumed and decayed by bacteria and fungi from the surrounding environment, eventually drying into a sheet, which he hung up and exhibited. He also cooked these experiments with heat and flames, creating *Incendiary Wafers* (1970/71).

For Matta-Clark, cooking was much more than preparing a meal; it was a social, scientific and artistic experiment. And although he only ran Food for a couple of years, he introduced new and innovative concepts to the worlds of both food and art. Which, in his mind, were always one and the same.

Gordon Matta-Clark, *Incendiary Wafers*, 1970–1971
Agar and algae, mixed media
112 Greene Street, New York

KOMBUCHA

—

Inspired by Matta-Clark, this recipe experiments with growing bacteria but with a result that is both delicious and very good for you. The kombucha scoby may look a bit gross, and the prospect of working with it might be intimidating, but the more you make kombucha, the more you'll begin to understand it and the magical world of fermentation. You can order a kombucha scoby in kombucha starter online; one scoby will make infinite brews.

MAKES 1 ½ L (6 CUPS)

100 g (½ cup) caster sugar (superfine sugar)
1½ L (6 cups) just-boiled water
2 black tea bags
1 organic kombucha scoby in kombucha starter

In a large saucepan or heatproof bowl, dissolve the caster sugar in the just-boiled water. Don't be freaked out by the amount of sugar – this is what the yeast and bacteria feed on to ferment the tea and you end up with very little in the final drink. Add the tea bags, stir and let steep for 1 minute, or until the tea is amber coloured. Don't leave the tea bags in there for too long, or the tea will be bitter. Remove (but don't squeeze) the tea bags and discard them. Let the tea cool to room temperature.

Once the tea is cool, skim off any thin oily film from the top and transfer the tea to a 2 L (8 cup) jar. Tip in your scoby with 100 ml (⅓ cup plus 1 tablespoon) of the starter liquid (this will be included in the package). Secure a piece of muslin or thin cloth on top of the jar with an elastic band as a lid and use a piece of masking tape to label the jar with the date you started it.

Pop the jar into a dark but airy corner of your kitchen to work its magic for 5–7 days for the first ferment – do not put it in a cupboard, as it needs good air circulation. Try not to move the jar during this time; the less you handle it, the better the result will be.

After about 5 days, a thin film may have formed on the surface of the tea – this is a new scoby. There might be some odd bubbles or weird-looking yeasty strings floating around. This is almost always good stuff, but if you're unsure, there are plenty of helpful websites with photographs confirming what is and isn't normal, which can be very helpful for beginners!

Use a straw to gently move the scoby aside, so you can taste the kombucha. By now, it should taste a little zingy but not vinegary. If it is too vinegary, you may have left it to ferment for a little too long. Fermentation time depends on the scoby and the temperature of the room – the warmer it is, the quicker the fermentation. If the kombucha is too sweet, leave it to ferment for another day or so. If it tastes bitter, this is likely because your teabags were steeped for too long. The more you make kombucha, the more you will learn how it behaves. Again, there are many resources online to help you identify any issues with your brew and how to fix them.

If you're happy with your kombucha at this stage, transfer the scobies to a jar. Give the kombucha a stir with a wooden spoon and pour 100 ml (⅓ cup plus 1 tablespoon) of the kombucha over the scoby. This is the starter liquid for your next batch. You can either start making more kombucha straightaway or you can store the scoby and starter liquid in a jar with a fabric lid at room temperature until you're ready to make more.

Pour the rest of the kombucha through a fine-mesh sieve into glass bottles to remove any yeasty bits, leaving a 5 cm (2 in) gap at the top of each bottle. Seal with clip top or screw top lids. You can either drink the kombucha flat now or allow it to ferment further to create more complex flavour and carbonation. Label the bottles with the bottling date and place them back into the dark, airy spot for another 2–7 days (keep tasting to see when you're happy with the flavour). Put the kombucha in the refrigerator to chill for serving – chilling makes the kombucha refreshing and helps it hold carbonation better.

Strain again before serving. Bottled kombucha will keep in the fridge for 1–3 months.

MENU
PLANNER
—

The aim of *Painting the Plate* is to encourage readers to not only get more creative in the kitchen but also to spark conversations about art among experienced art lovers and newbies alike. For those not on the 'inside', the art world can seem intimidating. But transfer that conversation to the dinner table – a safe and familiar place with friends – and it suddenly becomes much more approachable. Most people have the confidence to say what they do and don't like on their plate, and I think this is also the perfect place to start expressing opinions about art.

These menus are a gentle nudge in the right direction and a way to structure conversations around a theme, whilst also making the most out of the recipes. Of course, you can combine any recipes you wish to create your perfect menu. Look at each recipe to see how many it caters for and adjust the measurements for your number of guests. But most importantly, have fun – it's a dinner party, after all!

INFLUENTIAL WOMEN
—

This show-stopping menu is inspired by an impressive roster of female artists. Each of these women had a significant impact on both the art world and the feminist movement and offer a plethora of topics to spark conversation at a dinner party. Read the artists' pages to learn more about their practices and the movements they influenced and discover how these women were innovators, not only in the studio but in the kitchen, too.

Starter | Cherry and jambon de Bayonne bruschetta with homemade ricotta | *Les Fleurs*, 2007, Louise Bourgeois | **Page 12**

Main | Beetroot, halloumi and chicory salad with tahini-yoghurt dressing and pomegranate molasses | *Vernal Yellow*, 1980, Lee Krasner | **Page 32**

or

Singaporean-inspired laksa with fish balls | *Rambutans*, c. 1965, Georgette Chen | **Page 94**

Dessert | Lemon curd and raspberry trifle | *Red Hill and White Shell*, 1938, Georgia O'Keeffe | **Page 164**

COCKTAILS AND CANAPÉS

—

These recipes are as delicious as they are beautiful and can be made in advance, with only a bit of assembly required before your guests arrive. I suggest reading Lowell Blair Nesbitt's page for inspiration on elaborate ways to present hors d'oeuvres.

Canapés

Beetroot-pickled devilled eggs | *Let it All Hang Out*, 1973, Judy Chicago | **Page 20**

Cherry and jambon de Bayonne bruschetta with homemade ricotta | *Les Fleurs*, 2007, Louise Bourgeois | **Page 12**

Beetroot-cured salmon with homemade blinis | *Pink Orchid*, 1989, Lowell Blair Nesbitt | **Page 48**

Chocolate-dipped meringues with a salted pecan and rosemary crumb | *View of the 'Grossglockner' Mountain (The Great Bellringer),* 1857, Markus Pernhart | **Page 172**

Chocolate truffles with cocoa powder and smoked sugar | *Pyramid, Sphere, Cube*, 1997–1998, David Nash | **Page 148**

Cocktails

Blue martini | *Blue Sponge*, c. 1961, Yves Klein | **Page 210**

Pear and ginger Champagne cocktail | *Élisabeth Philippine Marie Hélène de Bourbon, dite Madame Elisabeth*, 1788, Adélaïde Labille-Guiard | **Page 218**

LIGHT FRENCH FARE

—

A celebration of French food and art, this selection of artists spans two centuries, from the French Revolution to post World War II. It's an era of dramatic change, as reflected in their work.

I recommend starting with the Champagne cocktails as an apéritif and accompanying the rest of the menu with a French white wine from Bordeaux, Normandy, Provence or Île-de-France to embrace the artists' homeland.

Apéritif | Pear and ginger Champagne cocktail | *Élisabeth Philippine Marie Hélène de Bourbon, dite Madame Elisabeth*, 1788, Adélaïde Labille-Guiard | **Page 218**

Starter | Oysters with a pickled ginger and shallot dressing | *The Birth of Venus*, c. 1912, Odilon Redon | **Page 16**

Main | Moules marinières with herb-salted French fries | *Jardin Nacré*, 1955, Jean Dubuffet | **Page 106**

Dessert | Saffron and cardamom poached pears | *Three Pears*, c. 1888-1890, Paul Cézanne | **Page 152**

A FLORAL FEAST

—

From seventeenth-century Dutch still life to the iconic *Sunflowers* of Post-Impressionism to vast Photorealist blooms, these edible bouquets showcase the astounding development of painting over the course of four centuries.

Starter | Beetroot-cured salmon with homemade blinis | *Pink Orchid*, 1989, Lowell Blair Nesbitt | **Page 48**

Main | Five-spice duck legs with plums and kale | *A Bouquet of Flowers*, c. 1612, Clara Peeters | **Page 74**

Dessert | Orange custard tart | *Sunflowers*, 1889, Vincent van Gogh | **Page 160**

AN ARTFUL BRUNCH

—

This artistic breakfast spread is inspired by the work of artists spanning a century of art history, each with their own unique connection to food.

If you're expecting a lot of guests, I suggest reading Claude Monet's page for inspiration on extra breakfast treats to fill the table.

Crusty bread | *Oval Sculpture*, 1943, Barbara Hepworth | **Page 44**

Shakshuka | *Lovers*, 1984–1992, Howard Hodgkin | **Page 102**

or

Spinach pancakes with eggs and feta | *Sleeping Leaves*, 1991, Gabriel Orozco | **Page 138**

French breakfast muffins with honey and thyme butter | *Wheatstacks, Snow Effect, Morning*, 1891, Claude Monet | **Page 156**

Dill-infused Bloody Mary | *L'Atelier rouge*, 1911, Henri Matisse | **Page 214**

A PAINTERLY PICNIC

—

These colourful recipes are perfect for a meal *en plein air*. Each dish can be made and cut into portions in advance and only a fork is needed to eat the salad, making them ideal for a picnic in the great outdoors.

Turmeric hummus with black sesame and seaweed crackers | *The weather project*, 2003, Olafur Eliasson | **Page 36**

Roasted pepper tart with a Parmesan crust | *Orange and Yellow*, 1956, Mark Rothko | **Page 82**

Green orzo salad | *Make a Salad*, 2008, Alison Knowles | **Page 130**

Chocolate brownies | *Autumn Rhythm (Number 30)*, 1950, Jackson Pollock | **Page 196**

MINIMAL EFFORT, MAXIMUM IMPACT: THE EFFORTLESS DINNER PARTY

—

Delicious, beautiful, and oh-so-easy, this menu presents a variety of movements and mediums for discussion. All the recipes are quick and simple to give you maximum time with your guests. Prepare the dessert the night before to make it even more effortless.

Apéritif | Blue martini | *Blue Sponge*, c. 1961, Yves Klein | **Page 210**

Starter | Chipotle prawns | *Vampiros Vegetarianos*, 1962, Remedios Varo | **Page 40**

Main | Cheese fondue with potatoes, radishes, pickled cornichons and chicory | *Seville Series No. 3, Fondue Meal*, 1991, Daniel Spoerri | **Page 118**

Dessert | Chocolate salami | *Literature Sausage (Martin Walser: Halbzeit)*, 1967, published 1961–70, Dieter Roth | **Page 192**

or

Saffron and cardamom poached pears | *Three Pears*, c. 1888–1890, Paul Cézanne | **Page 152**

LIGHT AND FRESH: A MENU FOR PABLO PICASSO

—

This menu is light and refreshing, just as Pablo Picasso would have wanted it. Read his artist page to learn more about his diet and the important impact he felt it had on his artistic practice.

Starter | Watermelon, radish and cucumber salad with goat's cheese | *Untitled*, 1979, Helen Frankenthaler | **Page 24**

Main | Whole roasted sea bream with Spanish pisto | *Still Life, Fish and Frying Pan*, 1936, Pablo Picasso | **Page 134**

Dessert | Goat's cheese ice cream with honey and sea salt | *The Persistence of Memory*, 1931, Salvador Dalí | **Page 180**

SEEING YELLOW: A MENU FOR VINCENT VAN GOGH

—

This menu covers a huge variety of artistic eras, with very different artworks, each featuring its own shade of yellow. Although it may be an odd concept to centre a menu around a colour, it could make for an interesting dinner party series. Make sure to read Vincent van Gogh's artist page to learn more about his infatuation with this sunshiny shade to get started.

Apéritif | Pear and ginger Champagne cocktail | *Élisabeth Philippine Marie Hélène de Bourbon, dite Madame Elisabeth*, 1788, Adélaïde Labille-Guiard | **Page 218**

Starter | Turmeric hummus with black sesame and seaweed crackers | *The weather project*, 2003, Olafur Eliasson | **Page 36**

Main | Lamb cutlets with yoghurt sauce and a saffron dressing | *La Troupe de Mademoiselle Eglantine*, 1895, Henri de Toulouse-Lautrec | **Page 78**

Dessert | Orange custard tart | *Sunflowers*, 1889, Vincent van Gogh | **Page 160**

BIBLIOGRAPHY
—

Louise Bourgeois (1911–2010) | Page 10
Citations: Conway, Madeleine, and Nancy Kirk. *The Museum of Modern Art Artist's Cookbook.* New York: The Museum of Modern Art, 1977.
Januszczak, Waldemar. 'How To Peel an Orange'. *Hauser & Wirth*, 18 December 2020. https://www.hauserwirth.com/ursula/31163-how-to-peel-an-orange-louise-bourgeois/.
Sources: Cooke, Rachel. 'She'll put a spell on you.' *The Observer*, 14 October 2007.
The Easton Foundation. *Biography.* http://www.theeastonfoundation.org/biography.
Weaver, Ben. 'Destruction of the Father.' *The London List*, 3 January 2020.

Odilon Redon (1840–1916) | Page 14
Citations: Larson, Barbara. 'Odilon Redon and the Pasteurian Revolution: Health, Illness, and *le monde invisible.*' Science in Context, Vol. 17, No. 4. Cambridge: Cambridge University Press, December 2004.
Sources: Civitello, Linda. Cuisine and Culture: *A History of Food and People.* Hoboken, NJ: John Wiley & Sons, 2011
Domaines Barons de Rothschild (Lafite). *Château Peyre-Lebade.* https://lafite.vin.co/1692D1BOLW.
Hauptman, Jodi. *Beyond the Visible: The Art of Odilon Redon.* New York: Museum of Modern Art, 2005.
McKendrick, Jamie. 'Perchance to dream.' *The Independent*, 11 February 1995.
National Galleries of Scotland. *Odilon Redon 'The Temptation of Saint Anthony'. 'Et toutes sortes de bêtes effroyables surgissent'* (Plate VIII). Inv.P 2446. https://www.nationalgalleries.org/art-and-artists/38119/.
Roman, Gabrielle. 'A History of Pasteurization.' *Culture Cheese Magazine*, 18 April 2015.

Judy Chicago (b. 1939) | Page 18
Citations: Brooklyn Museum. 'The Dinner Party: Place Settings.' https://www.brooklynmuseum.org/eascfa/dinner_party/place_settings.
Judy Chicago: The Dinner Party. YouTube, San Francisco Museum of Modern Art, 2000. https://www.youtube.com/watch?v=tskczrGpESA.
Kleiner, Fred S. *Gardner's Art Through the Ages: A Concise Global History.* Ebook. Boston: Cengage Learning, 2022.
Simmons, Amelia. *American Cookery.* Kansas City: Andrew McMeel Publishing, 2012. First published by Simeon Butler in 1796.
Pollan, Michael. *Cooked: A Natural History of Transformation.* London: Allen Lane, 2013.
Sources: Ristanovic, Viktoria. 'The Art Warriors of the Second Wave of Feminism.' *The Untitled Magazine*, 16 August 2019.
Weiss, Sasha. 'Judy Chicago, the Godmother.' *The New York Times Style Magazine*, 7 February 2018.
Williams, Stacy J. 'A Feminist Guide to Cooking.' *American Sociological Association.* 'Contexts', Vol. 13, No. 3, August 2014. https://doi.org/10.1177/1536504214545763.

Helen Frankenthaler (1928–2011) | Page 22
Citations: Conway, Madeleine, and Nancy Kirk. *The Museum of Modern Art Artist's Cookbook.* New York: The Museum of Modern Art, 1977.
Homer. *The Iliad.* Translated by Rodney Merrill. University of Michigan Press, 2007. Book 11: 638.
Sources: Chalaby, Cora. 'Artwork in Focus: Helen Frankenthaler's Madame Butterfly (2000).' *Dulwich Picture Gallery*, 22 November 2021.
Cumming, Laura. 'Helen Frankenthaler: Radical Beauty review – the most sublime show of the year?' *The Guardian*, 19 September 2021.
Currey, Mason. *Daily Rituals Women at Work: How Great Women Make Time, Find Inspiration, and Get to Work.* London: Pan Macmillan, 2019.
Fedele, Frank. *The Artist's Palate: Cooking with the World's Great Artists.* New York: DK Publishing, 2003.
Greenberger, Alex. 'Helen Frankenthaler's Liberated Abstractions Charted a New Path for Painting.' *Art in America*, 12 March 2021.
Nemerov, Alexander. 'How a Moment of Crisis Led Helen Frankenthaler to Create an Iconic Artwork'. *Art in America,* 12 March 2021.
Roman, Gabrielle. 'Tech-savvy Ancient Cheesemakers.' *Culture Cheese Magazine*, 26 March 2015.
Bronze grater. British Museum. Inv.1975,0804.20. https://www.britishmuseum.org/collection/object/G_1975-0804-20.
Thompson Hill, Kathleen. 'Really Grate: The Kathleen Thompson Hill Collection of Cheese Graters.' *The Cheese Professor,* 17 March 2021.

Marina Abramović (b. 1946) | Page 26
Citations: Abramović, Marina. 'The Art of Harmony.' *The Purist Online*, April 2019.
'Lips, Stars and Warrior Crests – Marina Abramović's Misfits for the Table.' *The Untitled Magazine*, 2 February 2015.
Abramović, Marina. *Spirit Cooking.* Santa Monica: Edition Jacob Samuel, 1996. https://www.moma.org/collection/works/portfolios/143945.
Chan, T.F. 'Marina Abramović's recipe for diet soup.' *Wallpaper**, 13 August 2021.
Sources: *Abramović Method, Misfits for the Table – Marina Abramović and Bernardaud.* YouTube, Marina Abramović and Bernardaud, 5 February 2015. https://www.youtube.com/watch?v=6ZIqkXICORO.
Arikoglu, Lale. 'Talking With Marina Abramović About Loneliness, and Dinner Plates.' *The Observer*, 5 February 2015.
Currey, Mason. 'Marcel Proust, Gustav Mahler, Marina Abramović: Is the secret to artistic success a light lunch?' *Slate Magazine*, 24 April 2013.
Garrett, Natalie Eve, ed. *The Artists' and Writers' Cookbook: A Collection of Stories with Recipes.* New York: PowerHouse Books, 2016.
'Marina Abramović's dishes.' *Abitare*, 27 February 2015.
MoMA. *Marina Abramović, Spirit Cooking*, 1996. https://www.moma.org/collection/works/143945.
MoMA. *Marina Abramović: The Artist Is Present.* https://www.moma.org/calendar/exhibitions/964.
Saner, Emine. 'Marina Abramović: "I'm an artist, not a satanist!"' *The Guardian*, October 7, 2020.

Lee Krasner (1908–84) | Page 30
Citations: Lea, Robyn. *Dinner with Jackson Pollock: Recipes, Art & Nature.* New York: Assouline, 2015.
Sources: Cooked, Rachel. 'Reframing Lee Krasner, the artist formerly known as Mrs Pollock.' *The Observer*, 12 May 2019.
Gabriel, Mary. 'How Lee Krasner Made Jackson Pollock a Star.' *Literary Hub*, 2 October 2018.
McCabe, Katie. 'The Painter Lee Krasner Has Long Been Eclipsed by Her Much More Famous Artist Husband. Now, a New Book Is Rewriting Art History on Her Terms.' *Artnet News*, 6 May 2020.
Wichmann, Natalie. 'Lee Krasner's New York City II: The Hood.' *Schirn Mag*, 4 November 2019.

Olafur Eliasson (b. 1967) | Page 34
Citations: Eliasson, Olafur, Asako Iwama, Andreas Koch, Alice Waters, and Daniel Weismann. *Studio Olafur Eliasson: The Kitchen.* London:

Phaidon Press, 2016.

Bottura, Massimo. *The Kitchen Studio: Culinary Creations by Artists*. London: Phaidon, 2021.

Sources: Hanly, Gavin. 'Studio Olafur Eliasson Kitchen comes to the Tate alongside his exhibition.' *Hot Dinners*, 10 July 2019.

Jampel, Sarah. 'This Artist Cookbook Has a Recipe for "Rain After Cloud".' *Food 52*, 26 April 2016.

Keller, Julia. 'From Studio to Dining Table: Olafur Eliasson.' *Schirn Mag*, 18 December, 2020.

Nunes, Andrew. 'A Look Inside Olafur Eliasson's 368-Page Vegetarian Cookbook.' *Vice*, 2 June 2016.

O'Loughlin, Marina. '"It's not just food being shared, but ideas": lunch with Olafur Eliasson.' *The Guardian*, 9 April 2016.

Remedios Varo (1908–63) | Page 38

Citations: Pottenger, Dennis. *Alchemy, Jung, and Remedios Varo: Cultural Complexes and the Redemptive Power of the Abjected Feminine*. London: Routledge, 2021.

Sources: Carson, Margaret. 'Three Letters by Remedios Varo.' *BOMB Magazine*, No. 143, April 11, 2018.

Frye, Carrie. 'How To Be Old: Two Women, Their Husbands, Their Cats, Their Alchemy.' *The Awl*, 5 April 2013.

Garza, Virgilio. '"My highlight of the year" – Vampiros Vegetarianos by Remedios Varo.' *Christie's*, 16 December 2015.

Hatfield, Zack. 'Remedios Varo's *Letters, Dreams & Other Writings*.' *The Brooklyn Rail*, February 2019.

Tate: Look Closer. *Love, friendship & rivalry: Surreal Friends*. https://www.tate.org.uk/art/artists/leonora-carrington-7615/love-friendship-rivalry-surreal-friends.

Barbara Hepworth (1903–75) | Page 42

Citations: Valentin, Curt. Letter to Barbara Hepworth, 6 October 1948, Museum of Modern Art Archives, New York, III.A.13.[5].

Campbell-Johnston, Rachel. 'Carving her mark: the life and art of Barbara Hepworth.' *The Times*, 8 May 2021.

Hepworth, Barbara. Letter to E.H. Ramsden, undated. *Tate Archive*, TGA 9310/1/1/7.

McIntosh, Malcolm. *In Search of the Good Society: Love, Hope and Art as Political Economy*. London: Routledge, 2018.

Sources: Curtis, Penelope. *Barbara Hepworth (St Ives Artists)*. London: Tate Publishing, 1998.

Wilkinson, David. *The Alfred Wallis Factor: Conflict in Post-War St Ives Art*. Cambridge: Lutterworth Press, 2017.

Lowell Blair Nesbitt (1933–93) | Page 46

Citations: Conway, Madeleine, and Nancy Kirk. *The Museum of Modern Art Artist's Cookbook*. New York: The Museum of Modern Art, 1977.

Greene, Gael. 'Holiday Entertaining: Great Parties Around the Clock.' *New York Magazine*, 25 October 1982.

Desimone, Mike, and Jeff Jenssen. 'Drink Like an Emperor.' *Wine Enthusiast*, 4 October 2010.

Sources: Hanina Fine Arts. Lowell Nesbitt. http://www.haninafinearts.com/artists/lowell_nesbitt/biography.

Kron, Joan. 'Studio in a Stable.' *The New York Times*, 19 May 1977.

Raynor, Vivien. 'Art: Lowell Nesbitt Tends His Garden'. *The New York Times*, 24 March 1978.

George Segal (1924–2000) | Page 50

Citations: Keyishian, Marjorie. 'Chicken Farmers Who Became Artists.' *The New York Times*, 5 July 1992.

MMoCA. George Segal. https://www.mmoca.org/learn/teaching-pages/george-segal/.

Sources: Civitello, Linda. *Cuisine and Culture: A History of Food and*

People. Hoboken, NJ: John Wiley & Sons, 2011.

Friedman, Martin. 'George Segal.' *Art Forum*, Vol. 45, No. 5, January 2009.

Jill Newhouse Gallery. *George Segal*. http://www.jillnewhouse.com/artists/george-segal2.

Medaris, David. '"Depression Bread Line" by George Segal coming to MMoCA.' *Isthmus*, 10 January 2008.

Segal Foundation. *George Segal: Biography*. http://segalfoundation.org/about_bio.html.

Man Ray (1890–1976) | Page 54

Citations: Turner Sachs, Barbara, and Beryl Barr, eds. *The Artists' & Writers' Cookbook*. Sausalito: Contact Editions, 1961.

Bouhassane, Ami. *Lee Miller: A Life with Food, Friends & Recipes*. Lewes, Sussex: Lee Miller Archives Publishing, 2021.

Sources: Beggs, Alex. '"A Surrealist Banquet" Is a Must-See Art Show for Food Lovers.' *Bon Appétit*, 4 May 2017.

Borrelli-Persson, Laird. 'Haute Cuisine: Surrealist Man Ray's Tangerine Cream and Other Recipes from the Pages of Vogue.' *Vogue*, 4 December 2014.

Caws, Mary Ann. *The Modern Art Cookbook*. London: Reaction Books Ltd, 2013.

Farrell, Aimee. 'Lee Miller: model, writer, war photographer … Cordon Bleu cook.' *Financial Times*, 17 November 2017.

Marks, Thomas. 'Guests and gadgets – in the kitchen with Lee Miller.' *Apollo*, 1 June 2020.

'Muse, Conflict Photographer and … Celebrity Chef: Lee Miller's Recipes.' *The Arts Society*, 25 June 2018.

Andy Warhol (1928–87) | Page 60

Citations: Conway, Madeleine, and Nancy Kirk. *The Museum of Modern Art Artist's Cookbook*. New York: The Museum of Modern Art, 1977.

Warhol, Andy. *The Philosophy of Andy Warhol (From A to B & Back Again)*. New York: Harcourt Brace Jovanovich, 1975.

Smith, Stephen. *A Day in the Life of Andy Warhol*. YouTube, BBC, 29 August 2015. https://www.youtube.com/watch?v=IfPv6RtNTRQ.

Norwich, William. 'Warhol Cookbook Co-Author Tells All.' *The Observer*, 12 January 1997.

Warhol, Andy, and Suzie Frankfurt. *Wild Raspberries*. Boston: Little, Brown and Company, 1998. First published in 1959 by Seymour Berlin, New York.

Sources: Keener, Katherine. 'Satirical cookbook by Andy Warhol, including recipes like "Omelet Greta Garbo", heads to auction.' *Art Critique*, 10 March 2021.

Lesser, Casey. 'What Andy Warhol Really Ate'. *Artsy*, 8 February 2019.

Popova, Maria. 'Wild Raspberries: Young Andy Warhol's Little-Known Vintage Cookbook.' *The Marginalian*, 20 November 2013.

Gustav Klimt (1862–1918) | Page 64

Citations: Koja, Stephen. *Gustav Klimt: Landscapes*. Munich,: Prestel, 2006.

Sources: Gotthardt, Alexxa. 'What you need to know about Gustav Klimt.' *Artsy*, 26 March 2018.

Wolfe, Shira. 'The Life and Paintings of Gustav Klimt.' *Artland Magazine*. https://magazine.artland.com/gustav-klimt-life-paintings/.

Sakai Hōitsu (1761–1829) | Page 68

Sources: Dougill, John. *Kyoto: A Cultural and Literary History*. Oxford: Signal, 2006.

Ehara, Ayako. 'The Diet of the Common Townspeople of Edo.' *Kikkoman, Vegetables and the Diet of the Edo Period, Part 3*. Tokyo Kasei-Gakuin University.

Oji, Makiko. 'Culinary Basics of Japan: The Taste that the "Edo-kko" Loved.' *Google Arts & Culture, in cooperation with National Foundation of*

Japan's National Park Association, SAVOR JAPAN.

PBS. *Japan: Memoirs of a Secret Empire*. https://www.pbs.org/empires/japan/enteredo_2.html.

The Metropolitan Museum of Art. *Persimmon Tree*, 1816, Sakai Hōitsu. https://www.metmuseum.org/art/collection/search/45392.

Thompson, Jessica. 'Fast Food Nation: Edo Dining Culture.' *Metropolis Japan*, 26 August 2017.

Warbuton, Toni. 'Toni Warburton focuses on themes of spring and summer in Japanese 17th Edo period ceramics in her response to the ceramics in the exhibition Seasons at the Art Gallery of NSW in 2003. https://www.toniwarburton.com.au/artist-talks/'.

Seco, Irene. 'How samurai, statesmen, and scholars shaped the Japanese tea ceremony.' *National Geographic*, 19 November 2021.

Shin-Yokohama Ramen Museum. https://www.raumen.co.jp/english/.

Willman, Anna. *The Japanese Tea Ceremony*. The Metropolitan Museum of Art. https://www.metmuseum.org/toah/hd/jtea/hd_jtea.htm.

Clara Peeters (1594–after 1957) | Page 72

Citations: Forster, *Stuart*. 'The Significance of the Still Life During the Dutch Golden Age.' *Culture Trip*, 8 August 2019.

Sources: Civitello, Linda. *Cuisine and Culture: A History of Food and People*. Hoboken, NJ: John Wiley & Sons, 2011.

Murphy, Katherine. 'More to cheese than meets the eye?' *Apollo Magazine*, 11 March 2017.

Rahusen, Henriette. 'Dutch Burghers and Their Wine: Nary a Sour Grape.' National Gallery of Art, 19 October 2017. https://www.nga.gov/audio-video/audio/rahusen-wine.html.

Rose, Peter G. *Explorers, Fortunes, and Love Letters: A Window on New Netherland*. Albany, NY: New Netherland Institute / Mount Ida Press, 2009.

Henri de Toulouse-Lautrec (1864–1901) | Page 76

Citations: Toulouse-Lautrec, Henri, and Maurice Joyant. *The Art of Cuisine*. New York: Holt / Rinehart and Winston 1966.

Sources: Gillis, James. *The Toulouse-Lautrec Walking Stick*. M.S. Rau, 3 August 2017. https://rauantiques.com/blogs/canvases-carats-and-curiosities/toulouse-lautrec-walking-stick.

Sooke, Alastair. 'How to cook like Henri Toulouse-Lautrec.' *BBC Culture*, 29 July 2014.

Mark Rothko (1903–70) | Page 80

Citations: Breslin. James E. B. *Mark Rothko: A Biography*. Chicago: University of Chicago Press, 2012.

Carmean, E. A. 'The Sandwiches of the Artist.' *Art World Follies*, October, Vol. 16, (Spring, 1981). The MIT Press, 1981.

Sources: Banville, John. 'Temple of mysteries: Mark Rothko.' *Tate Etc*, 1 May 2006.

Jones, Jonathan. 'Feeding Fury.' *The Guardian*, 7 December 2002.

Pace Gallery. *Mark Rothko*. https://www.pacegallery.com/artists/mark-rothko/.

Schjeldahl, Peter. 'The Dark Final Years of Mark Rothko.' *The New Yorker*, 8 December 2016.

Wolfe, Shira. 'Stories of Iconic Artworks: Mark Rothko's Seagram Murals.' *Artland Magazine*.

Frida Kahlo (1907–54) | Page 84

Sources: Keller, Julia. 'From Studio to Dining Table: Frida Kahlo.' *Schirn Mag*, 13 April 2020.

Rivera, Guadalupe, and Marie-Pierre Colle. *Frida's Fiestas: Recipes and Reminiscences of Life with Frida Kahlo*. New York: Clarkson N. Potter, 1994.

Slaughter, Jane. 'A guide to Diego Rivera and Frida Kahlo in the kitchen.' *Detroit Metro Times,* 4 March 2015.

Umberto Boccioni (1882–1916) | Page 88

Citations: Marinetti, Filippo Tommaso. *The Futurist Cookbook*. London: Penguin Books Ltd, 2014. First published in Italian as *La Cucina Futurista*, 1932.

Sources: Brickman, Sophie. 'The Food of the Future.' *The New Yorker*, 1 September 2014.

David, Elizabeth. *Italian Food*. Revised Edition. London: Penguin Books Ltd, 1989.

McCouat, Philip. 'The Futurists Declare War on Pasta.' *Journal of Art in Society,* 2014.

Georgette Chen (1906–93) | Page 92

Citations: *The Worlds of Georgette Chen, Episode 3*. Tan Lek Hwa. Wong Mai Yun. National Gallery Singapore, 2014.

Gary Hume in the Studio. YouTube, Matthew Marks Gallery. Interviewer, Hettie Judah. Director, Jesse Watt. 5 November 2013. https://www.youtube.com/watch?v=bv8K7eL5N3g.

Chen, Georgette. Letter to friends dated 7 June 1951. Collection of National Gallery Singapore Library & Archive, RC-S16-GC1.2-69, 70, 71. In *Georgette Chen: At Home in the World*, edited by Russell Storer, National Gallery Singapore, 2021.

Sources: 'Georgette Chen's Singapore: A True Paradise for the Artist.' *Sotheby's*, 24 August 2022.

National Gallery Singapore. Russell, Storer, ed. *Georgette Chen: At Home in the World*, National Gallery Singapore, 2021, Singapore.

Roots. National Heritage Bond. *The History and Evolution of Singapore's Hawker Culture*. https://www.roots.gov.sg/stories-landing/stories/Serving-Up-a-Legacy.

Sood, Suemedha. 'Singaporean food's past and present'. *BBC Travel*, 15 December 2010.

'Singapore in the Spotlight.' *The Telegraph* and Visit Singapore. https://www.telegraph.co.uk/travel/discover-singapore/history-timeline/.

Richard Long (b. 1945) | Page 96

Citations: Wroe, Nicholas. 'No stone unturned.' *The Guardian*, 28 June 2003.

Cole, Ina. 'Ideas Can Last Forever: A Conversation with Richard Long.' *Sculpture Magazine*, 1 July 2016.

Long, Richard. *WHITE LIGHT WALK, 1987*. http://www.richardlong.org/Textworks/2011textworks/22.html.

Sources: Barkham, Patrick. 'Taking a Walk.' Podcast. *The Oldie*.

Bramley, Ellie Violet. 'Wild garlic, nettles and berries … how foraging went mainstream.' *The Observer*, 14 March 2021.

Cooke, Rachel. 'Does anyone get the feeling that he's just going round in circles?' *The Observer*, 7 June 2009.

Macfarlane, Robert. 'Walk the line.' *The Guardian*, 23 May 2009.

Muchnic, Suzanne. 'Romanticism Can Go Take a Hike.' *Los Angeles Times*, 6 February 2000.

The Hepworth Wakefield. *Artists: Richard Long*. https://hepworthwakefield.org/artist/richard-long/.

Howard Hodgkin (1932–2017) | Page 100

Citations: *Sir Howard Hodgkin on his life, work and mortality (2014)*. YouTube, BBC Newsnight Archives. Presenter, Stephen Smith. November 2014. https://www.youtube.com/watch?v=QOKR3-KLpTw.

Absent friends – Howard Hodgkin's final paintings; Robert Indiana remembered. Host, Ben Luke. Producers, Julia Michalska and David Clack. *The Art Newspaper Podcast*, Episode 33, 25 May 2018.

Sources: McKenzie, Janet. 'Howard Hodgkin.' *Studio International*, 27 July 2006.

Seal, Rebecca. 'Breakfast of champions: Howard Hodgkin's poached eggs.' *The Guardian*, 30 May 2015.

'Sir Howard Hodgkin: Turner winner who "hated painting" dies at 84.' *BBC News*, 9 March 2017.

Stonard, John-Paul. 'Howard Hodgkin: "Too much is enough."' *The Guardian*, 8 October 2016.

Wullschlager, Jackie. 'Lunch with the FT: Howard Hodgkin.' *Financial Times*, 20 January 2012.

Jean Dubuffet (1901–85) | Page 104
Citations: Gascoigne, Laura. 'Raw Materials.' *The Spectator*, 14 October 2017.

Dubuffet, Jean, Mildred Glimcher, and Marc Glimcher. *Jean Dubuffet: Towards an Alternative Reality*. New York: Pace Publications, 1987.

Sources: Avgikos, Jan. *Jean Dubuffet: Will to Power (Volonté de puissance)*. https://www.guggenheim.org/artwork/1102.

Dapena-Tretter, Antonia. 'Jean Dubuffet & Art Brut: The Creation of an Avant-Garde Identity.' *Platform: Journal of Theater and Performing Arts*, Vol. 11, 'Authenticity', Autumn 2017.

Finn, Claro. 'Transgressive Technique – Jean Dubuffet: Brutal Beauty' *The Critics' Circle*, 31 May 2021.

Hirshhorn Museum. 'Collection Highlights: Jean Dubuffet.' https://hirshhorn.si.edu/explore/collection-highlights-jean-dubuffet/.

'Jean Dubuffet: Founding Father of Art Brut.' *Sotheby's*. 3 June 2019.

Perry, Rachel E. '"Le Contre-pied des Rites Bibliophiliques": Dubuffet's Art Brut Books.' *Artists' Publishing Practices*, Université d'été 2018, Bibliothèque Kandinsky MNAM, 2018.

Smart, Alastair. 'Brut Strength.' *Bonhams Magazine*, No. 55, Summer 2018.

Lucio Fontana (1899–1968) | Page 108
Citations: Archivo Storico Barilla. *Una Pasta Fatta Ad Arte: Farfalle Al Taglio Di Salmone – Lucio Fontana*. Young & Rubicam Italia. https://www.archiviostoricobarilla.com/en/scheda-archivio/una-pasta-fatta-ad-arte-farfalle-al-taglio-di-salmone-lucio-fontana-2/.

Brickman, Sophie. 'Massimo Bottura's Edible Art, Served Amidst Million Dollar Paintings.' *Saveur*, 10 November 2015.

Bottura, Massimo. *Never Trust a Skinny Italian Chef*. London: Phaidon Press, 2014.

Sources: Braun, Emily, Enrico Crispolti, Andrea Giunta, et al. *Lucio Fontana: On the Threshold*. New York: The Metropolitan Museum of Art, 2019.

Cheshes, Jay. 'Chef Massimo Bottura's Feast for the Eyes.' *The Wall Street Journal*, 27 May 2014.

Goldstein, Andrew M. 'The Picasso of Pasta? Massimo Bottura on Elevating Cuisine to the Status of Art.' *Artspace*, 13 December 2014.

Gottschaller, Pia. *Lucio Fontana: The Artist's Materials*. Los Angeles: Getty Conservation Institute, 2012.

Meares, Joe. 'Food for thought: Italian chef Massimo Bottura on his obsession with contemporary art.' *The Sydney Morning Herald*, 7 November 2014.

Nechvatal, Joseph. 'Lucio Fontana's Proto-Technologism.' *Hyperallergic*, 26 May 2014.

Peers, Alexandra. 'The Art of Food: Sotheby's Woos Top Collectors With Top Chef.' *The Observer*, 11 October 2015.

Tate. *Lucio Fontana: Nature*. https://www.tate.org.uk/art/artworks/fontana-nature-t03588.

Gary Hume (b. 1962) | Page 112
Citations: Chan, T.F. 'Artist's Palate: Georgie Hopton and Gary Hume's Pasta Liguria.' *Wallpaper**, 12 November 2020.

Sources: *Gary Hume in the Studio*. YouTube, Matthew Marks Gallery. Interviewer, Hettie Judah. Director, Jesse Watt. 5 November 2013. https://www.youtube.com/watch?v=bv8K7eL5N3g.

Ingram, Lyndsey. *Georgie Hopton, Gary Hume, Hurricanes Hardly Ever Happen*. Exhibition catalogue. London: Lyndsey Ingram, 2020. https://issuu.com/lyndseyingram/docs/hopton-hume-catalogue-pages.

Katz, Marisa Mazria. 'Hume with a view.' *Monocle*, No. 107, October 2017.

Needham, Alex. 'Gary Hume: the half-an-hour-a-day man.' *The Guardian*, 17 January 2012.

O'Hagan, Sean. 'Gary Hume: "I couldn't hold down a job. That's why I became an artist."' *The Observer*, 18 May 2013.

Tyson, Nicola. 'The Artist Georgie Hopton.' *Upstate Diary*, No. 8, April 26, 2019.

Dniel Spoerri (b. 1930) | Page 116
Citations: Keller, Julia. 'From Studio to Dining Table: Daniel Spoerri.' *Schirn Mag*, 29 September 2021.

Novero, Cecilia. *Antidiets of the Avant-Garde: From Futurist Cooking to Eat Art*. Minneapolis: University of Minnesota Press, 2010.

Sources: Marks, Thomas. 'The frozen dinners of Daniel Spoerri.' *Apollo Magazine*, June 9, 2021.

Spoerri, Daniel. 'Menu of the Galerie J. Restaurant and table reservation. 1963.' National Library of Switzerland. http://www.civico103.net/en/archive/15/menu-of-the-galerie-j-restaurant/#.YzrkHXbMK5f.

Spoerri, Daniel. *Mythology & Meatballs: A Greek Island Diary/Cookbook*. Berkeley: Aris Books, 1982.

József Rippl-Rónai (1861–1927) | Page 120
Sources: Berend, T. Iván. *An Economic History of Nineteenth-Century Europe: Diversity and Industrialization*. Cambridge: Cambridge University Press, 2012.

Byrd Hollar, Melanie, and John P. Dunn, eds. *Cooking Through History: A Worldwide Encyclopedia of Food with Menus and Recipes* [2 volumes]. Santa Barbara: ABC-CLIO, 2020.

Christie's. 'József Rippl-Rónai, Pink Orchids.' Christie's Impressionist and Modern Art Day Sale, 21 June 2006. https://www.christies.com/en/lot/lot-4733727.

Civitello, Linda. *Cuisine and Culture: A History of Food and People*. Hoboken, NJ: John Wiley & Sons, 2011

Edelstein, Sari, ed. *Food, Cuisine, and Cultural Competency for Culinary, Hospitality, and Nutrition Professionals*. Sudbury, MA.: Jones & Bartlett, 2011.

Koller Gallery. 'Rippl-Rónai, József.' https://www.kollergaleria.hu/artist/rippl_ronai_jozsef-1269-en.

Jacob Lawrence (1917–2000) | Page 124
Sources: Dickinson, Stephanie. *Jacob Lawrence: Painter*. New York: Cavendish Square Publishing, LLC, 2016.

Freeman, Deb. 'The Great Migration and Black Food.' *Setting the Table podcast*, Episode 1, 9 March 2022.

Harkins Wheat, Ellen. 'Jacob Lawrence and the Legacy of Harlem.' *Archives of American Art Journal* 30, No. 4, 1990.

Harris, Jessica B. 'Migration Meals: How African American Food Transformed the Taste of America.' *Eating Well*, 8 February 2021.

Miller, Adrian. 'An Illustrated History of Soul Food.' *First We Feast*, 25 August 2015.

MoMA. Kedmey, Karen. *Jacob Lawrence: American*, 1917–2000. https://www.moma.org/artists/3418.

MoMA. *One-Way Ticket: Jacob Lawrence's Migration Series*. Museum of Modern Art. https://www.moma.org/interactives/exhibitions/2015/onewayticket/panel/11/.

Sen, Mayukh. 'She Was a Soul Food Sensation. Then, 19 Years Ago, She Disappeared.' *Food 52*, 2 February 2017.

Strobel, Pamela. *Princess Pamela's Soul Food Cookbook*. New York, Rizzoli International Publications, Inc., 2017. First published by Signet Books, New York 1969.

The Phillips Collection. *Jacob Lawrence: The Migration Series*. https://lawrencemigration.phillipscollection.org/artist/about-jacob-lawrence.

Alison Knowles (b. 1933) | Page 128
Citations: Maciunas, George. *Fluxus Manifesto*. 1963. https://www.moma.org/collection/works/127947.

Knowles, Alison. Event Scores from *A Great Bear Pamphlet*. 1965. https://www.aknowles.com/eventscore.html.

Higgins, Hannah B. 'Food: The Raw and the Fluxed.' In *Fluxus and the Essential Questions of Life*, edited by Jacqueline Baas. Chicago: Hood Museum of Art / University of Chicago Press, 2011.

Sources: Knowles, Alison. *Alison Knowles – 'I'm Making a Giant Salad'*. YouTube, TateShots. Tate, 3 September 2008. https://www.youtube.com/watch?v=lmqvnIXnmyM.

Knowles, Alison. *Alison Knowles: Identical Lunch*. YouTube, FEAST: *Radical Hospitality in Contemporary Art*. The University of Chicago, 28 March 2012. https://www.youtube.com/watch?v=2tWVaOMlaEY.

MoMA Library. *Experimental Women in Flux: Selective Reading in the Silverman Reference Library*. Exhibition, The Museum of Modern Art Library, 2010. https://www.moma.org/interactives/exhibitions/2010/womeninflux/.

Novero, Cecilia. *Antidiets of the Avant-Garde: From Futurist Cooking to Eat Art*. Minneapolis: University of Minnesota Press, 2010.

Pablo Picasso (1881–1973) | Page 132

Citations: Currey, Mason. *Daily Rituals: How Great Minds Make Time, Find Inspiration, and Get to Work*. London: Pan Macmillan, 2013.

Cook, William. 'A feast for the eyes: What Picasso's Kitchen reveals about his art.' *BBC Arts*, 12 June 2018.

Sources: Borrelli-Persson, Laird. 'Haute Cuisine: Picasso's Recipes from the Pages of *Vogue*.' *Vogue*, 16 October 2014.

Conrad, Peter. 'The many faces of Pablo Picasso.' *The Observer*, 8 February 2009.

Lott, Lavigna. 'I Ate Like Picasso in Hope of Becoming an Artistic Genius.' *Vice*, 5 April 2018.

Richardson, John. *A Life of Picasso, Volume I: 1881–1906*. London: Pimlico, 2009.

Gabriel Orozco (b. 1962) | Page 136

Sources: Bonami, Francesco. 'The early adventures: Gabriel Orozco I.' *Tate Etc.* (No. 21: Spring 2011) January 1, 2011.

Gabriel Orozco. YouTube, Art Basel, 30 March 2018. https://www.youtube.com/watch?v=tdkuHDbcZY4.

Gerlis, Melanie. 'Gabriel Orozco on art and branding.' *Financial Times*, 29 March 2018.

Huen, Eustacia. 'Why Does The World's Most Expensive Steak Cost $3,200?' *Forbes*, 31 December 2015.

Jones, Jonathan. 'The Da Vinci mystery: Why is his $450m masterpiece really being kept under wraps?' *The Guardian*, 14 October 2018.

'"Tuna King" Kiyoshi Kimura on his most expensive fish.' BBC News, 5 January 2019. https://www.bbc.co.uk/news/av/world-asia-46767850.

'"You Have to be Confronted With Reality All the Time": Watch Artist Gabriel Orozco Explain Why the Street Is His Studio'. *Artnet News*, 13 September 2018.

Victor Vasarely (1906–97) | Page 142

Citations: Fedele, Frank. *The Artist's Palate: Cooking with the World's Great Artists*. New York: DK Publishing, 2003.

Sources: Castelow, Ellen. 'Food in Britain in the 1950s and 1960s.' Historic UK. https://www.historic-uk.com/CultureUK/Food-in-Britain-in-the-1950s-1960s/.

Deutsche Bundesbank Eurosystem. *Bundesbank sends Vasarely dining room on a journey*. 1 August 2018. https://www.bundesbank.de/en/tasks/topics/bundesbank-sends-vasarely-dining-room-on-a-journey-760610.

Foundation Vasarely. *Victor Vasarely*. https://www.fondationvasarely.org/en/victor-vasarely/.

Grey, Sarah. 'A Social History of Jell-O Salad: The Rise and Fall of an American Icon.' *Serious Eats*, 10 August 2018.

Grovier, Kelly. 'Victor Vasarely: The art that tricks the eyes.' *BBC Culture*, 5 March 2019.

Jones, Claire. 'Bundesbank dining room served up for 'Op Art' show.' *Financial Times*, 3 August 2018.

The Guggenheim Museums and Foundations. *Victor Vasarely*. https://www.guggenheim.org/artwork/artist/victor-vasarely.

David Nash (b. 1945) | Page 146

Citations: *The British Library, National Life Stories: Artist's Lives: David Nash*, Interviewed by Denise Hooker (transcript) – REF C466/32. June 7, 1995. https://sounds.bl.uk/related-content/TRANSCRIPTS/021T-C0466X0032XX-ZZZZA0.pdf.

Sources: Berger, Michele W. 'From 2,800-year-old charred food lumps, a window into past civilizations.' *Penn Today: School of Arts & Sciences*, 8 February 2022.

Kinsman, Kat. 'Francis Mallman Is Grilling Vegetables Now.' *Food and Wine*, 20 May 2020.

Nosrat, Samin. *Salt, Fat, Acid, Heat: Mastering the Elements of Good Cooking*. Edinburgh: Canongate Books Ltd, 2017.

Pollan, Michael. *Cooked: A Natural History of Transformation*. London: Allen Lane, 2013.

Rupp, Rebecca. 'A Brief History of Cooking with Fire.' *National Geographic*, 2 September 2015.

Paul Cézanne (1839–1906) | Page 150

Citations: Raymond, Michael. '"The Apple of my Eye": Artists on Cézanne.' *Tate Etc*, No. 56, Autumn 2022, 8 September 2022.

Naudin, Jean-Bernard, Gilles Plazy, and Jacqueline Saulnier. *Cézanne – A Taste of Provence*. London: Ebury Press London, 1995.

Sources: Danchev, Alex. *Cézanne: A Life*. London: Profile Books, 2012.

Elderfield, John. 'Hail Cézanne.' *The National Portrait Gallery (Australia)*, 19 December 2017.

Pearlman Collection. *Three Pears, ca. 1888-90. Paul Cézanne (French, 1839–1906)*. https://www.pearlmancollection.org/artwork/three-pears/.

Shulman, Martha Rose. 'Garlic Soup That's in a Rush.' *The New York Times*, 18 September 2015.

Claude Monet (1840–1926) | Page 154

Citations: Baxter, John. *Eating Eternity: Food, Art and Literature in France*. New York: Muyeson, 2017.

Sources: Joyes, Claire. *Monet's Table: The Cooking Journals of Claude Monet*. New York: Simon and Schuster, 1989.

Rosen, Michael J. 'Cuisine Art'. *The New York Times*, 20 May 1990.

Waldek, Stefanie. 'Forget the Gardens: The Best Part of Giverny is Monet's Kitchen.' *Architectural Digest*, 29 May 2017.

Vincent van Gogh (1853–90) | Page 158

Citations: Van Gogh, Vincent. Letter to his brother Theo Van Gogh, Saint-Rémy-de-Provence, Thursday, 22 August 1889. https://vangoghletters.org/vg/letters/let797/letter.html.

Sources: 'A real squeeze: Paint in tubes.' *Art World News*, 1 July 2015.

Bailey, Martin. 'Van Gogh's suicide: Ten reasons why the murder story is a myth'. *The Art Newspaper*, 6 September 2019.

Baxter, John. *Eating Eternity: Food, Art and Literature in France*. New York: Museyon, 2017.

Harkup, Kathryn. 'It was all yellow: did digitalis affect the way Van Gogh saw the world?' *The Guardian*, 10 August 2017.

MacPherson, Cory. *Inventions in the Visual Arts: From Cave Paintings to CAD*. Ebook. London: Cavendish Square Publishing LLC, 2016.

Marrack, Eleanor. *Van Gogh*. London: Chartwell House, 1992.

St Clair, Kassia. *The Secret Lives of Colour*. London: John Murray, 2016.

Thomas, Denis. *The Age of Impressionists*. London: Reed International Books Ltd, 1987.

Georgia O'Keeffe (1887–1986) | Page 162

Citations: Wood, Margaret. *A Painter's Kitchen: Recipes from the Kitchen of Georgia O'Keeffe*. Santa Fe, NM: Red Crane Books, 1991.

Chadwick, Whitney. *Women, Art, and Society*, 3rd ed. London: Thames and Hudson, 2012

Sources: Baranyk, Ashley. 'Friendship and Food: Georgia O'Keeffe's recipe binder.' Georgia O'Keefe Museum, 22 May 2020. https://www.okeeffemuseum.org/friendship-and-food/.

Keller, Julia. 'From Studio to Dining Table: Georgia O'Keeffe.' *Schirn Mag*, 11 August 2020.

Melouney, Carmel. 'Georgia O'Keeffe, health food devotee: the pioneer of modernism's favourite recipes.' *The Guardian*, 26 June 2017.

Nierenberg, Amelia. 'Own the Recipes of Georgia O'Keeffe.' *The New York Times*, 7 February 2020.

Plummer, Todd. 'Now You Can Cook Like Georgia O'Keeffe.' *Vogue*, 21 March 2017.

Syme, Rachel. 'Cooking from Georgia O'Keeffe's Recipes.' *The New Yorker*, 6 March 2020.

Tico Studeman, Kristin. 'Artist Georgia O'Keeffe Was Drinking Green Juices and Tiger's Milk Way Before It Was Trendy.' *W Magazine*, 30 March 2017.

Roy Lichtenstein (1923–97) | Page 166

Citations: Conway, Madeleine, and Nancy Kirk. *The Museum of Modern Art Artist's Cookbook*. New York: The Museum of Modern Art, 1977.

Nayeri, Farah. 'Roy Lichtenstein's Widow recalls macro diet, love for jazz.' *Bloomberg UK*, 20 February 2013.

Davies, Lucy. 'Inside Roy Lichtenstein's Studio.' *The Telegraph*, 5 February 2013.

Sources: Christie's. Works from the Collection of Ileana Sonnabend and the Estate of Nina Castelli Sundell. Roy Lichtenstein (1923–1997) Ceramic Sculpture 13. 2015. https://www.christies.com/en/lot/lot-5895998.

'Pop Art: Aesthetics of Consumption.' *Cardi Gallery Magazine*. https://cardigallery.com/magazine/pop-art/.

Markus Pernhart (1824–71) | Page 170

Sources: Davies, Evitt. 'The tragic true story of "beauty queen", Empress Elisabeth of Austria.' *Tatler*, 30 September 2022.

Dorotheum. *Marcus Pernhart*. https://www.dorotheum.com/en/k/marcus-pernhart/.

Edelstein, Sari, ed. *Food, Cuisine, and Cultural Competency for Culinary, Hospitality, and Nutrition Professionals*. Sudbury, MA.: Jones & Bartlett Learning, 2011.

Gutenbrunner, Kurt. 'The Chef; Kurt Gutenbrunner.' *The New York Times*, 30 January 2002.

Leo Baeck Institute. Simonson, Michael. *Kaiserschmarrn*. https://www.lbi.org/collections/Mahlzeit/kaiserschmarrn/.

National Gallery of Slovenia. *Marko Pernhart – Biedermeier and Romanticism*. https://www.ng-slo.si/en/304/marko-pernhart?tab=collections&authorId=503.

Jean-Michel Basquiat (1960–88) | Page 174

Citations: *Jean-Michel Basquiat: The Radiant Child*. Tamra Davis. Arthouse Films, July 2010.

Pellerin, Ananda. 'Mr Chow: How a Chinese restaurant became an art world mecca.' *CNN Style*, 5 April 2018.

Clement, Jennifer. *Widow Basquiat: A Memoir*. Ebook. New York: Crown, 2014.

Sources: '21 Facts About Jean-Michel Basquiat.' *Sotheby's*, 21 June 2019.

Basquiat: Rage to Riches. David Shulman. BBC Studios Documentary Unit production, a co-production with PBS, 7 October 2017.

Delap, Josie. 'American fried chicken has its origins in slavery.' *The Economist*, 2 July 2021.

Endolyn, Osayi. 'Fried Chicken is Common Ground.' *Eater*, 3 October 2018.

Giacobbe, Alyssa. 'Mr. Chow – Iconic Restaurateur to the Stars – Looks Back on 50 Years at the Top.' *Architectural Digest*, 14 February 2018.

Hosking, Taylor. '"Basquiat: Rage to Riches" Is the Last Doc We Need on the Iconic Artist.' *Vice*, 21 September 2018.

John, Arit. 'Making Fried Chicken and Watermelon Racist.' *The Atlantic*, 6 February 2014.

Jones, Kellie, et al. *EyeMinded: Living and Writing Contemporary Art*. Durham: Duke University Press, 2011.

Miss Rosen. 'How restaurateur Mr Chow became the unlikely hero of the art world.' *Dazed*, 15 February 2018.

'Mr. Chow: Recipe for a Painter.' *Whitewall*, 29 December 2014.

Sawyer, Miranda. 'The Jean-Michel Basquiat I knew…'. *The Guardian*, 3 September 2017.

Vanderhoof, Erin. 'Andy Warhol, Jean-Michel Basquiat, and the Friendship That Defined the Art World in 1980s New York City.' *Vanity Fair*, 31 July 2019.

Ward, Alvin. 'Explore the Fascinating History of Soul Food.' *Mental Floss*, 22 April 2020.

Wullschlager, Jackie. 'Basquiat in Paris.' *Financial Times*, 19 November 2010.

Salvador Dalí (1904–89) | Page 178

Citations: Dalí, Salvador. *Les Dîners de Gala*. Cologne: Taschen, 2016. First published by Draeger, Paris in 1973.

Schoenholz Bee, Harriet, ed. *MoMA Highlights: 375 Works from The Museum of Modern Art, New York*. New York: The Museum of Modern Art, 2019.

Dalí, Salvador. *The Secret Life of Salvador Dalí*. Ebook. New York: Dover Publications, 2013. First published by Kessinger in 1942.

Vincent, Alice. '11 surreal facts about Salvador Dalí.' *The Telegraph*, 23 January 2014.

Conway, Madeleine, and Nancy Kirk. *The Museum of Modern Art Artist's Cookbook*. New York: The Museum of Modern Art, 1977.

Sources: Baxter, John. *Eating Eternity: Food, Art and Literature in France*. New York: Museyon, 2017.

Dalí, Salvador. *Dalí: The Wines of Gala*. Cologne: Taschen, 2017. First published in French as *Les Vins de Gala* in 1977.

Hall, Jake. 'How to Throw a Dinner Party Like Salvador Dalí.' *AnOther Magazine*, 3 November 2016.

Hall, Luke Edward. 'The parties we will throw when this is over…'. *Financial Times*, 18 December 2020.

'Salvador Dalí's Dizzying Dinner Party (VIDEO).' HuffPost. 19 January 2012. https://www.huffpost.com/entry/salvador-dalis-dizzying-d_n_1216384.

Whitmore, Hope Estella. 'Death, Sex, and Dinner Parties'. *The Awl*, 2 November 2016.

Bridget Riley (b. 1931) | Page 182

Citations: Gómez, Edward M. 'Bridget Riley's Razzle-Dazzle Career.' *Hyperallergic*. 14 September 2019.

Makris, Christina. *Aesthetic Dining: The Art Restaurant Around the World*. London: Cultureshock, 2021.

Sources: *Bridget Riley – Painting the Line*. Presenter, Kirsty Wark; Director, Sophie Deveson. BBC, 2021. https://www.bbc.co.uk/programmes/m0011psx.

'Brummel Recommends: Core by Clare Smyth.' *Brummell Magazine*, 28 September 2017.

Da Silva, José. '"I wish I had bought a Banksy": Inside the collection of Mark Hix.' *The Art Newspaper*, October 5, 2019.

Fedele, Frank. *The Artist's Palate: Cooking with the World's Great Artists*. New York: DK Publishing, 2003.

Hancock, Alice. 'Chef Mark Hix: "More people will see good art in a restaurant than a gallery."' *FT Magazine*, 26 October 2018.

Waldek, Stefanie. 'Bridget Riley's The Ivy Painting Is on the Block.' *Architectural Digest*, 28 February 2015.

René Magritte (1898–1967) | Page 186
Citations: The Getty Research Institute. *Getty Research Journal, Number 12, 2020*. Los Angeles: Getty Research Institute, 2020.
Phillips. 34. *René Magritte, Le Choeur des Sphinges*. https://www.phillips.com/detail/rene-magritte/NY010720/34.
Sources: Beggs, Alex. '"A Surrealist Banquet" Is a Must-See Art Show for Food Lovers.' *Bon Appétit*, 4 May 2017.
Danchev, Alex. *Magritte: A Life*. Ebook. London: Profile Books, 2021.
Catalano, Janine. 'Distasteful: An Investigation of Food's Subversive Function in René Magritte's *The Portrait* and Meret Oppenheim's *Ma Gouvernante—My Nurse—Mein Kindermädchen*.' *Invisible Culture*, No. 14: *Aesthetes and Eaters – Food and the Arts*. University of Rochester, 2010.
Cripps, Ed. 'Party Animals: The Rothschild Surrealist Ball.' *The Rake*, December 2016.
Margaritoff, Marco. 'Black Tie, Long Dresses, And Surrealist Heads: Inside The 1972 Rothschild Ball.' *All That's Interesting*, 28 December 2020.
Novero, Cecilia. *Antidiets of the Avant-Garde: From Futurist Cooking to Eat Art*. Minneapolis: University of Minnesota Press, 2010.
Skelton, Charlie. 'Why Magritte was like a standup comedian.' *The Guardian*, 23 February 2015.
The Menil Collection. *René Magritte, Belgian, 1898–1967. This is a Piece of Cheese (Ceci est un morceau de fromage)*, 1936 or 1937. https://www.menil.org/collection/objects/2333.

Dieter Roth (1930–98) | Page 190
Citations: Tzara, Tristan. *Dada Manifesto*. 1918.
Sources: Goldstein, Andrew M. 'MoMA Curator Sarah Suzuki on How Dieter Roth Invented the Artist's Book.' *Artspace*, 20 June 2013.
Grow, Sharra. 'A Sweet Result: Saving a Dieter Roth chocolate sculpture from becoming food.' *International Institute for Conservation*, 18 February 2022.
Novero, Cecilia. *Antidiets of the Avant-Garde: From Futurist Cooking to Eat Art*. Minneapolis: University of Minnesota Press, 2010.
Roth, Dieter. *Literature Sausage (Literaturwurst)*, 1969: Inv.944.2010. In *MoMA Highlights: 375 Works from The Museum of Modern Art, New York*. Edited by Schoenholz Bee, Harriet. New York: The Museum of Modern Art, 2019.
Walsh, Colleen. 'A feast for the eyes, sort of.' *The Harvard Gazette*, 2 April 2021.

Jackson Pollock (1912–56) | Page 194
Citations: Lea, Robyn. *Dinner with Jackson Pollock: Recipes, Art & Nature*. New York: Assouline, 2015.
Sources: Hirsch, Jesse. 'How to Eat Like Jackson Pollock.' *Vice*, 20 May 2015.
Jones, Jonathan. 'Jackson Pollock review – this is art as nervous breakdown…and it's majestic.' *The Guardian*, 29 June 2015.
Melouney, Carmel. 'Jackson Pollock's secret prize-winning recipe for apple pie discovered.' *The Guardian*, 30 April 2015.

Rirkrit Tiravanija (b. 1961) | Page 198
Citations: *Rirkrit Tiravanija. Untitled (Free/Still). 1992/1995/2007/2011-*. David Shuff, Calvin Robertson, Ben Coccio. The Museum of Modern Art, February 3, 2012. https://www.youtube.com/watch?v=0xRx2s3FpSg.
Mayyasi, Alex. 'The Oddly Autocratic Roots of Pad Thai.' *Atlas Obscura*, 7 November 2019.
Sources: Bröcker, Felix, Anneli Käsmayr, and Raphaela Reinmann. 'Food as a Medium Between Art and Cuisine: Rirkrit Tiravanija's Gastronomic Installations.' In *Culinary Turn: Aesthetic Practice of Cookery*. Edited by Nicolaj van der Meulen, Jörg Wiesel. Transcript Verlag, 2017.
Chan, Bernice. 'History of pad Thai: how the stir-fried noodle dish was invented by the Thai government.' *South China Morning Post*, 28 April 2019.

Fox, Dan. 'Welcome to the Real World.' *Frieze Magazine*, No. 90, 12 April 2005.
Melasniemi, Antto, and Rirkrit Tiravanija. *Bastard Cookbook*, New York: Finnish Cultural Institute in New York / Garrett Publications, 2019. http://garret.fi/books/antto-melasniemi-and-rirkrit-tiravanija-bastard-cookbook.
Newell-Hanson, Alice. 'Artist Rirkrit Tiravanija Cooking Pad Thai with his Students.' *The New York Times Style Magazine*, 21 April 2022.
Sukphisit, Suthon. 'History discovered in a staple dish.' *Bangkok Post*, 16 February 2014.
Superflex. *Social Pudding*. https://superflex.net/works/social_pudding.
Tsui, Enid. 'Rirkrit Tiravanija defends his pad thai performance art piece ahead of its revival at Hong Kong gallery.' *Post Magazine*, 15 May 2021.
Yao, Pauline J. 'The Lives of Objects: Rirkrit Tiravanija in Conversation.' *M+ Magazine*, 24 June 2019.

Edward Burne-Jones (1883–98) | Page 202
Citations: *Where else do they give you £100,000,000 worth of objets d'art free with every egg salad?* From the campaign series 'V&A – An ace café with a nice museum attached'. Produced by Paul Arden and Jeff Stark for Saatchi and Saatchi Ltd., London, 1988. V&A Museum Inv.E.515-1988.
'The World's First Museum Café.' V&A Museum, from the exhibition *Designing the V&A*, 6 May 2017 to 7 January 2018. https://www.vam.ac.uk/articles/a-first-of-its-kind-history-of-the-refreshment-rooms.
Burne-Jones, Edward. Letter to Katie Lewis. From the album 'Letters to Katie'. The British Museum Inv.1960,1014.2.72. https://www.britishmuseum.org/collection/object/P_1960-1014-2-72.
Sources: 'Britain is built on sugar: our national sweet tooth defines us.' *The Guardian*, 13 October 2007.
Broomfield, Andrea. *Food and Cooking in Victorian England*. Westport, Conn.: Praeger Publishers, 2007.
Victorians: Food and Health. English Heritage. https://www.english-heritage.org.uk/learn/story-of-england/victorian/food-and-health/.
Graham, Kelley. *'Gone To The Shops': Shopping in Victorian England*. Westport, Conn.: Praeger Publishers, 2008.
'William Morris and the V&A.' V&A Museum. https://www.vam.ac.uk/articles/william-morris-and-the-va.

Yves Klein (1928–62) | Page 208
Sources: Banai, Nuit. *Yves Klein (Critical Lives)*. Ebook. London: Reaktion Books, 2014.
Hitchcock, Alfred. *Alfred Hitchcock: Interviews*. Edited by Sidney Gottlieb. Jackson: University Press of Mississippi, 2003.
Martin, Hannah. 'How Yves Klein's Blue Cocktail Table Became a Cult Favorite.' *Architectural Digest*, 11 November 2016.
Reilly, Samuel. 'Feeling blue: Yves Klein at Blenheim Palace.' *1843 Magazine*, 25 July 2018.
Schuster, Clayton. 'Yves Klein's Signature Blue Paint Is Now for Sale, So It's Easier Than Ever to Recreate a Priceless Artwork.' *The Observer*, 16 March 2019.
Sotheby's. 9, *Yves Klein*. https://www.sothebys.com/en/auctions/ecatalogue/2012/contemporary-art-evening-auction-l12020/lot.9.html.
Spence, Charles. 'What is so unappealing about blue food and drink?' Crossmodal Research Laboratory, University of Oxford, March 2018. *International Journal of Gastronomy and Food Science*, 1 December 2018.
St Clair, Kassia. *The Secret Lives of Colour*. London: John Murray, 2016.
Weitemeier, Hannah. *Klein*. London: Taschen, 2001.
White, Kathleen. '21 Facts about Yves Klein.' Sotheby's, 26 June 2018.

Henri Matisse (1869–1954) | Page 212
Sources: Baxter, John. *Eating Eternity: Food, Art and Literature in France*. New York: Museyon, 2017
Cumming, Laura. 'Not just a man of the cloth.' *The Observer*, 6 March 2005.

Fedele, Frank. The Artist's Palate: Cooking with the World's Great Artists. New York: DK Publishing, 2003.

Hart, Kim. 'The Story behind One of Matisse's Most-Painted Objects.' *Artsy*, 5 September 2017.

Jones, Jonathan. 'Matisse in the Studio review – genius crowded out by bric-a-brac.' *The Guardian*, 31 July 2017.

Krull, Kathleen. *Lives Of The Artists: Masterpieces, Messes (and What the Neighbors Thought)*. San Diego: Harcourt Brace & Company, 1995.

Motherwell, Robert. *The Writings of Robert Motherwell*. Edited by Dore Ashton. Berkeley: University of California Press, 2007.

Spurling, Hilary. *The Unknown Matisse – A life of Henri Matise: The Early Years, 1869–1908*. Berkeley: University of California Press, 1998.

Watkins, Nicholas. 'Matisse's studio: "an interior world of his own making."' RA Magazine, 9 August 2017.

Wheeler, Monroe. *The last works of Henri Matisse: large cut gouaches*. Exhibition catalogue, Museum of Modern Art / Art Institute of Chicago / San Francisco Museum of Art. New York: Museum of Modern Art, 1961.

Adélaïde Labille-Guiard (1749–1803) | Page 216

Citations: Civitello, Linda. *Cuisine and Culture: A History of Food and People*. Hoboken, NJ: John Wiley & Sons, 2011.

Sources: Baxter, John. *Eating Eternity: Food, Art and Literature in France*. New York: Museyon, 2017.

Bramen, Lisa. 'When Food Changed History: The French Revolution.' *Smithsonian Magazine*, 14 July 2010.

Branko, Milanovic. 'Level of income and income distribution in mid-18th century France, according to Francois Quesnay.' *World Bank Policy Research Working Paper No. 10545*, 26 December 2010.

Jeffares, Neil. 'Labille-Guiard, Adélaïde.' In *Dictionary of pastellists before 1800*. London: Unicorn Press, 2006. http://www.pastellists.com/articles/labilleguiard.pdf.

Mann, Charles C. 'How the Potato Changed the World'. *Smithsonian Magazine*, November 2011.

McPhee, Peter. 'Hidden women of history: Adélaïde Labille-Guiard, prodigiously talented painter.' *The Conversation*, 7 February 2019.

The Metropolitan Museum of Art. *Self-Portrait with Two Pupils, Marie Gabrielle Capet (1761–1818) and Marie Marguerite Carreaux de Rosemond (died 1788)*. https://www.metmuseum.org/art/collection/search/436840.

PBS: American Experience. *The French Revolution*. https://www.pbs.org/wgbh/americanexperience/features/adams-french-revolution/.

Quinn, Bridget. *Broad Strokes: 15 Women Who Made Art and Made History (in That Order)*. San Francisco: Chronicle Books, 2017.

Standage, Tom. 'When potatoes were the height of fashion.' *1843 Magazine*, 15 July 2019.

Wittmeier, Melissa M. 'The Art of the Table in Eighteenth-Century France.' *Journal of the Western Society for French History*, Vol. 38. Ann Arbor: Michigan Publishing, 2010.

Gordon Matta-Clark (1943–78) | Page 220

Citations: Lee, Pamela M. *Object to Be Destroyed: the work of Gordon Matta-Clark*. Cambridge, MA.: MIT Press, 2000.

Kennedy, Randy. 'When Meals Played the Muse.' *The New York Times*, 21 February 2007.

Sources: 'Food for Thought: Gordon Matta-Clark's Restaurant for Artists Changed the Culinary Discourse.' *Autre Magazine*, August 24, 2022.

Harris, Laura. 'Displacement and Ferment: Gordon Matta-Clark and Vicky Alvarez in the South Bronx.' *Living Commons*. http://livingcommons.org/laura-harris.

Hinojosa, Lola. 'Food.' Museo Nacional Centro de Arte Reina Sofia. https://www.museoreinasofia.es/en/collection/artwork/food.

Nemser, Cindy. 'From the Archives: The Alchemist and the Phenomenologist.' Art in America, 25 September 2017.

Novero, Cecilia. *Antidiets of the Avant-Garde: From Futurist Cooking to Eat Art*. Minneapolis: University of Minnesota Press, 2010.

Rian, Jeff. 'Rocking the Foundation.' *Frieze Magazine*, No. 11, 5 June 1993.

ABOUT THE AUTHOR

—

Felicity Souter is a writer, artist and cook based in London. With a passion for blending the arts together, she believes good food should look as beautiful as it tastes and that every mouthful should be savoured like a work of art. She ultimately believes a great meal is defined by who shares it and regardless of the menu, she's never happier than she is at the dinner table, with family, friends and extra gratings of parmesan.

ACKNOWLEDGMENTS

—

The idea for *Painting the Plate* first came to me about fifteen years ago, while I was having a cup of tea with my dad. The title came shortly after and now after years of on-off planning, testing, writing and eating, it's finally here – a printed book!

But ultimately, no matter how brilliant you think your idea is, you need like-minded people to believe in it too, for that dream to become a reality. Luckily for me, I had just that and to all those incredible people, I want to say a huge (HUGE!) thank you.

THANK YOU

To my wonderful agent Imogen Pelham, for taking a chance on this project and patiently helping me to refine and perfect my proposal.

To my brilliant and encouraging editor Julie Kiefer, for not only understanding my vision but for whole-heartedly sharing my enthusiasm for it and making the entire process an absolute joy. I will never forget that.

To Kerstin Pecher and Andrea Weißenbach, for tackling the complicated logistics of finding and licensing the artwork images. Your dedication and perseverance really made this project.

To Lauren Salkeld and Hannah Young for editing the text with such precision and skill.

To Heidi Kral for creating such a beautiful book design.

To Cilly Klotz, your amazing production team and everyone at Prestel for creating such a beautiful finished product.

To Stefanie Adam and Melanie Schirdewahn for expertly translating the book into German.

To Susanne Philippi for copyediting the German edition with such care.

To all of the image libraries and artist estates for granting us permission to use the artworks.

And, of course, to the artists past and present for providing inspiration through their extraordinary work.

THANK YOU

The biggest thanks of all go to my wonderful family and friends for supporting me through the ups and downs of writing a book, even testing the recipes to make sure they work outside of my kitchen. I don't have space to name each of you individually, but you know who you are!

Particular thanks to my amazing sister Anna, for not only being my biggest cheerleader, but my first (and utterly brilliant!) editor. Your talent never ceases to amaze me.

To Rosemary, for encouraging me to turn our flat into a test kitchen during the endless months of lockdowns.

To Mummy, for your infinite love and support (both practical and emotional!).

To Abi, for helping me find the bravery to pursue this.

To Patch, for being my photography guru.

And to my Alex – chief taste-tester and my absolute rock.

Photo credits

Editorial direction: Julie Kiefer
Picture editor: Andrea Weißenbach, Kerstin Pecher
Copyediting and proofreading: Hannah Young
Copyediting recipes: Lauren Salkeld
Design and layout: kral & kral design
Production management: Cilly Klotz
Separations: Helio Repro, Munich
Printing and binding: Grafisches Centrum Cuno GmbH & Co. KG

Penguin Random House Verlagsgruppe FSC® N001967
Printed in Germany

ISBN 978-3-7913-8877-9

www.prestel.com